Let's Move to China, Ma Cherie!

Let's Move to China, *Ma Cherie!*
An Ex-Pat's Tale

Susan McDonald,
As told to her by Adela Chávez

MOUNTAIN ARBOR PRESS
Alpharetta, GA

Some names and identifying details have been changed to protect the privacy of individuals.

The author has tried to recreate events, locations, and conversations from his/her memories of them. In some instances, in order to maintain their anonymity, the author has changed the names of individuals and places. He/she may also have changed some identifying characteristics and details such as physical attributes, occupations, and places of residence.

Copyright © 2017 by Susan McDonald

All rights reserved. No part of this book may be reproduced or transmitted in any form or by any means, electronic or mechanical, including photocopying, recording, or any information storage and retrieval system, without permission in writing from the author.

ISBN: 978-1-63183-078-5
Library of Congress Control Number: 2016921528

This ISBN is the property of Mountain Arbor Press for the express purpose of sales and distribution of this title. The content of this book is the property of the copyright holder only. Mountain Arbor Press does not hold any ownership of the content of this book and is not liable in any way for the materials contained within. The views and opinions expressed in this book are the property of the Author/Copyright holder, and do not necessarily reflect those of Mountain Arbor Press.

10 9 8 7 6 5 4 3 2   0 1 2 6 1 7

Printed in the United States of America

∞ This paper meets the requirements of ANSI/NISO Z39.48-1992 (Permanence of Paper)

Dedication

Susan:

To Adela, for having the courage to tell her story
and the tenacity to see our project through to the end.

Adela:

To my father, who taught me passion for life
To my mother, forever strong
To my amazing sister
To my kids, who are my reason
To Miguel-san, my inspiration
To Tía Susan, for her patience and hard work

Epigraph

Omnia mutantur
Omnia fluunt
Quod fuimus aut sumus
Cras non erimus

Everything changes
Everything flows
What we were or are
Tomorrow we will not be

—Ovid (43 BC–17 AD)

Contents

Preface ... xi

Part 1 – First Steps into China
Chapter 1 – My Husband's Big Plan for Our Future ... 3
Chapter 2 – First Day in Shanghai ... 10
Chapter 3 – My New Neighborhood and New Auntie ... 15
Chapter 4 – Adventures in Grocery Shopping ... 19
Chapter 5 – Strawberries and Chinglish ... 23
Chapter 6 – Chinglish Is Not Enough ... 27
Chapter 7 – Lessons from Xiao Tian and the *Tai-Tais* ... 32
Chapter 8 – Michel, the Model Frenchman ... 41

Part 2 – Settling into Life in Shanghai
Chapter 9 – We Visit Beijing ... 47
Chapter 10 – My Mother-in-Law Comes for a Visit ... 56
Chapter 11 – China Days, or Lifestyles of the Ex-Pat ... 66
Chapter 12 – First Trip to Thailand ... 74
Chapter 13 – Weekends with Felix ... 78
Chapter 14 – Weddings and Asian Beauty Secrets ... 88
Chapter 15 – Thursdays with Mr. Wu ... 94

Part 3 – How Felix and I Found Each Other
Chapter 16 – I Ace My Interview ... 103
Chapter 17 – The Vista Way of Life ... 108
Chapter 18 – A Prophecy Come True ... 118
Chapter 19 – More Mexicans Arrive ... 123

Part 4 – Storm Clouds Gather over Shanghai
Chapter 20 – Felix's Love/Hate Relationship with China ... 135
Chapter 21 – Raising a Global Child ... 147
Chapter 22 – Deeper Problems with Felix ... 154
Chapter 23 – The Real Reason We Moved to China ... 164
Chapter 24 – Birth of Sebastian ... 168
Chapter 25 – Leaving Shanghai Behind ... 180

Part 5 – Life in Malaysia

Chapter 26 – Hasty Arrival in Kuala Lumpur	189
Chapter 27 – Getting Acquainted with K-L	193
Chapter 28 – Too Much Change, Much Too Fast	199
Chapter 29 – Felix at Work in Malaysia	202
Chapter 30 – Our Chinese Uncle and a Mexican Serenade	206
Chapter 31 – Finally, I Make a Friend	214
Chapter 32 – Asian Influences	222
Chapter 33 – Asian Oddities	227
Chapter 34 – Pilar's Wedding	234
Chapter 35 – I Get to Drive Again	238

Part 6 – The Beginning of the End of Asia

Chapter 36 – Our Trip to Penang and Its Aftermath	251
Chapter 37 – Advice from Friends and Relatives	258
Chapter 38 – The Agony of Defeat	267
Chapter 39 – My Asian Adventure Comes to an End	271
Epilogue	276
About the Author	277

Preface

This story is true. It happened to my niece, and I watched as it unfolded, first in Mexico and then in Asia, from my home in the US. Adela began to write her memories in Spanish a few years after she returned to Mexico, and she showed them to me at the beginning of 2012. I speak Spanish fairly well, but have read very little in my husband's mother tongue, so it took me a long time to wade through eighty pages of recollections. In fact, I did a lot of the reading in between patients at the dentist office where I was working part time. The more I read, the more I was captivated by her adventures and her incredible memory for detail. As a former journalist, I knew she had the beginnings of a great story, but I just did not have the necessary grasp of Spanish to be her editor.

Then, on New Year's Day 2013, I woke up with a much bigger and better idea! I would translate into English what she had written so far about China, then add a prequel and a sequel—the story of her fairy-tale romance at Disney World and her final Asian residence in Malaysia. I proposed this idea to Adela when my husband and I visited her family six weeks later, and she agreed. Three years and many dozens of e-mails later, I finished the story you are about to read.

Adela's memoir is the product of a true and deep collaboration between the two of us. The memories are all hers, and I tried to retain as many of her words and phrases as I possibly could. Her memory truly is amazing, isn't it? While rewriting her adventures, I researched China and Malaysia to add more depth to her descriptions of the places she visited, and I took a pair of scissors to her manuscripts to reassemble the stories in chronological order. Names and identifying details have been changed for Adela's friends and family members to protect their privacy, but aside from that we have recounted all events as truthfully as memory allows.

Adela and I hope you enjoy reading about her life and her adventures in the early days of China's modernization, and we hope the story of her too-good-to-be-true husband will help enlighten other women about the dangers of falling "blindly in love." If you enjoyed our book, please tell your friends, family, and book club members about *Let's Move to China,* Ma Cherie*!* All proceeds will go to Adela and her financial struggle to raise two kids, one with special needs, without any child support payments from her charming French ex-husband.

—Susan McDonald

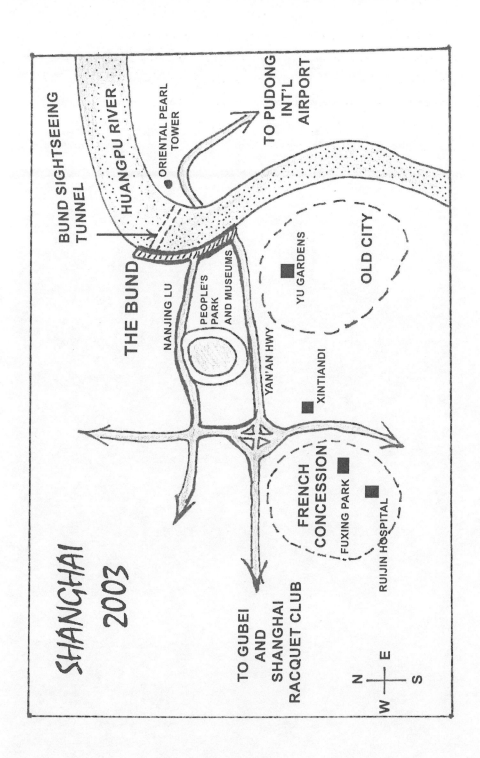

Part 1

First Steps into China

Chapter 1
My Husband's Big Plan for Our Future

It all began in 2002, when I was six months pregnant.

Like most women in my condition, I was busy creating my "nest" and preparing for the birth of my first child. My free time was spent shopping for cute little baby clothes or dreaming about a better apartment for our growing family, maybe even a rental house close to my parents. I could never have imagined that in just a few days my life would change completely. My destiny, and that of my child, would never be the same.

My husband came home from work one night that December and announced he had something very important he wanted to discuss. The tone of his voice told me it was something very serious, and he had a determined look in his eyes that I had not seen before. So I stopped what I was doing and gave him my full attention. We had been married for four years and had known each other for six. We were very happy together, and I was deeply, almost blindly, in love with him. Glancing at the expression on his face that evening, I could imagine any number of important things he might want to talk about. But *never*, in my wildest dreams, could I have guessed the request he was about to make of me.

My name is Adela, but my friends and family call me Adelita. My husband Felix and I were, I guess you could say, typical yuppies—young, urban professionals. We both studied business in college, we lived in a large metropolitan area, and each morning we commuted to work in the offices of the same international corporation.

What may surprise you is that we lived in Mexico. Yes, Mexico has a middle class of urban professionals; it's not all beaches and Aztec pyramids.

We lived in the city of Puebla, which has been home to several generations of my family. It is a large, peaceful city located about two hours away from the urban frenzy of Mexico City. Our employer was one of the biggest in town, and its work force included several hundred other *poblanos*, which is what residents of my city are typically called.

A group of businessmen from China had recently come to Puebla to tour the factory and administrative headquarters of our employer. In those days China was industrializing rapidly, and these visitors wanted to incorporate more Western business and manufacturing methods into our company's facility in China. My husband had been part of the team showing them around. Felix could be a very charming man when he chose to be, and apparently they liked his style. In fact, they liked it so much that before they returned to China, they discussed his transfer to a position in their offices in Shanghai—*Shanghai!* Even the name conjures up visions of mystery and danger in the Orient!

Felix was very enthusiastic about this idea, saying it could be a wonderful new avenue for our life together. He was convinced that our best future lay in Asia. But, the more he talked about it that evening, the more my head swam. To be honest, the only image I had of Shanghai at that point in my life came from the opening scenes of an Indiana Jones movie. As Felix kept talking, that jazzy blond nightclub singer kept dancing and spinning around in my mind singing "Anything Goes" over and over again. That's all that Shanghai meant to me in 2002. Later on, I would realize just what an omen that was, but at the time I could barely comprehend what Felix was trying so earnestly to tell me.

Now, I have always loved a good adventure, and I've traveled widely in both Europe and North America, but Felix's proposal left me stunned. China is, literally, on the other side of the world! For several days, I felt completely overwhelmed by Felix's grand plans. Surges of morning sickness and nausea, which I had not felt since the end of my first trimester, came swirling back to haunt my days and nights.

With the responsibility of a new life growing inside me, I could not share my husband's enthusiasm, not at first. However, seeing him so excited and so convinced that this would be a great move for our family, I began to yield. Within two weeks he had me convinced, and I said yes to his proposal. Yes! I would leave my homeland of Mexico. Yes! I would leave behind a very good job and the family I loved, and I would fly with him toward this new horizon. I would support the husband I adored and continue our happy married life on the other side of the world!

This is how I—a young wife and mother-to-be—came to spend five years of my life in Asia. Sometimes I can hardly believe it myself, but the story I am about to tell you is true. It all really happened to me and my family. It is a love story. It is a travel-and-adventure story, and it is a cautionary tale about what can happen if one doesn't remain true to oneself.

The first people Felix and I told about our grand plan were my parents. To say they were unenthusiastic is to wallow in understatement—they were devastated by our news. Not only would they be losing their eldest daughter for who-knows-how-many years, they would also miss watching their first grandchild grow up. "You don't speak even one word of Chinese," they kept telling us, "and you have no idea what life there will be like, for you or your newborn!"

True enough. But we had made the decision, and no words, no matter how logical, would change our minds. I knew it would be a tremendous challenge to give birth in two months and then move across the globe, and I also knew I would be the one responsible for making all the arrangements to dismantle our life in Mexico and reassemble it in China. But I had confidence in my husband, and I knew that whatever path we chose, it was vital that we stick together. Looking back on it now, however, I doubt that I was thinking very clearly in those days, so bombarded was I by the hormones of pregnancy and my husband's visions of the future.

Barely one month after he made that incredible proposal, Felix left for China to sign his three-year contract and begin work. I could not even consider going with him. By then, I was in my seventh month of pregnancy, and no airline would risk letting me on a plane for such a long journey.

I did not see Felix again until he returned to Mexico one day before my scheduled Cesarean. Scheduled because I am a real chicken when it comes to pain, and I just could not imagine myself lying in bed for hours and hours suffering from contractions. However, there was another, more important reason for carefully scheduling the birth. Felix needed a target date in order to fly in from China and then return to work in Shanghai within two weeks.

So, on March 11, 2003, our daughter Julia was brought into this world, right on schedule.

Julia and I could not join Felix in China as soon as I had hoped, however. This time, it was not the airline regulations that prevented our travel, but fears of pandemic. The respiratory disease SARS, caused by an influenza virus, had been brewing in China that winter and spring. China found itself enveloped in a growing health crisis, and the international news was full of warnings about this impending global epidemic.

Of course, I began to pay close attention to any news coming out of China. Mexican television reported that China was officially acknowledging only a few cases of SARS. But from Shanghai, Felix told us he saw lots of ambulances speeding through the city, often followed by trucks carrying men dressed like astronauts. Many Chinese took to wearing face masks in public, and everyone would step away quickly from anyone who sneezed or coughed. Even Felix admitted to having had a panic attack when someone standing behind him in an elevator sneezed.

Most of Shanghai's foreign residents fled to their home countries, and the doctors affiliated with Felix's company prohibited any personnel from traveling to China, which, of course, included Julia and me. Felix had returned to work before the travel restrictions were announced, and then decided he would stay put, not willing to allow even an epidemic to get in the way of our destiny. Meanwhile, back in Mexico, I waited and worried. I remember praying often and to any saint whose name I could remember. "Please," I begged them, "do not let me become a widow with a newborn child."

In retrospect, perhaps it was a good thing that Felix left me with so much to do, since it gave me precious little time to sit around and fret. In addition to monitoring the quarantine in China and learning to care for a newborn, I had to get passports and visas for China, pack and inventory our cargo container, empty our apartment, sell our furniture and cars, and finally return to my office—not to reenter after a relaxed maternity leave, as I had originally planned, but to resign my job, a task that left me with very mixed emotions. I lost weight quickly due to the stress of our big move—forty pounds in three months—but that too was for the best since I had gained over sixty pounds during my pregnancy.

By midsummer the SARS epidemic had waned, and Felix's employer decided that it was once again safe for employees and their families to enter China. In spite of the suspiciously low estimates by the Chinese government, world health experts estimated that the epidemic had sickened eight thousand people around the world, and of those, eight hundred had died.

Felix took only a few days off from work to come home to Mexico and accompany Julia and me on the trans-Pacific flight to Shanghai. Julia was just over four months old on our departure date, July 18, 2003. Before we left, we took the opportunity to have Julia christened by our Catholic priest. Although not a terribly religious man, my father had insisted on that, telling us he "could not rest if you take her to China unchristened."

I remember as if it were yesterday the torture of saying goodbye to my parents at the airport in Mexico City. My initial enthusiasm for our great adventure in China had dwindled to zero, and I could hardly speak the words to tell them goodbye. I could not hold back my tears as Felix and I passed through security and the silhouette of my parents disappeared into the crowd. Tears clouded my vision, fogged my glasses, and rained down on Julia's face and blue blanket. Walking like a zombie down that long corridor toward the departure gate, I decided that the second-saddest place on this earth, after a cemetery, must surely be an airport, where so many people come to say goodbye to the loved ones and the community they are leaving behind.

The next day Felix and I spent our fifth wedding anniversary on a plane traveling from San Francisco to Shanghai. It was not an auspicious beginning. I spent the ten-hour flight wrapped in a blanket, alternating between bouts of vomiting and diarrhea. We were both sick due to something, obviously bad, that we had eaten in the airport restaurant the night before. A very kind stewardess noticed how sick I was and helped Felix care for our daughter. She was truly an angel of the skies. Then, two hours before landing, as I was beginning to feel better, my husband took his turn with the motion-sickness bag. Thank goodness Felix had had the foresight to purchase some aspirin in the airport before we departed. Although it had little effect on how we felt, the aspirin did manage to camouflage any fever we might have had from the infrared monitors that scanned all arriving passengers in Shanghai. Those with fevers were put in quarantine until it could be determined whether they had SARS or not, which would have been a total nightmare.

That long, awful flight finally ended, and we arrived at Shanghai's new Pudong Airport. The international-arrivals terminal was thronged with people that night, many of them carrying signs written in Chinese characters. At first I thought it must be some sort of a demonstration, or maybe a crowd awaiting the arrival of a celebrity, but no. What I interpreted as an unruly mob was just a typical evening at an airport in the most populous country in the world. Outside it was a hot summer night. We waded through dense crowds of people to reach the taxi stand and, two hours of heavy traffic later, arrived at our new home.

The three of us had been traveling for thirty-one hours. Even so, I could not take my eyes away from the window of the taxi as we traversed the city. My impressions of that ride are still so vivid—the brilliant colors of the Chinese characters on neon signs, the oh-so-foreign faces of the pedestrians who crowded the sidewalks and crosswalks, and the constant river of people flowing by on bicycles, motor scooters, and in cars. They seemed to come and go without ever stopping, as if they were ants at work. I was fascinated, but also a bit intimidated. It was all so new and different, but I knew one thing—I wanted to learn everything I could about my new home.

The move to China was a decisive moment in my life. As a child growing up in Puebla, the only connection I had to China was the stories I heard about our city's folk heroine, *La China Poblana*, or in English, the Chinese Lady of Puebla. According to legend she was a Chinese girl of noble birth who was kidnapped by pirates and brought to Mexico several centuries ago. She somehow made her way to our city and became the toast of the town. Puebla even has a colorful statue and fountain in her honor. I could not help but think of her as we drove through Shanghai that night. By coming from Mexico to China I was traveling the path of *La China Poblana*, but in reverse! It was hard to comprehend all that had happened to make it so, but now *my* feet were stepping into the land of the Mandarins!

Chapter 2
First Day in Shanghai

It was late in the evening when the taxi pulled up to our apartment. We were completely exhausted and tumbled straight into bed. The next morning, as if nothing out of the ordinary had happened, Felix got up early and went to work. I was so tired from the long journey, bad food, and getting up to feed Julia during the night that I did not even hear him leave. When I finally did wake up, I spent several moments just staring at the empty spot on the bed beside me wondering where he could be before I got up to check on Julia.

I soon realized that Felix must have left to go to work, but I had no idea where that was. I had forgotten to ask him for the phone number of his office, or even his cell phone. I did not know my phone number, my address, or even in what part of town our apartment was located. It slowly dawned on me that here I was, somewhere in the enormous metropolis of Shanghai, in the very foreign (to me) People's Republic of China, all alone—and with a baby in my arms.

The first thing I did was check the kitchen for food. I found a single box of cornflakes and a small bottle of milk. Well, at least I had breakfast. I walked over to look out the window, and immediately my spirits soared. Spread out before me was a lovely view. From my vantage point at the window, I could see a large section of my new neighborhood, the Shanghai Racquet Club and Apartments. Several nice apartment buildings were located near mine, and we were surrounded by lawns and lovely gardens with ponds and fountains. I vaguely remembered getting out of the taxi the night before and noting with considerable surprise that the buildings, bathed in a soft glow from the streetlights, were Mediterranean in style. But we saw no other people that night, and there was no one in sight now.

I turned back around to explore the apartment. It was certainly spacious. My new home contained a living room with a dining area, kitchen, laundry room, four bedrooms, and four baths, plus a nice little triangular terrace. We were on the second floor. My footsteps echoing on the wooden floors made the apartment seem even larger since the rooms contained only the most basic pieces of furniture, which were included in the rental. The walls were painted creamy white and totally bare. One of the bedrooms was full of boxes to be unpacked. Fortunately, our cargo container had arrived a week earlier.

After eating my cornflakes and feeding Julia, I decided to go out. I was anxious to explore and to see where and how my new life was going to unfold. I also needed to buy some basic food items to get us to the weekend, when Felix said he could take me shopping. Searching around the apartment, I found two pieces of Chinese paper money lying on a table. They were red, worth one hundred yuan, and displayed the face of Mao Tse-tung. How much money was it? I had no idea, but I smiled as I opened my wallet and exchanged my Mexican bills, with the face of Aztec poet Nezahualcoyotl, for the new red ones with Chairman Mao. Hopefully they would buy me the basics, at least. I prepared a diaper bag with four bottles of milk for Julia, in case we got lost, and put her in her stroller. Together we left the building.

We walked out into a sweltering 40°C. That's 102°F. Shanghai was in the middle of a heat wave during the summer of 2003, with temperatures the highest in over forty years. I could see waves of heat rising from the pavement. We did not encounter one single person during the walk from our apartment building to the entry gate of the Shanghai Racquet Club. It seemed as if human beings had disappeared from the face of the earth, and Julia and I were the only ones left. On the other side of the gate, however, I could see that things were quite different. With a mixture of excitement and fear, we stepped out to explore our little corner of Shanghai. I felt sure that Felix would be proud of us that evening when I told him all about our first adventure in China.

Just a few steps beyond the gate I saw stores, businesses, and people—lots of people, many on bicycles circulating at great speed. The people all looked astonishingly alike, and the small businesses weren't that different one from another either, at least to my untrained eyes. I couldn't tell what street I was on because, of course, all the signs were in Chinese. So as we ventured forward, step by step, I tried to note the landmarks and any special details about the places we passed so that I could find my way back. I joked to myself how much I could have used a ball of yarn or handful of bread crumbs to mark the way home.

We could not proceed very rapidly, however, due to the reactions we were getting from the Chinese pedestrians. People on the street were openly staring at us as we walked along, craning their necks to get a better look at my daughter and staring at her with their eyes wide open in surprise. People even stopped us to take photos with their cell phones and cameras. The first few times I gave the photographers my best Colgate smile, but after a little while I began to feel uneasy at the excessive attention we were drawing. It was apparently obvious to everyone that we were *waiguoren*, or foreigners. Since my hair is dark and straight, I think it was probably my clothes that gave me away so easily, and of course, Julia's blond hair. People even stepped up to touch Julia or caress her hair, saying, "*Hen piaoliang, hen piaoliang.*" Judging by their expressions and tone of voice, I assumed they were saying "very pretty, very pretty," but it still made me nervous. Part of me wanted to just turn around and run back to the apartment, but I kept reminding myself that Felix had said China was a very safe country. He had already spent four months here, and I really wanted to believe him, especially now. According to Felix, Julia and I could have taken a taxi at two o'clock in the morning and still be perfectly safe, but on my first day in this huge city I wasn't quite ready to try it. Besides, where would I go? I didn't know where to find a taxicab, and even if I did, I wouldn't be able to tell the driver anything. I didn't even know my own address. Besides that, we needed food, and I had not yet found what we needed, or even any food that I recognized.

After walking a long way in the heat and seeing only people who appeared to have come from the same mold, I saw in the distance a silhouette that grabbed my attention and filled me with hope. Walking down the street toward me was someone who looked Western, not Asian—a tall, slender young woman with chestnut-brown hair. And what's more, she was pushing a baby stroller! Never in all my life have I been so happy to see a familiar face, even though it belonged to a total stranger. Without hesitation, I walked right up and introduced myself. And that is how I met Agnes, a young French woman to whom I will always be grateful.

Agnes walked with Julia and me to buy some fruits and vegetables at a market nearby. She knew where to go to find some I would actually recognize. Then she showed me the way back to the Shanghai Racquet Club. It turned out she was heading that way herself. Thank goodness, because I was ready to collapse from the heat, jet lag, and anxiety. Agnes and her husband had recently purchased a membership at the club. Her son was actually having a swimming lesson there right now, and she was using her free hour to go out strolling with her infant daughter and do a little shopping.

God had indeed been kind to me that day and had sent me the perfect guide! Agnes had been living in Shanghai for over two years. Now that it was summer, she told me, she came to the club almost every day. She told me the Racquet Club community had a small convenience store and showed me where it was located. I was able to buy some meat and other staples and charge them to our apartment rental account. My two Chinese bills might have been enough to purchase food for dinner that night, but not much more. We agreed to meet the next day for coffee.

That evening I prepared a simple chicken-and-vegetable soup. They say that chicken soup is good for the soul, and I really craved some of that comforting broth after my first foray alone into the teeming streets of Shanghai. Back in my own kitchen, however, I soon discovered that even the chickens are different in China. My boiled chicken made a broth that looked like soapy water, with lots of gray foam on top. Not at all like the clear-yellow broth you get from a Mexican chicken. But hunger is powerful, and we ate it anyway.

When he returned home, Felix was quite surprised to learn that I had gone outside the apartment community to go shopping. When he left for work so early that morning, he had completely forgotten about dinner and whether we had any food to cook at home. Felix promised we would go to a real grocery store on Saturday, and we did. But that's another story.

Chapter 3
My New Neighborhood and New Auntie

As promised, the next morning Agnes was waiting for me in the lobby of the Shanghai Racquet Club. She was very kind and gave me lots of good information about the club and its facilities. She also explained why "the compound," as everyone called the Racquet Club and Apartments, seemed like such a ghost town. It was all due to SARS, of course. She expected that many people would be returning in the next month or two now that the peril of epidemic had passed, and time proved her correct. She also introduced me to two other young mothers who were among the few female "ex-pats" remaining in Shanghai in spite of SARS. Ex-pat is short for expatriate, which means a foreigner residing in China. (Like me now!) Kayla and Janette were both American, very friendly, and outgoing. They both had older children, but like Agnes, each had a second child, a baby just about Julia's age. Their families both lived within the compound. I was very glad to meet them and hoped we would become friends.

While talking with Agnes that morning, I was surprised to find that she already knew my husband Felix; and she knew that he was not Mexican, but French like herself. I had not mentioned that detail yesterday because there had been just too many other things (food, directions, shopping assistance) to deal with first. Felix had moved from France to the USA for a year, and then on to Mexico. He came to my hometown of Puebla about a year before we got married. In fact, Agnes had met Felix two months earlier at a dinner party for ex-pats from France. I would soon learn just how small a world Shanghai's ex-pat community could be, at least the one populated by folks from Europe and the Americas. It gave Agnes and me one more thing in common—French husbands, who are in a category all their own. Agnes's husband worked for a chain of sporting-goods stores. Although his office was located on the other side of Shanghai, the family lived near our compound so that their son could attend the French school located nearby.

During the next few days I did a lot of exploring in and around our compound, and I decided that Felix's choice of residence had been a good one. Life in our compound would put me in contact with lots of people and give me a better social life. Plus, I could tell that living here meant we would have a prestigious address. Our apartment rental was four thousand dollars per month, which Felix's company paid. Penthouses in the compound rented for up to eight thousand. Felix had gotten a good deal, he said, due to the panic brought about by the SARS epidemic, which caused so many foreigners to leave in haste. Rental prices were typically quite high, in part because the international companies paid nearly all the costs of their ex-pat employees' living expenses. This, I would learn, gave ex-pat families plenty of spending money, which was considered part of the bonus ex-pat employees received to compensate them for uprooting their families and moving abroad to work.

The compound was big and completely fenced in. In 2003, it contained nine apartment buildings, which were surrounded by beautiful gardens with streams, ponds, statues, and fountains. The sports club at the center of the compound was really great and included a restaurant, three swimming pools, a gymnasium, and courts for both tennis and squash. The club's tennis school was highly regarded. It brought in foreign instructors, and its frequent tennis tournaments attracted professional players to the stadium in the center of the club. There was a nice playground for small children, and even a kindergarten for preschool ex-pats.

The compound was a true Eden for the foreign families who sought a little peace and tranquility inside the busy, vibrant city of Shanghai. When my father came to visit us several months later, he christened it The Golden Cage. It seemed a very suitable place for Julia to spend her first years. Almost all the residents were foreigners, or ex-pats like us, who came to work for various international corporations or teach at the American school or the French school, both located just a few blocks away. There were also a number of foreign men living here who were married to Chinese women.

Two days after our arrival in Shanghai, Xiao Tian entered our lives. She was a maid/nanny/housekeeper whom my husband had hired without even meeting her. Her one and overwhelming qualification in Felix's mind was that she had worked four years for a French family who had just returned to Europe. This French family had been friends with one of Felix's boyhood buddies from France, named Michel. By one of those quirks of destiny, Michel had been living in Shanghai for three years. Felix was so happy to encounter his friend again, and we felt doubly blessed that this friendship had led us to Xiao Tian. She was a wonderful, capable person who made our life in China much, much better in so many ways.

Chinese domestic workers must have an amazing communications network because they all seem to know just when a new family moves into the neighborhood. Our arrival immediately brought a parade of hopeful housekeepers knocking at our door. I didn't know what to do with so many applicants, nor did I know what to say since I couldn't understand a single word they said. I could only say, "I'm sorry, I don't understand," and with an embarrassed smile close the door. The only reason I could tell that Xiao Tian was the *ayi* selected by my husband was because she handed me one of his business cards. The word *ayi* actually means "aunt" in Chinese, but that is the word everyone used for housekeepers and maids.

Xiao Tian crossed the threshold of our new home with a big smile and the wonderful attitude that our different languages would be only a minor inconvenience. She had a very round face, long hair, and small eyes that seemed to take in everything around her. She was fairly young, about thirty-two years old. Once inside the door, she gave me a short little speech and then a pleasant, open smile. I looked at her and could not help but smile in return. I couldn't really speak to her or give her any instructions, but my instincts told me that she was a good person. Plus, she was just delighted when she saw Julia. Later on, I learned that *ayis* are well known to boast among themselves about the children in their care. Apparently, the blonder the child, the higher the *ayi's* prestige among her peers. Curly hair adds another notch up the bragging ladder. So Julia, with her curly, blond hair, was a real prizewinner for Xiao Tian.

She arrived every morning on her bicycle, which was so rusty that it looked as if it would disintegrate at any moment. When she got off her bicycle, she would remove her cone-shaped hat, woven from palm leaves, and her long-sleeve cotton gloves, which protected her arms from the sun. It took her about fifty minutes to cover the seven kilometers to our apartment, but even in the fierce heat of that first summer she always arrived with a happy smile and a ready-to-work attitude. She was a self-starter and showed true initiative, which I came to find unusual in the Chinese. They are much more likely to wait for orders and then follow them without questioning. Lucky for us, Xiao Tian was not like that. She could think of things to do around the house that had not even occurred to me yet, and she was always looking for ways to help us and take good care of us.

Xiao Tian always paid careful attention when I cooked, and it was probably food that truly brought us together. Learning to cook Western dishes is an important job skill for Chinese domestic workers, but I think Xiao Tian truly enjoyed sampling new foods and learning to cook them. For my part, I loved her fried rice, stir-fried vegetables, Chinese noodles, and smoked tofu.

Sometimes when I am feeling nostalgic for those days in Shanghai, I cook myself something Chinese, something that I learned to cook by watching her, and I feel comforted.

Chapter 4
Adventures in Grocery Shopping

During our first few days in Shanghai, Felix and I ate mostly food purchased from the compound's convenience store. While the shop was certainly convenient, it was also small, rather expensive, and its limited supplies often ran low by midafternoon. As promised, Felix took me grocery shopping on our first weekend in Shanghai. I was really looking forward to my first big trip outside our compound. He had made some inquiries with other ex-pat families and learned there were several Western-style supermarkets located "near" us in Gubei, our section of the city and the area where most of the foreigners lived. In Shanghai, a city of sixteen million registered inhabitants (and probably five million unregistered), "near" is a relative term. With the city's intense and incessant traffic, it took our taxi over an hour to reach Carrefour, a French-owned supermarket that was automatically Felix's first choice.

That day it took us over three hours to buy just the basic supplies for our meals and simple housekeeping. Why so long? First of all, the store was huge, two floors and an escalator, and it was just packed with people that day—and every other day, as I would soon learn. The labels on almost all of the products were written in Chinese characters, so I could not tell what was inside a can or box, unless it had a picture on it, which many did not. All the brands were completely new to me, so I had to analyze each product very carefully. I ended up actually having to smell each of the containers of detergents and soaps—the individual aroma of each product was the only way I could determine whether it was for cleaning clothes, washing dishes, or bathing Julia.

Buying fresh fruits and vegetables was easier since we could at least recognize some of them from our former life, but the fish-and-seafood display looked like something out of a science-fiction movie—what they had for sale resembled nothing I had seen in any market or grocery store in Mexico or Europe. Large tubs and tanks held live turtles, squiggling eels, and scary-looking crabs, all waiting to be individually selected by some shopper for her dinner that night. Several of these unfortunate animals had apparently jumped out of their tanks and lay trampled to death on the supermarket floor. One of the turtles almost made his escape and managed to cross the floor and hide behind a stack of boxes. But then a store employee scooped him up and returned him to the tank with his brothers. There was a wide selection of fish, many of them unrecognizable to me.

To my surprise, the inventory of dairy products was small and very expensive. They were almost all imported from Australia, New Zealand, or Europe. Even powdered milk was in very short supply. I would soon learn this was the case in all the grocery stores because the Chinese do not consume much dairy at all. Apparently their bodies lack an enzyme to properly digest milk, and it makes many of them feel ill. True or not, Xiao Tian avoided milk entirely. Paper products for personal hygiene were also in short supply and expensive.

As we made our way around the huge store, searching for items I considered essential and investigating aisle after aisle of things I neither recognized nor needed, I became more and more concerned. My mind flashed back to the time in Mexico when I was packing our container of goods to ship to China. I distinctly remembered asking my husband by phone, and later in person, if we would be able to purchase all the household items we would need in China for daily living. That blockhead, macho to the core, responded that I shouldn't worry about that at all. Of course I would be able to find everything I needed in Shanghai. It's a very modern city, he said over and over.

Never believe a man when he says this, I learned that day. Everything that you might need was available—if you were a businessman. Cheap electronics and computers were no problem. Had I known the real situation, I would have packed huge supplies of baby formula, diapers, and baby food. As it turned out, we had to buy expensive Japanese Huggies for the ridiculous price of fifty dollars, which definitely made me think twice about how often to change Julia's diaper. (I would later learn that Chinese toddlers generally wear trousers with a long opening between their legs from front to back. They "do their business" wherever, so parents teach them at a very young age to control their eliminations.)

Commercially prepared baby foods, like Gerber's, were actually available at Chinese stores, but Agnes and her two friends had warned me about them. The ingredients were not what I might expect, they said. Bone marrow, liver, and pork tongue were common components in the bottled baby foods, as well as fish head and mushrooms. When I inspected the jars of baby food on Carrefour's shelves, I must admit I did not find them very appealing. Now, I have always tried to be open-minded when it comes to food, but when I thought of my child's tender age I decided I'd better stick to what I knew. For this reason, I would just have to do as my mother had done with me—liquefy my own cooked meals in a blender, and then freeze small portions for Julia.

While I did not anticipate finding such immense crowds of people that day inside Carrefour, I was *totally* unprepared for the manners of the Chinese shoppers themselves. From the moment we exited our taxicab, I noticed that the Chinese seemed to have no sense of personal space like we do. They are accustomed to tightly packed crowds and are not embarrassed at all to be pressed up against another person. Several times that afternoon I had to seek out a less crowded aisle in the store and sit cross-legged with my eyes closed, breathing deeply until I got over a mild panic attack. (I've always felt uncomfortable in crowds.) It didn't help that the Chinese shoppers would bang their shopping cart into mine over and over again without ever saying "excuse me," or the equivalent, or even looking me in the eye. And I couldn't believe it when I saw someone inspect and then take an item right out of my own cart. (What? They couldn't find it themselves?) But the worst moment came when I was inspecting a small box of some sort of soap or detergent. A woman walked up, took the box right out of my hand, and, walking away, dropped it into her own shopping cart.

In China, grocery shopping is truly an extreme sport, and after three hours of competition we emerged from the store tired and battle-fatigued. Felix hailed a taxi. It stopped for us, and while we were preparing to load our purchases inside, a Chinese couple got in our taxi and away it went. I couldn't believe it. Felix hailed another taxi, and, wiser now, we fended off all comers as we scrambled to load our bags in the car and not dump Julia on her head. Then it was only an hour-and-a-half taxi ride back through Gubei to our "nearby" Shanghai Racquet Club compound.

Golden cage?! You bet, and that day I thanked God for it.

Chapter 5
Strawberries and Chinglish

On our fifth day in Shanghai, all three of us—Felix, Julia, and I—went to have the medical exam that was required of all foreigners in order to get a permit to live in China. Up to that point I knew just three phrases in Chinese: *nihao* (hello), *xie-xie* (thank you) and *hen piaoliang* (very pretty). But I am certain the fourth Chinese word I learned—*caomei* (strawberry)—is one that I will never, ever forget because of all the mayhem it caused that day.

The exam, performed at the Center for Infectious Diseases, was supposed to be a quick, routine physical. The CID was not impressive, just a large, old building covered in square, white tiles, but it could easily have been mistaken for an embassy headquarters considering all the security that surrounded it, probably due to the recent SARS epidemic. Once inside, we saw people dressed in hazard suits just like in the movies about epidemics. Even the people without those suits were wearing surgical-style face masks that covered their nose and mouth. From behind their masks, we could hear the security people saying in English, "Come in, come in."

Wow, I thought, *it's really great that they speak such good English here—that should make things a lot easier.* I could not have been more wrong.

The first thing they did was escort Felix in one direction and Julia and me in another. We followed our guide down what seemed like miles of hallways, all harshly lit and bare. It was not just a simple physical. They gave me several different types of blood tests, took a chest x-ray, and examined me gynecologically, which included checking the scar from my recent Cesarean section. It seemed to take a very long time.

Finally, they got to the personal interview and asked me various questions about my health. The doctors were speaking to me in a strange mix of English and Chinese words, but I tried my best to answer as clearly and honestly as I could. Later on, I would learn that this mix of the two languages is so commonly encountered in Chinese-Western interactions that it even has a name—Chinglish, and it really pays to learn the basic words and phrases if one wants to get along in Shanghai. I thought that the interview was going pretty well, and we seemed to be nearing the end of the ordeal when they asked me if I was allergic to anything. I answered in English, "Yes, strawberries."

I couldn't believe the horrified look that crossed the doctor's face, and I was even more startled when he jumped up and literally ran out of the room to get another doctor. After being so thoroughly manhandled and probed by various medical practitioners, I was about to have a nervous collapse, and now there were new people checking me over again and again, as if I were some rare specimen. Finally, someone had the bright idea to go get a Chinese-English dictionary, and after a tense minute or two they all let out a sigh of relief—Ayooo! That, I soon learned, is the typical Chinese expression for "Whew!" or "Everything is okay!"

I never found out what it was they thought I said that day. But I did learn the word for strawberry (*caomei*), and I never again said the English word "strawberry" in front of any Chinese person if I could help it. When Julia and I were finally allowed to go, we found Felix waiting anxiously for us. His exam had been quite short, and he breathed a sigh of relief when he saw us exiting with our approved medical certificate—Ayooo!

The day after the medical exam I decided to get my new life in order, and I wrote out a list of personal goals. The first one was to get physically fit and lose the last ten pounds of my pregnancy weight. An ideal way to accomplish this, it seemed to me, would be to join the sports club at the

First Steps into China

center of our compound. In addition to tennis and other racquet sports, the club offered morning classes in aerobics, water aerobics, yoga, and tai chi. Unfortunately, these classes wouldn't begin for another few weeks. I was impatient to get started, so I decided to just go ahead and hire one of the club's personal trainers. Justin Wu had been a professional swimmer, and with his aggressive training I reached my weight goal in just a few months.

Justin actually had a Chinese first name, but he got tired of repeating it and having foreigners struggle to remember it, so he chose a Western name to use at the club. He spoke almost no English, and I knew only four words of Chinese, but to implement his torture trials, language was hardly necessary. He set up a series of cardiovascular exercises using weights, and with all the repetitions he demanded, I quickly learned to count to twenty in Chinese.

Justin was the first of many Chinese I met who used Western names with foreigners. This was quite common in restaurants and stores, as it helped make interactions with Westerners go more smoothly. They each chose their own name, and I often wondered just how they came up with them. I remember meeting one fellow named Brownie, and another who called himself Cookie. One guy even called himself Cruise, after Tom I imagine. But the real winner for me was the technician who came to install the internet connection in our apartment. When I opened the door, he greeted me in a deep, serious voice saying, "Hello, my name is Pan, Peter Pan."

Sean Connery himself could not have done it better.

Since it was summertime and very hot, I was really looking forward to the water aerobics classes held in the club's beautiful outdoor pool, and I signed up within a week or two of my arrival. The first two classes were so pleasant that I couldn't understand why there were just three participants—a Brazilian, a Spaniard, and me. We were then informed that, due to popular demand, the class would be moved to the indoor pool. Imagine my surprise when I arrived for the third class and found that eight Asian women had joined our group! And that's how I discovered just how much the Chinese hate the sun.

Apparently sun-tanned skin is associated with low-class manual labor, and both men and women cover up to avoid it. They frequently use gloves to protect their hands while driving and often wear long, removable cotton sleeves when they go outside to shield their arms from the sun, as Xiao Tian did every day on her ride to and from our apartment. Plus, they will always, *always* carry a hat with them to shade their face in case they must be outdoors for more than a minute or two. Whenever I went to the compound's outdoor pool, I noticed that the Chinese women were usually wearing white jackets to cover up, and they always chose a seat in the shade, never the sun. I quickly came to realize that beauty, at least in the eyes of the Chinese, required fair skin, and the women went to great lengths to protect theirs, not only by hiding from the sun but also by applying various types of creams and lotions, some even made of ground-up pearls. Did they have beauty secrets unknown to Western women? It piqued my curiosity, and I decided it was definitely something I would have to investigate while I was here.

Chapter 6
Chinglish Is Not Enough

My first several outings with Felix into downtown Shanghai left me dazzled. The city has two distinct and incredible skylines—one historic and one ultramodern. They face each other on opposite banks of the wide Huangpu River. I could never decide which one appealed to me more.

The Pudong section of town is located along the eastern bank of the river and includes the main financial district, called Lujiazui. In 2003, this area was filling up with amazing new skyscrapers, some of them among the tallest buildings in the world. Several were constructed in fantastic, modern shapes or had roofs topped by huge circular or pyramidal sculptures. During the day the skyscrapers here were *very* impressive, but at night this incredible scene really came alive. Most of the buildings were (and still are) illuminated at night and glow brilliantly against the dark night sky. Their silhouettes are punctuated by a million glowing signs advertising famous brand names from around the world. The Pudong skyline is a-*maz*-ing, and the first time we saw it, Felix and I stood and stared in awe for several minutes without speaking.

In 2003 Pudong was connected to the older, mainland section of the city, called Puxi, by a highway tunnel that went right under the Huangpu River and by several ferries and bridges. Here on the west bank of the river is the historic "Old Shanghai," with its world-famous Bund waterfront district. Well known as the financial center of China before its Communist revolution, the Bund is a mile-long line of beautiful old buildings in British, art deco, and French designs. Most of them now house banks, consulates, or posh hotels. Many high-end restaurants are located on the top floors of these architectural treasures. They face the modern Pudong area across the river, treating diners to a breathtaking view, day or night.

A park and wide, paved walkway run parallel to the Bund along the river. The first time Felix and I walked along this promenade I could hardly believe that this incredible city, such a blend of old and new, European and Chinese, was my new home. What would life in China bring for me and my family? I couldn't help but wonder. Hand in hand, we strolled along the riverbank pondering our future and accompanied, as always, by literally thousands of other pedestrians, all Chinese of course.

I was pleased to learn that my side of town, Puxi, contained the famous Nanjing Lu, the most important shopping street in Shanghai and surely one of the busiest streets in the world. A half mile on the eastern end of Nanjing Lu had become a pedestrian-only street shortly before we arrived in 2003. It was a marvelous place to window shop, and included the popular Pearl City shops, which displayed world-class examples of the oysters' art. A couple of my earliest acquaintances at the Racquet Club were from Singapore, and they were just crazy about pearls. When they invited me to go shopping with them about a month or so after my arrival, I eagerly accepted. It was my first visit to Nanjing Lu, and we spent several hours just at Pearl City.

Nanjing Lu was great during the daytime, but it too became so much more vibrant when the lights come on at night. Each step down the street revealed a new and wonderful sensory overload for my eyes. It was along Nanjing Lu that I discovered the No. 1 Shanghai Department Store and the No. 1 Shanghai Pharmacy. Their names seemed peculiar to me. I had never seen stores numbered like that, so ever curious, I asked Felix to take us there on our next outing. True to its name, the department store was indeed the first state-owned department store to open in post-revolutionary China. Famous for its exotic window displays, this store was huge (eight stories) and an amazing place to shop. But it was a rat race inside and very difficult to navigate due to the never-ending crowds. I have read that on a busy day, one hundred *thousand* shoppers might enter its doors.

First Steps into China

I would have to say that the No. 1 Pharmacy truly was the biggest and best in town. The catch was, unfortunately, trying to be understood when we didn't speak any Chinese. It was hard enough to make everyday purchases during those first few weeks in China. Trying to buy medicines or get medical care was far more challenging, as I would soon learn all too well.

We had been in Shanghai only a month or so when Julia developed a high fever. Then she began vomiting frequently and filling her diaper with diarrhea. I was frightened and decided that I must take her to a doctor immediately.

Never will I forget that hot, sweltering day in August or the long taxi ride along one of Shanghai's double-decker highways. I wasn't even sure the driver understood my words for "hospital," and I was sweating profusely, partly because I was so frightened and partly because I was sitting under a big towel to avoid getting splashed with baby vomit.

"Whatever am I doing here?" I kept asking myself. "Why did I ever agree to go so far away from home and family?" My husband, of course, was at work.

Somehow, the driver must have understood a bit of my fractured Chinglish because after an hour of driving, he dropped us off at Ruijin Hospital, the only place I knew to go in those early days in Shanghai. Inside it was very crowded, but that was normal. In China, I was learning, there were always crowds of people everywhere, as if they flowed from some unseen fountain nearby. I made my way to the registration desk, but was told by pointing and other hand gestures to go upstairs to the section for foreigners. *That's a good sign!* I thought. Surely in the section for foreigners I would find someone—doctor or patient, I didn't care which—with whom I could communicate. After all, I do speak English, German, and French.

But my hopes were dashed. When we arrived at the international clinic I was handed a registration form written in Chinese characters only. I put on an inquisitive face and said, "What???" to show that I did not understand what they needed. No help. I tried showing the form to people passing by in the corridor, saying, "I need help, please." Everyone just ignored me, including a group of nurses walking up and down the hall. I did not encounter anyone who wasn't Chinese. All the while Julia was crying and growing ever more restless in her stroller.

My desperation finally gave me the key to getting help. I picked Julia up out of her stroller and held her up so that she was visible to everyone nearby. The novelty of a blond Western infant did the trick. The nurses who had totally ignored me before decided that I was now worth their attention, and one of them finally pointed to the form I was holding and said, "Put name patient, here birthday." I did so and took the form back to the registration desk.

I don't know whether the person they took us to was a pediatrician, a nurse, or what, and I couldn't even tell him what was the matter with my daughter. Using English words, lots of hand gestures, and even some Pictionary-type drawings, I did my best to explain my daughter's symptoms, and I showed him a sample of the diarrhea in her diaper. Did the doctor understand? Maybe. At least he kept nodding his head and saying, "Okay, okay. Baby not okay!" He then wrote out an impressive page of Chinese characters on a piece of paper. I paid fifty yuan and walked out of the examination area holding tightly to a fretful Julia and what I hoped was a prescription for an appropriate medicine.

Now I needed to locate the hospital's pharmacy, but how? I tried showing my prescription to people in the hallways, but got no helpful responses at all. I was growing frantic once again when I finally noticed that most of the people in a particular area of the hospital were holding little bags of medicine. I walked toward this area and saw that the people holding the bags of medicine were exiting from a corridor I had not noticed before. I followed this stream of people and soon reached the hospital's pharmacy. What a relief! In exchange for my prescription slip, the pharmacist gave me a handful of little bags containing either pink or orange powder. He then started speaking rapidly in Chinese, probably, I reasoned, giving me some directions on how to administer the medicines.

Here we go again! I thought in despair. I looked at him sadly and said for the umpteenth time that day, "I'm sorry, I don't speak Chinese." This time it worked. He walked to the rear of the pharmacy and came back with a much younger woman. She read the prescription, and then told me in fairly comprehensible Chinglish to mix two bags of different colors together with water and give it to my daughter three times a day. And so I did, and she recovered, although to this day I have no idea whatsoever what it was in all those little bags.

You have no idea just how much I would have liked to have my mother, or even a friend, with me on that afternoon, someone to come with me and reassure me that everything was going to be all right. But I was completely alone in an alien world, and so I did the only thing I could. I got back into a taxi and endured another hot hour-an-a-half ride home to our compound. I could only put my trust in God that my little daughter would recover as I began the thrice-daily ritual of mixing those little bags of pink and orange powder.

Although my Chinese vocabulary at that time was practically nonexistent, I had at least been able to memorize the words to tell the taxi driver to take us home—"*Huaxiang Lu, Hua Cao, Minhang, Shanghai wanqiu julebu.*" But that, I realized, was not going to be enough to keep us healthy and safe. After the hospital experience I made sure I learned the words for medical terms, like fever, cough, cold, stomach, and diarrhea. I also rehearsed the numbers I was learning while doing all those torturous exercises with Justin Wu, as in *two* bags *three* times a day.

It was a start, but I was now determined to learn Chinese. Most Westerners, including Felix, said it would take years to accomplish what I wanted to do. But I didn't have years, not if I wanted my family to thrive, and not just survive, our sojourn in China. Was there any way I could jump-start my introduction to Chinese—and my knowledge of Shanghai?

Yes, there was, and I discovered it the next day right under my nose.

Chapter 7
Lessons from Xiao Tian and the *Tai-Tais*

The day after our harrowing trip to the hospital, I was thinking things over and suddenly realized that I already possessed two incredible tools for learning to understand Shanghai and its people. The first would be the other wives and mothers living in my compound—if and when they ever returned after the SARS scare. They had all faced the same struggles I was experiencing during my first weeks in Shanghai. Surely some of them could become friends and allies in my quest to make a good life for my family here in Shanghai.

My second and greatest asset was someone already hard at work helping me adapt to my new home, and that was the wonderful and irrepressible Xiao Tian, my housekeeper. From the very beginning I had been impressed with her pleasant personality and her can-do attitude. She was kind, compassionate, and truly concerned about the well-being of our family. But best of all, she was very creative in inventing ways to help us communicate with each other, and she had already begun to teach me a few words for everyday objects in Chinese. What I needed to do now, I suddenly realized, was to pay much closer attention to Xiao Tian's lessons. She could be the key to learning Chinese! Xiao Tian had a natural ability to teach, and I wanted so badly to learn. It was a match made in heaven, I realized, and I'd be a fool not to take advantage of it.

Initially, it was a bit intimidating because her first words to me sounded like nothing but noise. She uttered these strange sounds in the typical Chinese way, which is quite forceful, and at first it seemed that she was scolding me. But I soon realized from her facial expressions that she was not angry, that's just the way it sounds to a beginner. I think the very first word she taught me involved pointing at Julia's baby bottle and saying *niunai*! That is the word for milk, which, believe me, is an important one when you have an infant in the family. It was not easy for me to reproduce her words, but she was very patient and did not mind saying them over and over until I got it right—or sort of right, anyway. In this way I began to build a vocabulary of vital words and phrases, such as *pingguo* for apple and *huan niaupu* for "change the diaper." She began to pick up some words in Spanish too, from hearing me say them to Julia, and she would use them with her at appropriate moments. So little by little, we learned to understand each other and to communicate between ourselves and, to my delight, it was happening mainly in Mandarin! This is the dialect of Chinese spoken in most of mainland China, as opposed to Cantonese, which is spoken in the southern regions.

It did not take very long before I decided I needed a strategy for keeping all these words straight in my mind, so I got myself a notebook. Every time Xiao Tian taught me a word, I would write it down in my Mandarin notebook using whatever letters in the Spanish alphabet made the sound of the word to me. At night and when Julia was napping, I would practice my words, no matter how strange and crazy they sounded. I firmly believed that each day I would know more than the day before, and it would take me step by step toward a better understanding of not only Mandarin, but the Chinese people themselves.

My husband told me that I was completely crazy if I thought that I would ever be successful this way, but I did not let his pessimism deter me. It was simply a matter of doing the best I could with the resources I had. Since Xiao Tian and I were spending lots and lots of time together anyway, why not get started learning Mandarin at home? As the weeks passed, my notebook got thicker, Xiao Tian and I understood each other better, and she became ever more important to me and my family.

☼

The foreign families began to return to Shanghai about six weeks after my arrival, just as Agnes predicted. The panic over the SARS epidemic was fading, and I was soon able to meet many more of the ex-pat wives and children as summer turned into fall 2003. Fulfilling my lonely summertime hopes and dreams, these women were, in a word, wonderful. They were friendly and very open to newcomers, and so I quickly become incorporated into the *tai-tais*. That's the Chinese word for married lady, and it was the name the ex-pat community gave to the group's wives and mothers. By joining various exercise classes and meeting for regular coffee breaks with Agnes, Janette, or Kayla and their friends, I managed to acquaint myself with a dozen or more friendly *tai-tais* who visited or lived in our compound, and the experience was as richly rewarding as I had hoped.

They were a great group of women and everything this lonely, overwhelmed, first-time mother could have hoped for. We were truly a community whose members helped each other in every possible way, giving advice and sharing information on how to survive in China's fascinating yet very alien culture. Had the United Nations seen the warmth and cooperation within this group of Western ladies, they could have learned quite a bit about international cooperation! It did not matter whether you were Mexican, American, Australian, European, or South American. We knew we were all in the same boat, and together, we tried to move forward in the best manner we could for our families in a place that was difficult to understand and, sometimes, downright unfriendly.

Our group also included women from Southeast Asia, especially Malaysia, Singapore, and Thailand. The only ones who kept their distance were the Germans. Known among us as the German Gang, they were always together, always moving in their own circle. I had some access into that group since I speak German, but I found them unwilling to make even the slightest effort to join the other women, nor complicate their lives by speaking English, the lingua franca of the ex-pat community. Unfortunately for me, there were no other Mexicans, male or female, residing in the compound during our first year there, which left me with no choice but to reach out to others from around the globe. In hindsight, that was probably a blessing in disguise—I made so many friends from so many different backgrounds!

Living the life of a *tai-tai* in the posh and beautiful Shanghai Racquet Club could be glamorous and exciting. But it also meant living a life with many challenges, and I often wondered why God had put me on this path. At times I felt very isolated, even with the company of other *tai-tais*, and it really, really bothered me to be illiterate. Once outside the compound I could not read anything—not street signs, not newspapers, not labels on merchandise—nothing! In 2003, we were largely incommunicado with the outside world, and that's why the camaraderie and cooperation among the *tai-tais* was so vital and so cherished. In a way, it was as if we were all pioneers, banding together in our frontier fort preparing to enter unknown, and possibly hostile, territory.

Many of their best bits of information or advice probably sound mundane to an outsider, but I welcomed all the help I could get in this strange new world. For example, I learned from the *tai-tais* that there were actually three Western-style supermarkets in our part of Shanghai, not just the French one, Carrefour, where Felix took me on our first shopping trip. This was very important information because at Carrefour we could not find a baby formula that worked well for Julia, and we needed to check any other sources available. Felix and I searched the infant departments at one, named City Supermarket, and another, an Australian-owned business called Pines Supermarket, but luck was not with us. None of the few brands they had for sale helped Julia's tummy aches. Then, after we had been in China for a month or two, my parents called with the most amazing news. A friend of a friend of theirs in Mexico was flying to China on business. This wonderful man did us the huge favor of bringing along a suitcase full of NAN anti-reflux milk for our daughter. This was the formula she drank in Mexico, and we knew she could tolerate it well. This stash lasted until she was a year old, and we could start her on cow's milk.

Another time, after I had ruined several articles of clothing when attempting to launder them, I decided I'd better ask a more experienced *tai-tai* for help. My first choice was a neighbor from Australia, Sharon Lane, because she always appeared so beautifully dressed. She looked perplexed when I first approached her for this favor, but she eventually let me photograph all the cleaning, washing, and bathing products in her apartment. On my next shopping trip, I had my digital camera in hand and purchased exactly the same cleaning products she did. One more problem solved!

Early on, I was complaining to Janette about how completely stressed out and exhausted Felix and I were after our first few excursions outside the Shanghai Racquet Club. I was worried we might be getting sick or suffering from some strange vitamin deficiency or endemic disease. Once again an experienced *tai-tai* was able to diagnose our problem, and she reassured us both by admitting the same thing had happened to her. It's because you have to stay in a heightened state of mental alertness, she told me, in order to function in a safe and effective manner. As a foreigner, you can't understand what people are saying and you can't read the signs, she explained, so you are constantly operating outside your comfort zone, which takes a lot of extra energy and concentration. Plus, you have to develop a sort of sixth sense to avoid being run over by cars or bicycles on the streets and by people on the sidewalks.

She was right about that. Chinese pedestrians walk with a determination that makes them seem constantly in overdrive. They charge forward in an unyielding, direct path and will literally shove aside anyone who gets in their way. She also warned me that the Chinese do not see the logic in lining up for things. They don't ever organize themselves this way, she said. Even if there is a crowd waiting for something, they will never, ever form a line.

Another thing I learned from my new friends was that hardly any ex-pats drove their own cars. They all took taxis or had personal drivers, usually provided by their husband's employers. The incessant traffic and incomprehensible street signs made driving very difficult for foreigners. Add to that the immense size of the city and the chaotic rivers of bicycles and motor scooters running everywhere, and you begin to understand the huge risks involved for drivers unaccustomed to such a maelstrom. Unfortunately for us, Felix's employer was not as generous as most. It provided him with a car, but no chauffeur. So he was forced to drive himself back and forth to work every day, which took well over an hour each way—if the traffic was good. If the traffic was bad, it took longer, even though some of the newer highways had been built double-decker in an attempt to ease the traffic congestion.

Such was my worry for his safety that each morning before he left I made sure to ask the Virgin to bless him and watch over him until he could return safely home to Julia and me. By the time the weekend arrived, Felix was always exhausted and did not want to drive and fight with traffic on his days off. So I got to know my new city of Shanghai from the backseat of a taxi—which turned out to be pretty nice, actually. Taxi fares were cheap, and without exception, the taxi drivers were attentive, friendly, and very sympathetic to a foreign *tai-tai* attempting to exit their taxi with a stroller, packages, and small, blond child. Most of them spoke little—if any—English, however. I could hail a cab quite easily, they were plentiful everywhere, but I could not tell the driver where I wanted to go, something that had caused me so much distress on the day I had to take Julia to the hospital. So learning to communicate with taxi drivers became another urgent puzzle to solve.

Once again, my *tai-tai* friends showed the way. I quickly learned the most vital resource owned by each *tai-tai* was her collection of presentation cards. Each family tried to build up a sizable collection of the cards, just like a boy collects baseball cards, because their ability to move around in Shanghai depended greatly on this collection. To lose your cards was considered a disaster.

Just what were these precious presentation cards? Each business, restaurant, or shop in Shanghai that hoped to attract foreign customers created their own card, which was given out freely to visitors at their establishment. The cards were printed with the name, address, and phone number of the business in English *and in Chinese characters*. In most cases, there was a map on the reverse side of the card showing how to get there. Each time a *tai-tai* visited a business, store, or restaurant she liked, she made sure to ask for its presentation card, or *ming-pian*, because this would determine whether or not she would ever be able to find her way back in the enormous metropolis that is Shanghai. This card, when given to a chauffeur or taxi driver, told the driver exactly where to deliver his inept, incommunicado foreigner. Your cards were your passport to adventure, to good food, or even to the comforts of a familiar place, if that's what you were seeking. They were absolutely crucial.

Now, you might think that it would be sufficient just to give the taxi driver the name of some international company (like Xerox or Samsung) or to use a word that is recognized globally (like Coke or airport) to reach your desired destination. It definitely was not, at least not in 2003! If I said Sheraton Hotel, for example, the driver would not understand at all, and the same with Hilton, Hyatt, or even Carrefour. Each establishment had its own Chinese name, and it was imperative to learn to say it properly or give the aforementioned card. The Sheraton was known as Taiping Yang Pinguao, the Hyatt as Jin Mao Pinguao. And don't forget the most indispensable of them all, Carrefour, which in Chinese was Jalefour Gubei. We *tai-tais*, ever helpful and caring, regularly exchanged or photocopied each other's presentation cards. A great new restaurant or even a foreign-friendly pharmacy could set off waves of sharing or copying cards for friends and neighbors.

After I had been living in Shanghai for about six months, someone showed me a set of professionally produced presentation cards, which were called Taxi Cards. It was kind of like a Yellow Pages guide to Shanghai strung on a cord. It contained heavy-duty, laminated bilingual cards for dozens of the city's most popular shops, restaurants, hospitals, museums, parks . . . all kinds of wonderful places. The moment I saw that set of Taxi Cards I knew I wanted one. *What a great idea*, I thought. Whoever created those Taxi Cards was a genius, and I hope he or she made a million dollars!

The owner of the cards told me that she got them at a supermarket in downtown Shanghai, so Felix and I made a special trip there in search of the cards just as soon as we could. Felix held Julia and waited for me at the front of the store while I went to ask one of the cashiers where I could find the Taxi Cards. She did not understand me, but summoned a manager who supposedly spoke English. After I explained very carefully what I wanted, he disappeared for fifteen minutes or so. Julia was getting fussy and Felix was getting quite impatient by the time the manager finally reappeared—carrying a potato peeler and a big knife! I could not believe it! I was so frustrated that I didn't know whether to laugh or cry, and we left without getting our cards.

The language barrier was so hard for us to handle. Even with Xiao Tian's vocabulary lessons, I just wasn't progressing fast enough. To my surprise and delight, the very next day a Danish friend invited me to join her in her home for twice-weekly lessons in Mandarin Chinese! What a break! Another big step in my quest to learn Chinese had just fallen in my lap, and I eagerly accepted.

Her name was Hanna, and we had initially become friends because her son, Jasper, was the same age as Julia. We would get them together for playdates, joking that the two toddlers were becoming each other's first boyfriend and girlfriend. This relationship really helped smooth the way for our lessons since our kids and *ayis* already knew each other and got along well. All six of us (moms, kids, and *ayis*) came to look forward to the lessons, both for companionship and for learning.

Our teacher was named Nina Fu. She had an Australian boyfriend, so her English skills were excellent. Her lessons followed a textbook, but she was also happy to answer our many questions about how to incorporate Mandarin words and phrases into our daily lives. For example, how to talk to a Chinese pediatrician, or phrases that would help us at a tailor shop, restaurant, or beauty salon. The lessons were great. I added lots of new words to the ones I was learning daily from Xiao Tian. But most importantly, the lessons gave me the grammatical structure I needed to "glue" all my words together into sentences. It didn't take too long before I was able to have simple conversations with the Chinese people I was meeting every week. Despite what "everyone" had told me, I was on my way—speaking Mandarin was within my reach!

Chapter 8
Michel, the Model Frenchman

Sometimes life throws you such an incredible favor that it's hard to know whether it is just a wonderful coincidence or truly Providence at work. I believed it had to be the latter when Felix told me that a very good friend of his from childhood, named Michel, had been living in Shanghai for three years prior to our arrival. Michel worked for a French company and did a lot of traveling in China and throughout Asia.

When Felix first arrived in Shanghai, it was Michel who showed him around the Gubei area, predicting it would be a good place for us to live. His companionship kept Felix from feeling too lonely during those first few months when Julia and I were waiting back in Mexico for the SARS epidemic to subside. He invited Felix over to his house on weekends and introduced him to other French expatriates, which is how my first friend Agnes had made his acquaintance. For this I shall always be grateful to him.

Michel and Felix were thrilled to renew their friendship. They loved to laugh and joke around together, and they had gross and disgusting nicknames that they liked to use with each other. By the time I met Michel in Shanghai, he had been married for seven years to an American woman and had a six-year-old son. Unfortunately, theirs was not a happy marriage, and my hopes for making friends with his wife did not work out at all. The few times I met her she was aggressive, rude, and deeply angry at her husband. So it was Michel, and not his wife, who helped us get started in Shanghai, and it was Michel who arranged for Felix to hire our wonderful Xiao Tian from a French family that was leaving town. Michel was also the one who taught me to say "Ruijin Hospital" in Mandarin and told me that was the place to go if we ever had a medical emergency—which we did when Julia got sick a couple of weeks later.

To me, Michel did not fit the image of the handsome, debonair Frenchman at all. He was kind of nerdy looking, dressed sloppily, and was definitely overweight. But for some reason the Chinese found him incredibly cute—maybe it was because he had a large nose and big, blue eyes. A Chinese photographer had even hired him to model men's clothing in an advertisement. For many months after our arrival in Shanghai, Felix and I might be out walking or driving around town and come upon a giant picture of Michel up on a billboard. It was definitely weird, but I have to say that the Chinese photographer did an excellent job, because he looked much better on the billboard than he did in real life.

In those days there were a lot of Chinese photographers out wandering the streets of Shanghai looking for their next *waiguoren* (foreigner) model. This happened with children as well, so a lot of ex-pat moms enjoyed taking their kids to modeling agencies or were invited to do so while out with their youngsters. The blonder and more Nordic-looking the child, the better the chance of being invited to model.

My daughter was "discovered" while I was sitting with her in a coffee shop one day. She was six months old and modeled for a brand of children's clothing. We got about one hundred dollars an hour and Julia got her picture in a catalogue, but that was all. With Julia's curly, golden hair and steel-gray eyes, she got several callbacks, but it just did not work out. She was (and still is) a strong-tempered child who can't sit still for long and hated to have her picture taken. So at the tender age of nine months, her modeling career was over. Likewise, my sister Pilar was asked to model when she visited us about a year after we arrived. She does not have the typical Northern European look sought by most of the photographers, but has instead medium-brown hair, bronze skin, and beautiful big, brown eyes. When the makeup artists finished working on her, she looked gorgeous, but surprisingly Asian. The cosmetician enhanced her eyes to create a decidedly almond shape. The photo was taken for an ad promoting watches, and for a while we saw her picture in magazines and jewelry stores all over Shanghai.

Any foreigner, it seemed, could be a model and have their fifteen minutes of fame here—anyone but me, that is. I was never invited to be a model. I have long, black hair, green eyes, and a pale complexion. To Chinese eyes I appeared to be a "hybrid," the not-so-complimentary term for someone who was a mix of Chinese and Western parents. Everywhere I went, if I were wearing sunglasses and didn't say much, everybody thought I was Chinese. Sometimes this was an advantage since I could avoid getting overcharged at street markets. But the moment people saw my eyes, they would always stare and ask me what kind of hybrid I was. The Chinese were very curious about this. Many of them were completely unaware that a country called Mexico even existed, and they were quite sure that I must be half Chinese.

Part 2

Settling into Life in Shanghai

Chapter 9
We Visit Beijing

As our first summer in Shanghai turned into fall, the heat began to decline and the mosquitoes, which had truly been a plague, became a distant memory. This gave us a little time to enjoy life before what we heard would be a very cold winter, especially for a girl like me from Puebla, Mexico, where it is rarely ever very hot or very cold.

All our new ex-pat friends said that October and May were the months with the best weather and best air quality. So Felix decided that we should take advantage of the refreshing autumn weather and his upcoming week of vacation. "It's time for our first vacation together as a family," he announced, and it seemed perfectly obvious to him what our first destination should be. We would visit Beijing, China's capital city. What Felix did not realize, however, was that everyone else in China also had that same week off. It's an important holiday commemorating the birth of the People's Republic. We had *no idea* that at least half of these vacationing Chinese would also be planning to take a holiday trip to Beijing.

With the benefit of experience, we would learn that the best way to celebrate a national holiday in China is simply to leave the country. Go to Thailand, or Singapore, or any other nearby destination. But never, ever try to sightsee within China. Every spot, and the transportation to it, is incredibly crowded in a way that only the most populous country in the world can be. But Felix and I did not know this yet, and so we eagerly planned our trip to Beijing, the cultural and patriotic epicenter of the entire country.

We decided to hire a tour guide to lead us around the city's many famous sites, and with Simon Xing we got our money's worth and more. He was an excellent companion whose English was very, very good. On later trips, we often had to endure guides who had simply memorized their speech for each location but did not really understand what they were saying. If you asked them a question about something, they would just repeat their entire speech all over again, like a recording. Simon Xing was not like that and could answer our many questions with ease.

The first day we wanted to see Tiananmen Square and the Forbidden City. From all the TV news reports I'd seen from Tiananmen Square, I knew it was a vast, open, concrete plaza and the site of many political demonstrations, including the notorious one by students in 1989 that was so brutally put down. When we arrived at this huge square, it was full to overflowing with thousands and thousands *and thousands* of people. Wading through the masses of people with Julia in her stroller was a nightmare, and I was terribly nervous we might lose Simon in the crowd. I was not at all worried about losing Felix—he was tall, blond, and towered over the other tourists. Simon, on the other hand, blended right in. Losing him would have been a disaster. In fact, that entire day we did not see even one other Western foreigner.

Due to the crowds we did not pay our respects to Chairman Mao and skipped entering his refrigerated mausoleum in the center of Tiananmen Square. Instead, we waded through the crowds of people toward the Forbidden City, located across a wide boulevard just north of the Square. This huge complex of palaces and courtyards has been the symbolic heart of Chinese culture for over five hundred years. Twenty-four Chinese emperors ruled the land from this very spot.

Nine is considered a very lucky number in China, and it is said that the Forbidden City has 9,999 rooms. I wouldn't doubt it—it is *that* big. Its ornately decorated palaces, reception halls, and gardens are built as a series of ascending terraces reached by multiple sets of staircases. If you have seen the famous 1987 movie *The Last Emperor*, which won the Oscar for Best Picture, you may remember the many patios and staircases in this historic complex. With Julia in her stroller, Felix and I were obliged to carry her, stroller and all, up and down the multiple staircases—just as if she were a tiny empress herself, surrounded by a rolling sea of her many, many subjects.

Even though we were quite tired after our tour of the Forbidden City, we decided to end the day with a meal of Beijing's most famous dish, Peking duck. (Peking is the old-fashioned name Westerners used to use for Beijing.) The waitresses in the restaurant Simon recommended were dressed in gorgeous outfits modeled on the gowns worn by the concubines of the Chinese emperor. A quartet of musicians played typical Chinese melodies throughout the meal. The quartet included two Chinese violins, a type of mandolin, and a flute. I remember being surprised at the strong emotions their music evoked in me. As unfamiliar as I was with traditional Chinese music, some of the tunes made me feel happy and joyful, as if I could dance in the air. Others produced a melancholy that left me pining deeply for my family so far away and remembering scenes from my childhood. But then again, I remember how much Felix and I enjoyed the big bottle of local wine that came with our meal. Its label even featured a drawing of the Great Wall. Perhaps my nostalgia came more from the strong wine than the unfamiliar music. Who knows?

The highlight of the meal was watching the chef elegantly carve the duck and arrange it in a precise pattern on the serving dish. It was so pretty that I was actually reluctant to destroy his artistry by eating it. My attempts to carve a turkey with an electric knife at Christmas made me feel like a Neanderthal with a club compared to the finesse of this chef's movements. He went confidently and gracefully from table to table, giving every group of diners a beautiful show.

Each bite of this duck was a delight. The dark, shiny skin melted in your mouth like caramel, and the meat—it was so tender you barely needed to chew it. The classic way to eat the duck meat is to roll it inside a thin, crepe-style pancake, adding a bit of thinly sliced onion or other vegetable and a sweet, brown sauce. It was somewhat like a Mexican taco, and it tasted heavenly. To our surprise, at the end of the meal we were given a certificate stating that we had been served Duck Number XXXX of the thousands of ducks that had been prepared and served at the restaurant that year. I forgot the number of our duck. I lost the certificate almost immediately after stuffing it in among the diapers and bibs in Julia's diaper bag.

We ate so much that we decided to walk around a bit after dinner. Near our hotel was a street famous for its many food carts and exotic treats. Vendors were selling grilled silkworms, crunchy scorpions, fried starfish, and many other small creatures from both land and sea. What they had to offer was truly amazing, and the entire street looked like a scene from that Indiana Jones movie I remembered so well—and now here I was in the middle of it all! We had not seen anything like it in Shanghai, and I couldn't help but wonder if this bizarre bazaar wasn't set up more to amaze the tourists than to actually feed Beijing's visitors. People were taking pictures of the food and the vendors, and a few brave souls did sample these strange delights. I love trying new foods, and I really wanted to sample some of these, but for once I decided to be cautious. I was far from home and carrying a seven-month-old infant. If I got sick, it would be a disaster. So I decided to play it safe and save the silkworm kabob for another day.

Walking on, we came to a business offering many different types of massage, and we went inside to look around. Julia had already fallen asleep in her stroller, so Felix and I decided to treat ourselves to massages lasting an hour and a half. They told us to take off our street clothes and gave each of us a set of pajama-style pants and a shirt. For the next hour, the massages they gave us honestly felt more like torture than the pleasure we had anticipated. When the pummeling stopped, they finally left us lying faceup (and sore) on the massage table. Our therapist then approached each of us with a candle about the size of a pencil. Around the base of the candle was a cup that resembled a cupcake wrapper. Imagine our surprise when they put the candles *in our ears* and then lit the opposite end!

By this point I was getting very nervous, not knowing what was going on. But curiosity got the better of me, and I decided to close my eyes, try to relax, and just go with the flow. After about ten minutes, as the flame was approaching the base of the candle, the therapist removed the candle from my ear and inserted another one into my other ear, lit it, and left it to burn down as before. When the therapist extinguished the second candle, our massages were complete. We left the building feeling both confused and intrigued by what we had experienced.

Later, when we returned to Shanghai, I asked my neighbor from Taiwan what the candle in the ear was all about. She recognized it immediately and told me that "ear candling" is well known in traditional Chinese medicine. It is supposed to clear the ear canal of wax and other impurities, thus aiding in balance, relaxation, and well-being. *Wow*, I thought, *so now I know!* I did not want to repeat the treatment any time soon, however, because watching the flame approach my hair had been anything but relaxing to me!

The following morning Felix and I got up early to start our visit to the Great Wall, sections of which are located about forty miles north of the city. Our guide Simon recommended we visit the part located near Badaling. It was actually one of the last sections to be built, around the year 1505, and was carefully restored in the 1950s and again in the 1980s. We decided to be a little more practical that day and not take the stroller. Instead, we popped Julia into a fabric pouch called a Babybjörn. With Felix carrying Julia's diaper bag as a backpack and me carrying Julia strapped across my chest, we felt prepared to climb the innumerable steep steps and long passageways of this ancient military masterpiece. Our guide, Simon Xing, had seen it all before and wisely decided to wait for us near the entrance to the wall.

The Great Wall did not disappoint. It was very impressive as it snaked its way up and down the crest of the mountains. Yet even in its immense size, there were so many visitors hiking on the twenty-foot-wide road along the top of the wall that it looked like a running river of ants. Neither Felix nor I wanted to stop exploring the wall or admiring its ancient stonework, so we kept on going until we reached the farthest point allowed. But then, of course, we had to walk back, which took us an hour and a half.

About halfway into our hike, Julia needed some lunch and a diaper change, so we looked for a place to take a break. We soon found a small alcove in one of the wall's watchtowers, which let us get out of the main flow of traffic. The Chinese tourists, who kept streaming by just outside our open doorway, apparently found the sight of two foreigners attending their baby to be totally fascinating. Every single one of them, it seemed, stopped to look in, and most of them raised their cameras and took a picture of us at work. I doubt that ever in the long history of China has a diaper change ever been so well documented! By the time we got back from walking the wall, Felix and I were starving. As usual in China, food peddlers were there ready and waiting for hungry travelers. The typical Chinese street snack is either a cup of noodles, corn on the cob, or an egg boiled in black tea. Like any good Mexican girl, I was more than happy to bite into an ear of corn, but my husband dismissed all three choices, muttering that in France they only fed corn to their pigs!

On the drive back to Beijing, Simon suggested we stop at a jade factory because jade is so important to Chinese art and culture. I learned to my surprise that jade comes not only in shades of green, but also white, pink, purple, brown, and orange. In addition to lots of jewelry, the factory also sold lovely jade sculptures. The most popular images were cabbages (symbolizing abundance), horses (symbolizing strength), peaches (long life), and of course, the ever-popular Buddha. Just as every good Mexican girl wears a medallion of the Virgin of Guadalupe around her neck, every Chinese girl seems to require a bracelet of jade around her wrist. This bracelet must fit just so. It must *just barely* slide over her closed fist in order not to slide off again accidentally and get lost. A woman's jade bracelet is considered a very personal item, and it is said that the jade will lighten or darken depending on the personality of the woman who wears it.

Along the road running between the Great Wall and the city of Beijing are a great many restaurants, poised to take advantage of the hordes of tourists traveling to and from the wall. We chose one that looked good, went inside, and were astounded by the size of the place. The dining room was absolutely huge and contained, without exaggeration, hundreds of tables, all of them round. The service was super rapid and efficient, which was amazing considering the size of the place and the crowds of diners. After dinner, Simon suggested we attend either the Beijing opera, a classic art form renowned throughout China, or an exhibition of kung fu. Well, here we faced a dilemma. I was dying to see the spectacle that is Chinese opera, but Felix was more interested in martial arts. After considerable discussion we ended up seeing the kung fu, which was a real shame, if you ask me. Although it was quite an impressive show and I'm not sorry I saw it, I still feel bad about missing the opera that evening.

The next morning Felix and I woke up with aches and pains in muscles we did not even know we had. We both considered ourselves to be in pretty good physical condition, but climbing up and down the Great Wall carrying a child and her equipment taxed our bodies in ways we wouldn't have believed. We could barely crawl out of bed to begin our third day in Beijing, but we forced ourselves up and out the door. We spent the morning visiting the Summer Palace of the emperors, a beautiful place surrounded by water and wooded hills. It was designed to provide the emperors with a fresh, cool retreat and spare them the stifling summer heat of the Forbidden City. Although the palace complex dates from the eighteenth century, we learned that it had to be rebuilt twice, most recently after it was plundered during the Boxer Rebellion in 1900. The palace and its park were truly lovely, but what I remember most was having to run the gauntlet of vendors at the artists' market just outside the complex. The calligraphers and artists were very aggressive salesmen and pursued us at every step. It was really hard to tell them no, and there were so many of them! We finally succumbed to one's sales pitch and bought several nice paintings and linen hangings to decorate the bare walls of our apartment.

That afternoon we drove with Simon out to visit the Ming tombs, located about thirty miles northwest of Beijing. Along the way we passed orchards of peach trees that went on for miles and miles. The cultivation of peaches has its origin in China. In addition to being delicious, the peach is important as a symbol of long life. People often give peaches as gifts, either as edible fruit or as a decoration in metal or jade. This rural highway was heavily traveled with buses and tourists on their way to the tombs, so I was quite surprised when we drove by a troop of fifty or so Chinese soldiers marching in formation along the side of the road. Since the traffic was moving at fairly slow pace, I could see them well and noticed that these were definitely not the typical young men one sees on the streets of Shanghai, or Beijing either, for that matter. No, these fellows were much taller—a good six feet—and slender, but obviously very strong. Impeccably attired in their olive-green uniforms with red Communist accents, they were an impressive sight. I couldn't help but recall the old saying "There's just something about a man in uniform."

In general, I did not find the Chinese men particularly attractive, but these guys were something else entirely. I reached for my camera to snap a memory of this group, but our guide Simon immediately stuck his hand out to stop me. "We're not authorized to take photographs of soldiers," he warned me. "We could get in lots of trouble." The look on his face was enough to make me drop the camera back on the car seat. *Oh well*, I thought to myself. I'll just have to remember this moment and store it in my own mental archive—which I obviously have. Now, years later, I can barely recall our visit to the Ming tombs, impressive though they were. But those soldiers—now that's a memory I recall in exquisite detail!

That night, our last in Beijing, Felix and I invited Simon to join us for dinner. He had been such a great guide! We asked him to choose the restaurant, and we also asked him to invite his fiancée, who worked in the ticket offices at another of Beijing's major historical sites, the Temple of Heaven. He had talked about her a lot during our days together, and their wedding date was only a few weeks away. The four of us had a very pleasant dinner together and, knowing Simon pretty well by now, I wasn't surprised to hear her say how much she was looking forward to being married.

"How nice!" I said to myself when I heard her comment. "How nice that they are so much in love!" But love was not at all what she was talking about. She was looking forward to being married, she went on to say, because for the first time in her life she would have her own bedroom!

Well, that seemed really strange—until she explained that she had lived her whole life in an apartment that measured eighteen square meters, which is about twelve by fifteen feet. *Okay*, I thought to myself, *that might be a bit tight*. But she had not finished. In that apartment with her and her parents lived both her maternal and paternal grandparents—seven people! She slept on the floor in the main room (as opposed to the tiny kitchen), and it was often hard to get to sleep at night, she said, because her grandparents liked to watch television until late in the evening.

What an eye-opener that conversation was! It reinforced to me just how big a gap there was between the standard of living enjoyed by ex-pats and the vast majority of the Chinese people. During the years before the Communist revolution, many foreigners lived here quite luxuriously, especially in Shanghai, and now history was beginning to repeat itself as people like Felix and me moved into China. It's not surprising that this would provoke a certain resentment in the Chinese people against foreigners. More commonly, at least as far as I had been able to observe, it produced a fascination with foreigners and an intense curiosity into whatever we were doing, eating, or buying at the moment. I felt lucky that, so far, I had encountered only people who were simply curious and not openly antagonistic to their country's newcomers.

Chapter 10
My Mother-in-Law Comes for a Visit

Not long after we returned from our visit to Beijing that October of 2003, my French mother-in-law and her boyfriend arrived for a visit. They were only going to stay two months, she told us, because they had already made plans to spend the Christmas holidays back in France with friends from their dance club. *Thank heaven for Christmas!* was my silent reaction to that announcement. Felix's parents had divorced years earlier and each one had a new partner. This put me at a disadvantage since I had two pairs of in-laws to get along with while Felix had just one. I think that in my next life I should be allowed to marry an orphan since I've already paid double dues with in-laws in this one!

I had always gotten along well with my mother-in-law before. She called me "*la petite mexicaine*" and admired my long, black hair. In fact, the first time I met her she said how much she would like to have a granddaughter with hair like mine that she could weave into two long braids. She had always been easy to get along with, and I was happy to welcome her to meet Julia, even if my daughter, with her blond, curly hair, would never have the long, dark braids that her grandmother had envisioned. Felix was a masculine copy of his mother, something I had never noticed until one Halloween several years earlier when he dressed up in drag.

Even though I had only lived in Shanghai for four months and was still learning the ins and outs of caring for a small child, I now found myself drafted into the new roles of tour guide, translator, and shopping companion as well. I don't know whether it was my black hair or what, but my mother-in-law simply could not get it into her head that I did not speak much more

Chinese than she did. Each time we left the compound, she would constantly be asking me to "tell them this, tell them that, or what does this sign say?" She seemed to forget that I was her petite *mexicaine*, not her petite *chinoise*. No matter how many times I told her, it made absolutely no difference.

In addition, my mother-in-law had adopted some new and difficult habits since we last spent time together. She and her boyfriend were now eating a macrobiotic and vegetarian diet and wanted to stick closely to organic and whole-grain foods. Moreover, she was limiting herself to drinking only one glass of water a day, believing that more water was not only unnecessary but caused urinary tract infections. All this came at the advice of her daughter, Felix's sister, who had also convinced her that using deodorant was antinatural and caused breast cancer.

Well, the result of this return to nature was that, in spite of her liberal use of Paris perfume by Yves Saint Laurent, her body odor was, shall we say, quite pungent. I came to truly dread the moments at the beginning and end of each day when she would come to wish me "*bonjour, ma cherie*" or "*bonne nuit*" in the traditional French manner with three cheek-to-cheek kisses. I learned to just take a deep breath and hold it until the aromatic greeting was over.

It became a real nightmare to buy groceries and prepare meals for our French houseguests. She wanted me to ask whether each fruit or each vegetable was organic or whether each fish was wild or farm raised. She continued her inquiries every single time we bought groceries, no matter whether we were at Carrefour or a street market—and me with only the most basic vocabulary after just a few months' residence in China! Most of the Chinese vendors responded to our bumbling questions by saying, "*Ting bu dong*," which means "I don't understand." Whether they really didn't understand us or just didn't want to bother with two crazy foreign ladies, it really did not matter in the long run. If we wanted to buy, *this* is what the vendor had for sale, period.

My mother-in-law was firmly convinced that organic foods must surely be available in Shanghai because China is geographically close to Japan, and

Japan is where the macrobiotic diet originated. But no amount of Gallic logic could make it so. For the length of her stay with us, she and her boyfriend ate mostly boiled white rice and fruit. She would look up from her miserable meals and scold me for eating something like cheese or fish. Many times I would just flee to my room rather than listen to another lecture on my poor dietary habits. Finding any type of Western food was difficult enough in China in those days, and I told her in many different ways, some polite and some not, that she should be grateful for what we could find, but she never understood that. The second time she came to visit us in China she brought an entire suitcase full of "her food," and I was glad she did.

We did manage to pass some enjoyable moments with Felix's mother and her partner, especially the days we spent exploring the part of Shanghai called the French Concession. This large neighborhood was under French control during the late 1800s and early 1900s, when most of urban Shanghai was divided up between the Western powers of America, Britain, and France. The houses here are lovely and look very European, plus the verdant Fuxing Park, originally called the French Park, was a nice place to stroll and watch the local practitioners of martial arts, ballroom dance, or tai chi go through their paces. Some of the old buildings here were still in bad repair in 2003, but many had been renovated and served as *tres chic* restaurants, shops, or art galleries. Ex-pat couples from around the world who wanted to live in the most fashionable and lively district in Shanghai came here to live.

Ironically, it is in the French Concession that three important landmarks to twentieth-century Chinese Communism can be found, and visited, if one so desires. Homes belonging to Zhou Enlai and Sun Yat-sen are now museums and appear much as they did when these important Chinese leaders lived in them before revolution swept the country in the late 1940s. Another house commemorates the founding of the Chinese Communist Party, which occurred on that site in 1921. Mao Tse-tung was one of the twelve official delegates, all of whom had to flee when police arrived to break up the secret meeting.

I came to love this area of Shanghai more than any other. I always enjoyed exploring its streets and alleyways, and I used to wonder how the lives of the people here compared to our life in the foreigners' compounds. Beautiful plane trees, a legacy of the French, provided refreshing shade and lovely green spaces throughout this neighborhood, making the French Concession unlike any other part of Shanghai. I think my French in-laws felt more comfortable here than they did anywhere else in the city, which at least gave us something nice in common, something that was pleasant to recall about their visit.

One day late in their time in Shanghai, my mother-in-law's boyfriend asked if the three of us could go shopping together. He wanted to have two dresses made to order for her as a gift and wanted some help to find good-quality silk material from which she could make her choice. Of course, I said yes and, leaving Julia in the capable hands of Xiao Tian, off we went. I escorted them to various silk stores for the better part of a day, and I watched, patiently at first, as they discussed the fabrics up one side and down the other. After several hours they had purchased nothing but a small silk scarf—for a friend, they said. I finally took them to The King of Silk store on the famous shopping street, Nanjing Lu, and told them that if they could not find something they liked here, then I didn't know what else I could do for them. After some time, they decided that yes, they would order the dresses there. That was all, just two dresses. I told them we might not be able to return to the silk stores before they had to return home, so they should buy their silk goods *now*, but they said they wouldn't want more.

Of course, a few days later they decided that they should have purchased more of those nice scarves, and they wanted to go back to the boutique where we had found the one scarf they did buy. At that time I was still learning my way around downtown Shanghai, and I had no idea where that particular boutique was located. "Not a problem!" said my mother-in-law triumphantly. She had saved the small pink-and-gray plastic shopping bag from that store and pointed to what looked like a street address printed in one corner. I tried to explain to her in French that I had received that identical bag from various merchants around town, and the address was probably not from the store she wanted. My French vocabulary is reasonably good, but she claimed she did not understand me, or perhaps she just did not want to admit defeat. Anyway, nothing would do but that the three of us get in a taxi the next day and tell the driver to take us to the address on the bag. It was a long drive down crowded streets and through back alleys, but after an hour or so we finally arrived at the address on that bag, and voilà! It was not a chic boutique at all, but an old, rundown building far away from the fancy shopping district we had visited earlier in the week. I was so mad that I made the taxi driver take us to the nearest McDonald's (yes, there were several in Shanghai back then), and I ordered a McFlurry to calm my fraying nerves. I enjoyed it down to the very last drop, completely ignoring my mother-in-law's renewed warnings about the dangers of eating dairy.

Another great day in China with my mother-in-law was our visit to the famous Yuyuan Garden and Bazaar. The garden half of this historic complex includes two dozen classic Chinese buildings interspersed with ponds and connected by bridges and walkways. It is very beautiful and several hundred years old. Walls divide the garden into six distinctive areas, each with its own personality and special viewing pavilion. Walking along the crooked pathways, we felt as if we were inside a maze. We traversed the zigzag bridge that leads to the central teahouse, an architectural gem, and later on passed the huge Ming rockery, which is a natural garden sculpture designed to resemble the peaks, caves, and gorges of southern China.

Although the garden covers only five acres, its complicated layout makes it seem so much bigger. We built up quite an appetite long before we arrived at the bazaar section of the complex, which features dozens of small shops famous for their Chinese crafts and delicious snacks. The longer we walked through the bazaar, the more nervous my in-laws became. What to do? There was no Western-style food available in this classically Asian bazaar! Remaining as calm as possible, I announced that we had no alternative. We would just have to eat lunch in the bazaar, and that's what we did. I enjoyed a delicious noodle soup with vegetables and bits of spiced pork while my in-laws, looking quite miserable, ate their plates of steaming white rice in silence.

Sightseeing with my mother-in-law gave me more opportunities to be out and about in Shanghai than I had been able to manage earlier. I also felt quite comfortable by now leaving Julia in the care of Xiao Tian. She was proving to be a very capable caretaker; plus, it worried Felix to have his daughter subjected to the "dangers and dirt" one experienced outside our compound. That made my excursions as a tour guide child free, and I was able to go farther and be away from home longer than I had before. *That part of their visit I truly enjoyed.*

One thing that totally surprised the three of us was seeing so many Chinese pedestrians out on the street in their pajamas. At any hour of the day or night we might see a woman in a frilly nightgown or a man in brightly patterned flannel pants and top. One ex-pat friend told me they did this because many people had only one or two outfits, and if they were being laundered, wearing pajamas was a reasonable alternative. Other people said it was because Western-style pajamas were still a novelty in China and wearing them was a way to show how modern or wealthy one was. Either way, it was certainly a popular outfit to wear while doing one's morning shopping, and for us it soon became part of the daily panorama. After I returned home to Mexico, I would often go out of the house in my pajamas to visit the neighborhood drugstore or video store, even though it caused lots of stares from the people who passed me on the streets. I suppose a little part of me will always be Chinese.

When my mother-in-law and her partner finally returned to France, we could not believe how bad their room smelled. The odor of her body and his feet remained in the room long after they had departed. Even Felix recommended that we have the carpet and curtains cleaned and leave the windows open for a couple of weeks to ventilate the room. Nothing seemed to work, except time. It took a full month before we could enter the room without gagging.

☼

As I did my tour-guide duties with my in-laws week by week, I realized that Felix had been correct about at least one aspect of life in China. He had reassured me as I waited with infant Julia back in Mexico that China was a very safe place to live. There was very little crime, he said, and people were safe to walk the streets at any time in any neighborhood. This is very different from my home country, Mexico, where burglaries and muggings are unfortunately common events. Even during my travels in the US and Europe, my family and I were warned to stay out of certain high-crime neighborhoods and to be vigilant about our purses and jewelry at all times.

This was just never a problem in China during the years I lived in Shanghai. Felix and I could walk the streets at any hour and feel perfectly safe. I never worried about taking Julia in a taxi and going anywhere in town, even at night when I sometimes had to meet Felix in the evening after work. It was wonderful to have that sense of personal safety, and I really enjoyed it. But it came with a price.

The longer we lived in China, the more Felix and I came to understand the extreme control that the Chinese government exerts over its people, and its visitors as well. The Chinese people are subject to rules, regulations, and surveillance in every aspect of their lives, and they have learned that disobedience carries a very high price. So they obey the laws, and as visitors to their country we learned that we had better obey them, too.

The Chinese government begins its control over foreign visitors even before they enter the country, because no one enters China without having passed muster and obtained an entry visa. One employee of the company Felix worked for arrived from Europe without a visa. Whether he did this out of ignorance or pride, I do not know, but it became a nightmare for him. He was arrested at the airport and kept in custody for two days until he could be put on a return flight back home. During those two days he was kept under guard in a windowless room and not even allowed to take a shower. He was able to contact the consulate of his home country, but there was nothing they could do for him. The rules were clear. No visa, no entry.

Once inside China, visitors staying more than just a few days must pass a thorough medical exam to prove they are healthy and not a danger to the nation's safety. I will never forget my exam and its frightening strawberry incident! In addition, each and every foreign visitor that an ex-pat family receives in their home must be registered as soon as possible with the local police. This involved taking our visitors, with passport and visa in hand, to our local police station in Zhu Di. Each visitor got a yellow document covered with Chinese characters and stamped with a red star in the middle. If I did not register them within a week of their arrival, I would have to pay a fine and I would get in trouble with the authorities, so there was no point in not complying with this requirement.

Crime is very, very low because the Chinese government severely punishes those who commit crimes, even if the offense is nonviolent. Criminals could be sent to hard-labor camps in the cold northern parts of the country, or even be put to death, especially if the crime were committed against a foreigner. One of Felix's coworkers, a fellow from Germany, had his cell phone stolen. Because he knew who had stolen his phone, he reported it to the authorities. He was later horrified to learn that the thief had been sentenced to death. He said many times that had he known what was going to happen, he would never have reported it.

What China is most famous for, of course, is its huge numbers of people. Felix and I learned to expect large crowds of people no matter where we went or what hour of the day we left our compound. They were always there—filling the sidewalks and store aisles and cramming the buses and streets—people, people everywhere! In addition to centuries of high population density, the mid-twentieth century policies of Communist China's Chairman Mao served to increase the rate of population growth. He encouraged China's women to have as many children as possible because each new person would be an additional set of hands to work for the good of the country. Later on, after Mao's death, the government realized the dangers of such a burgeoning population and instituted its infamous one-child policy in 1978. Although the rate of population growth did slow down, in my opinion this policy was terribly harsh and has caused widespread killings and injustices toward women and girls.

When we lived in China twenty years after the one-child policy began, most couples were still allowed to have only one child, and they all wanted sons. In traditional Chinese culture a son will always remain a part of his family, work for the family, and care for his parents when they grow old. A daughter will ultimately marry into another family, and her value as a worker and bearer of children will accrue to her husband's family, not her birth family. With sons seen as so much more valuable than daughters, many baby girls were abandoned or even killed by their parents, and the orphanages in China were full of girls. It was very gratifying to me to see many of our friends and neighbors at the Shanghai Racquet Club adopt little Chinese girls, especially the Americans. A couple we knew well adopted a beautiful Chinese girl as their third child. They named her Nayia. She had been found abandoned in the snow. My French friend, Agnes, and her husband also adopted a Chinese girl a year or so after we met. At the time we lived in China, it was said that among young people there was just one woman for every four men.

What happened if a Chinese couple disobeyed the law and had a second child? Penalties were severe. The parents had to pay a huge fine, but even worse, the child could not be officially registered with the government and so had no legal standing. This meant the child could not access public services such as education or healthcare, nor could he or she legally marry or inherit property. I actually met one of these illegal children, or *heihaizi*, which literally means "black child." He was a very nice young man who worked for a family living in our compound. They called him *shu-shu* (uncle) instead of *ayi* (aunt), and they liked him very much. He was an excellent worker who helped them with childcare, like walking the kids home from the bus stop, and did lots of the heavier cleaning and housework, like washing the cars.

The couple who hired the *shu-shu* was one of the most interesting and entertaining pairs I met in Shanghai. The husband, Ralph, was an American who worked for an international furniture company. The wife's name was Adriana, and she was from Brazil. They met while Ralph was in Brazil learning to speak Portuguese—he liked his pretty young teacher so much that he married her! Adriana had a natural flair for interior decoration, which is a great talent to have if your husband sells furniture. She was very friendly and outgoing, and by clever networking managed to get herself hired by many of the *tai-tais* to decorate the bland, white apartments we all rented in the Shanghai Racquet Club. She was great at her job and was always escorting one *tai-tai* or another around to various shops and markets in search of the perfect furnishings for their homes.

Ralph and Adriana employed four people to keep their household running smoothly—an *ayi* to cook and do childcare, the *shu-shu* to do heavy cleaning and childcare, and two chauffeurs, one for Rick and one for Adriana and her decorating clients. They paid their *shu-shu* very well, which was extremely fortunate for him. Many *heihaizi* are forced into illegal jobs like prostitution or organized crime because they are not eligible for regular jobs. Working for a foreign family was one of the few ways this fellow could have a decent life. He was such a nice guy, very likable, and he had lovely smile. I remember reading that the Chinese census for the year 2000 estimated that there were eight million of these outlaw children in the population.

Chapter 11
China Days, or Lifestyles of the Ex-Pat

It did not take long for me to realize that the ex-pat community in Shanghai was divided into two groups, regardless of your sex, race, or national origin. Whenever ex-pats met in Shanghai, the third question they always asked each other (after what is your name and where are you from) was this one: Do you live in Puxi or Pudong? Your answer to that question pretty much determined whether or not the other person would want to get to know you. It was not prejudice or snobbery on their part, just simple geography. The Huangpu River cuts the city of Shanghai into two sections. With the intensity of city traffic and only a few roadways over or under the river, it was just too difficult to try to maintain any sort of relationship with someone living on the opposite side.

Luckily my side of town, Puxi, contained my favorite parts of Shanghai, the historic Bund business sector and the beautiful French Quarter, as well as the best-known shopping districts. So we *tai-tais* got to know the popular parts of Puxi pretty well, but rarely undertook the "journey" over to Pudong. We didn't really have to—just gazing across the river to its futuristic skyline was exciting enough!

As fall turned into winter and the weather turned cold, at least for this Mexican girl, I noticed that many of the families in our compound began to spend more time closer to home, inside our familiar walls. The club at the center of our compound organized social activities to help the international residents get to know each other, which was just great as far as I was concerned! When there were no organized activities, ex-pat families seemed to enjoy getting a taste of home by watching English-language television programs on the compound's cable TV network. I guess we all yearned for a little bit of our own world, the one we had left behind, and it felt really good to give ourselves a break from China, even if it was only for an hour or two. Certain programs became almost an addiction, and not just among the women. The men too watched the popular series at night. Everyone knew that these TV stories would be a big part of the conversation at the next party or get-together. Some of our favorites were *Sex and the City*, *Gray's Anatomy*, *Nip and Tuck*, and *24*. However, the TV show that nobody wanted to miss was *American Idol*, which was broadcast on Wednesday and Thursday nights. I can remember looking out my apartment window on those nights and seeing TVs in all the other windows with entire families gathered around them to watch the singers compete. Even the children were allowed to delay their bedtimes on those special nights in order not to miss this program.

The compound's cable TV network had about six English-language channels, plus lots of Chinese channels, which were unintelligible to foreigners like us. Local Chinese families living outside the compound could not subscribe to these foreign channels, and it was illegal for them to attempt to tap into the foreign cable TV lines. Sometimes when we were watching news networks like CNN or TV5, the picture or the sound—or both—would suddenly vanish. This usually happened when the discussion turned to controversial topics like Taiwan or Tibet. Chinese censorship extended even into the homes of foreigners.

When Felix and I arrived in 2003, the cinemas showed only Chinese movies, so most ex-pats purchased their own movies to watch at home. DVD movies in Western languages were widely available, incredibly cheap, and almost certainly pirated. It wasn't the quality of the DVD that made us suspect piracy, but the way you had to buy them. Only a few stores in Shanghai sold foreign DVDs, at least at first glance. Most such stores were disguised as bookstores or antique dealers. When you went inside to look around, an employee would approach you cautiously and whisper in English, "DVD? Come here, DVD." If you responded, they would lead you surreptitiously through a disguised door into the interior section of the store, and there you would find the real merchandise they had for sale. The pirated movies or video games were of excellent quality, and the packaging so good that it was very hard to tell whether they were originals or not. The inventories were from all parts of the world and included everything from the classics to the most recent releases.

Whenever ex-pat friends or neighbors traveled outside China, or had visitors coming from abroad, there was one thing everyone looked forward to. Foreign magazines like *People* or *Hello* were simply not available in China when we arrived in 2003, and everyone hoped that travelers would be bringing several back to China with them. Glossy magazines were as highly valued as a letter from home, and we passed them from one person to another. Everyone took extra good care of the magazines so they would remain in good condition as they made their way around the compound. About two years after we arrived, Western magazines began to appear at Chinese newsstands. However, foreign editions of popular magazines debuted at very high prices, and the government required that Chinese editions of magazines like *Cosmopolitan* be heavily edited—so as not to endanger the morals and values of the Chinese people. So we *tai-tais*, ever resourceful, continued our custom of sharing and circulating every magazine we could get our hands on.

An even bigger problem in China in those days was the scarcity of many common medications. Doctors had access to only a few types of antibiotics, for example, not the many different varieties available in the US or Mexico. The same was true of antihistamines, contraceptives, and something as simple as ear or eye drops. I remember that only one kind of eye drops was available in the stores, and they were not very helpful. I kept getting eye infections every couple of months, probably due to the polluted air, which was especially bad in the winter. Maybe a different kind of eye drop would have worked better for me, but since there was only one kind, I'll never really know for sure. And I almost flipped out when the doctors told me they had just one kind of birth control pill or one kind of contraceptive injection to offer me. I ended up having to ask my mother to please bring with her from Mexico the kind of birth control pill that suited me best. To make up for the few varieties of medicines available to us, most of the *tai-tais* cooperated with each other. Whenever possible, we consulted with each other and brought back our friends' preferred brands of medicine whenever we paid a visit to our home countries or went on vacation to a more Westernized country.

☼

Everyone in our compound experienced these deep differences in food, language, and customs over and over as we spent weeks, months, and often years living in such a profoundly non-Western country like China. Add to that the inability of most ex-pats to read or comprehend any of the signs we encountered in stores or along the roads and you may begin to understand how living day to day in China could sometimes be almost too much to bear. Among the ex-pat families in our compound, these moments of despair were often referred to as "having a China Day." A China Day could include any number of frustrations. Imagine the stress of being misunderstood time and time again when you are trying to accomplish even the simplest of daily tasks. Attending a business or social event could be very tricky because the basic assumptions that all Westerners take for granted are not *at all* how the Chinese structure their thoughts and deeds. Half of what you do or say turns out to be wrong, or not at all what you intended, or it simply gets lost in translation.

I once asked a small group of Felix's Chinese coworkers when I would have the pleasure of meeting their wives. They said nothing, just laughed nervously. I blushed, not understanding what I could possibly have said wrong, and Felix gave me a hard glare. One of the Chinese guys explained to me later that a wife's place was in the home, and it was unthinkable to invite them to a company party—yet here I was, so what did that say about me?!

"Anything can happen" was the constant theme of our lives in Shanghai. I can't tell you how many times I thought back to that Indiana Jones movie—the one that was my first reaction to the word "Shanghai" when Felix initially proposed that we move to China. Something happened every day, it seemed, to remind me of that singer and her jazzy rendition of "Anything Goes." What a perfect theme song to the uncertainty of our daily lives here!

In order to survive, an ex-pat in China had to develop both a sense of humor and an easygoing attitude about these constant frustrations. I had to learn to laugh at my own ineptitude or that of the Chinese when seen by my Western eyes. Everything depends on the lens through which one is looking. Life got so much better when we remembered to "expect the unexpected" and just relax because "anything can happen." We learned to prepare for the worst and hope for the best in every interaction with China and the Chinese people.

The *tai-tais* in general, and me in particular, were always seeking new coping strategies, or maybe even some trick we could use to keep going or even do a little better next time. I learned from one *tai-tai* friend, for example, how important it is to explain to your *ayi* the difference between the paper plates used at a party and ceramic plates—or she may put the paper ones in the dishwasher and flood the apartment. I learned that if I only needed a few items from the local market, it was better to send Xiao Tian shopping than for me to do it—I'd be charged triple the price that merchants charged her. I'd send her out to drop off and pick up our dry cleaning for the same reason. In fact, shopping for almost anything could be problematic. Most clothing shops, at least in 2003–04, carried items sized for only slender Asian bodies. The *tai-tais* told me I would be able to buy all the shirts I wanted here, but trying to find pants that fit Western hips was nearly impossible—and they were right. Most of us had to buy our pants while we were in our home countries or abroad.

☼

Xiao Tian continued to be my very best partner in learning to understand China. As we continued teaching each other how to prepare meals in our three cuisines (Mexican, French, and Chinese), we learned more and more of each other's language and culture. She paid very careful attention when I cooked typical Western dishes and would write down the recipes in a notebook using Chinese characters. Whenever we had some leftover food that she liked, she would ask to bring home samples for her family to try. Over time she became quite adept at making tortillas, Mexican-style soups, and a kind of Mexican lasagna called *chilaquiles rojas*. She also got pretty good at baking French pastries and cooking soufflés. For our part, we regularly ate and enjoyed many of her Chinese stir-fry dishes, her tofu creations, and her homemade Chinese noodles. We liked her cooking so much that eventually, when we were feeling adventurous, I would let her shop for and prepare whatever food she thought we might like. We had many wonderful meals that way, often with vegetables I didn't even recognize.

Many of the *ayis* who worked for Western families learned to cook foods taught to them by their employers. This helped them become a more desirable employee for ex-pat families in the future. But I soon noticed they often picked up much more than cooking from the lady of the house. Many of them also paid close attention to how their *tai-tai* dressed. This was so common that after a few years of employment with a particular family, an *ayi* could be easily matched to the woman who employed her because they would be dressed in a similar style.

The reverse was also true. Early in our relationship Xiao Tian purchased a hat and long-sleeve white cotton gloves for me. Although I did not understand at first, I came to realize that it was important to her that her *tai-tai* be pretty and fashionable, not marred by an ugly suntan. So she always insisted that I put on my hat before I left the apartment. But that did not mean I was always willing to do it, especially at first. She would rush to the door every time I said I was leaving to make sure I was properly protected from the *taiyang* (sun), and I would try to slip out the door before she got there, just like a naughty child. She would sometimes scold me for my unladylike behavior, and I would have to laugh because it reminded me so much of Mammy scolding Miss Scarlet in the movie *Gone with the Wind*. The funny thing is that even now, after having been away from Xiao Tian for almost a decade, I still try to remember my hat whenever I know I'm going to be outside for more than a few minutes. Xiao Tian would be so proud!

Most of the ex-pat women I met in Shanghai were not accustomed to having household workers since it is far too expensive in Europe and the US. They loved the idea of having someone else do the domestic chores, but they often told me it made them feel uneasy. They felt that having someone around all day gave them less privacy, as if they were under observation all the time. It did not bother me at all because in Mexico we are accustomed to having household servants, who often become an important part of the family.

That is how we felt about Xiao Tian. She was rapidly becoming someone very important and loved in our home. So I was surprised and angered to find Western families in Shanghai who treated their *ayis* very poorly. This seemed to be more common in the families from France and Germany, who would adopt attitudes of superiority and show little respect for the women they employed. No wonder they felt uncomfortable with these "strangers" inside their homes! Xiao Tian told me that *xiao* means "little" and *tian*, which was her father's family name, means "land." So her name literally meant "little piece of land" or "child of Tian." That first week in Shanghai it took me three or four days to be able to remember and then pronounce her name reasonably well, but I was quite proud of myself for this achievement. Many of the *tai-tais*, I later noticed, did not even bother to learn their *ayi's* name and simply called them "*Ayi.*"

Xiao Tian was married, and her one child had turned out to be a daughter, named Chi Moon, who was eleven years old in 2003. Although Xiao Tian was in every respect a hardworking woman, her husband, unfortunately, was not. He was always playing *mahjong* and losing lots of money betting on his games. *Mahjong* was very popular, and we often saw Chinese men, usually older ones, playing in the parks around Shanghai. Xiao Tian had to keep the money she earned hidden in secret locations around her apartment to keep it out of her husband's reach. Not surprisingly, their relationship was not very good. At times I saw her sad or quite worried that they would not be able to pay their rent or have enough money to buy the hexagonal bricks of charcoal that they burned to heat the room where the three of them lived.

Their apartment building had two floors, each divided into many, many single-room apartments of about eighteen square meters. One communal and unheated bathroom was located at the end of the long hall on each of the two floors. Going to the bathroom in the winter, she said, was not a pleasant experience. Since our apartment had four bathrooms, each with a heat lamp, I offered to let her take her showers in one of them whenever she wished, and she eagerly accepted. This wasn't the first or last time I would feel pangs of guilt while living in China. Why was I lucky enough to live with so many luxuries when literally millions and millions of people around me suffered in the heat and cold, often hungry and crammed into spaces where privacy and human dignity were almost impossible?

I came to admire Xiao Tian greatly. Her life was a struggle day after day just to survive, and yet she always greeted me with a smile and a sunny attitude. We were so happy to have her in our lives! When Christmas arrived, Felix and I wanted to do something special for her, so we bought her an electric motorbike at Carrefour. We hoped she would like it, but we totally underestimated the impact of our gift. When she saw it she started crying like no one I have ever seen cry before, and just kept hugging and kissing us. She was able to sell (yes, sell!) her terribly rusty old bicycle and ride to work comfortably on her new electric bike, which she charged up every three days using an outlet in our building.

Chapter 12
First Trip to Thailand

During our first winter in Shanghai, Felix and I decided to go someplace warm and tropical. We had heard good things about Thailand, so we decided to spend a week there—three days in Bangkok and three days at Koh Samui, an island off the east coast of Thailand. I loved the gorgeous temples in Bangkok. They looked as if they had precious stones decorating their walls and were home to some of the biggest golden statues of Buddha I had ever seen, or even imagined. Monks wrapped in bright-orange tunics were frequent sights on the streets. They are not supposed to work at all. Their sole mission in life is to pray, and it is the duty of the faithful to support them with charitable gifts of food or money.

Bangkok was a big, busy city, full of traffic, but that was okay because it was so much fun to ride around in the *tuk-tuks*. These three-wheeled motorcycles carried passengers around town just like taxicabs. They were fast and cheap, but best of all, open to the fresh air. I was surprised to find so many huge stores devoted solely to jewelry. We visited one that was two stories high and the size of a typical department store. Half of the store was devoted to jewelry with precious stones like emeralds, sapphires, and rubies, while the other half featured jewelry with semiprecious stones. The selection of merchandise was enormous. I was crazy about rubies in those days, so I headed for that section to look for some earrings to match my favorite red outfits. Felix was not very happy about this and rushed me out of the store before I could get a good look around. I suppose that was the best thing for our family budget, but I never quite forgave him for that lost opportunity!

I had not known that Thailand was so famous for its silk, but everywhere we went there were shops selling silk fabric in incredibly beautiful colors and textures. The shops all had in-house tailors who could complete a custom-made suit or dress in twenty-four hours. I had fallen in love with the traditional Thai dresses worn by the stewardesses on our Thai Airlines flight, so I had one made for me in gold and navy-blue silk. It looked so beautiful and elegant, or so I thought. Later on, when I modeled it for my mother during one of her visits to Shanghai, she said it would be a great costume for a Halloween party. Gee thanks, Mom! I think by that time Asia was really getting into my system. I was finding almost everything fascinating, and not so odd and "foreign" as before. I was totally embracing the clothes, the food, and my life as a *tai-tai*.

I have always been an early riser, like my dad. Felix, however, liked to sleep late on his days off. It took all the energy he could muster, he claimed, to keep up with his exhausting job, his long commute, and the inevitable "China Days." He could be very grumpy if awakened before he was ready, so I developed the habit of taking an early walk with Julia every morning. Julia would wake up about 5:00 a.m., I would give her a quick bottle of milk, and off we would go—unless it was raining, of course.

I continued this tradition of early morning walks even on our several vacations in Southeast Asia. To me, hanging out in the hotel room until late in the morning was a total waste of time, and I soon discovered that there is nothing more fascinating than watching a new day begin in an Asian village or town. In most places the wet market, or fresh-food market, sets up on certain mornings of the week at about 7:00 a.m., then closes up at about 9:30 as the heat of the day intensifies. Some merchants buy and sell live animals, while others stock their stalls with fresh seafood or fruits and vegetables, which vary in appearance as much as they do in taste and texture. Most of them were delicious! Several of my favorites were the mangosteen, the dragon fruit, the rambutan, and the volleyball-size green Thai grapefruit.

The most interesting part of the show for me was always the merchants themselves, who enticed shoppers with a virtual opera of loud cries announcing, I assumed, the freshness or superior quality of whatever it was they had for sale. Peddlers also walked up and down the market pathways competing with the more established merchants. They seemed to specialize in ready-to-eat treats and goodies. Many times I would stand nearby and watch as a cook prepared an individual plate of stir-fry for a customer. It was just fascinating to watch how they mixed and cooked the ingredients, adding strange plants and exotic spices that produced the most incredible aromas. I especially admired how certain cooks would begin with some sort of pasty dough and turn it into noodles of varying shapes and sizes with just the skillful movements of their handheld utensils.

By the time Julia and I got back to the hotel each morning, I already had a mental list of the foods we should try for breakfast or dinner—and I had already had a good, closeup look at the local people and their culture. What a show sleepy Felix missed! I really enjoyed pretending to be a local for a couple of days, and I continued these early-bird explorations whenever I could.

One of the things I noticed in many of the restaurants, hotels, and even the parks in Thailand were signs that forbade bringing a round, spiny fruit inside the establishment. I wondered what it could be and finally asked someone. The spine-covered fruit, I learned, was called a durian, and it is extremely popular, particularly among emigrants of Chinese descent, who call it the king of fruits. I would later learn that the shape of the roof of a famous concert hall in Singapore, called the Esplanade, was inspired by this spiny "king of fruits."

On my last morning in Thailand I finally came across a vendor with a big pile of durians for sale. Before I even laid eyes on the fruit I had noticed a very ugly odor in that section of the street market. I thought perhaps there was a dead animal nearby or maybe a toilet that wouldn't flush. When I noticed the display of durians and walked over to the stall, I realized that the smell was coming from the durian stand! The vendor was a friendly fellow. Like many Asians, he was fascinated by Julia and her blond, curly hair, so I was able to interact with him and get a careful look at the fruit.

It was about ten inches long and looked like a green hedgehog. When the vendor cut through the thick, hard shell to show me the yellow "marshmallow" sections inside, I had to try hard not to recoil at the intensified smell—it was awful!

At that moment my dad came to mind. He always taught me to be open to every gastronomic experience and to give every food a try. You can learn a lot about other cultures by their foods, he taught me, and sampling their food shows that you were well brought up. In Mexico, I had learned to eat and enjoy such unusual treats as agave worms, ant eggs, grasshoppers, and even bull testicle and penis. My dad's teachings had served me well on visits with my in-laws in France where "*la petite mexicaine*" ate everything she was given, including the famous escargot snails and river eels. So it wasn't such a big leap for me to sample this stinky and bizarre-looking fruit. In fact, once I found it, I knew I would have to give it a try.

The friendly vendor asked me where I was from and politely offered me one of the bright-yellow "marshmallows" on a stick. It looked so pretty, but I still had to pinch my nostrils closed just to bring it close enough to my mouth to pop it inside.

Oh my God, it was the most horrendous thing I have ever tasted in my life! The texture was like butter, and the flavor impossible to describe, except to say that it was terrible. For a few seconds I could neither breathe nor swallow—I did not know what to do! My eyes started watering, and I probably turned green as well. Then, with no conscious thought about it at all, I did something totally unexpected—I vomited.

I felt waves of nausea for the rest of the morning, something I had not experienced since I was pregnant, but at least I knew one thing. After my up-close and personal experience with the king of fruits, I now knew exactly why there were so many signs warning people not to bring their durians inside with them!

Chapter 13
Weekends with Felix

By the time weekends arrived, Felix always claimed he was exhausted, so he rarely wanted to go out and do things. It took a miracle for him to agree to leave the house and "have some fun" on a Saturday or Sunday. After serious campaigning on my part, we finally reached a compromise, and he agreed to take us on one family outing per weekend.

I remember we both enjoyed our "voyage" (or so it seemed) to Century Park in Pudong, the part of Shanghai located on the far side of the Huangpu River. To get there and back took practically the whole day, but it was worth it. We chose to take the ferry across the river that morning so we could get the best view of Pudong's futuristic skyscrapers. It is no coincidence that these ultramodern buildings are positioned to face the historic buildings of Shanghai's Bund, home of the city's colonial masters. The past and the future, the West and the East—all the parts of Shanghai's soul—confront each other here along the river. It was hard to believe that none of these ultramodern buildings—in fact nothing at all in modern-day Pudong—were more than fourteen years old. It had been nothing but a marsh and scattered villages in 1990, when China's leaders started their country on its pell-mell rush to modernize.

Now in 2004, this district had become the proud face of twenty-first-century Shanghai. Just like many other Shanghai tourists, we lined up along the railing on the north side of the ferry boat. That way we could use the famous Oriental Pearl Tower, which looks more like a space station than a building, as a backdrop for our family photos. Once we exited the ferry, our taxi drove us right past the Jin Mao Tower, the tallest building in China, at least in 2004. We then cruised down the wide, straight Century Boulevard to Century Park, also known as Shiji Gongyuan. The green belts along the boulevard and the park itself were designed by a French architect and are very picturesque. We put Julia in her stroller and walked leisurely along the landscaped paths of this eco park, through its forested sections and along the lake. We had a lovely day, and I hoped to return in a year or two when Julia would be old enough to enjoy Pudong's state-of-the-art aquarium and its zoo/museum devoted exclusively to insects—creepy, but certain to be fascinating!

For a quickie weekend outing I often asked Felix to take us for a walk through the Gubei flower market, which was located much nearer to our compound in the same section of Shanghai. In addition to whatever flowers were in season, vendors at this market also sold caged birds, lizards, chameleons, and fish for home aquariums. As far as year-old Julia was concerned, this was as good as a trip to the zoo. These small animals were so colorful and lively, and she could get up close and really observe them. She loved it!

Felix, however, found our sightseeing junkets somewhat tedious and soon grew tired of "wandering around and accomplishing nothing." He had his own ideas of what constituted a fun outing. For about a year he went through an intense period of collecting Chinese antiques for our apartment. With its four bedrooms and baths, the apartment did, I'll admit, have plenty of empty space to fill. We spent many of our weekends in 2004 on marathon shopping trips for old furniture, stone statues, paintings, musical instruments, and oriental carpets. For a while he decided we simply had to visit each of his favorite antique stores on the street Huaxiang Lu and in the Gubei district at least twice a month, and this was with me carrying an infant and all her gear in tow! It became like our family sport to spend the weekends rummaging through warehouse after warehouse of dusty old furniture. Most of the stuff dated from the Ming and Ching dynasties, and was imported, the dealers told us, from the northern province of Shaanxi or from Beijing and Tibet.

I must admit that it was interesting, some of the time, to learn about the original uses of these old pieces of furniture. Many of them had been renovated and repurposed for modern use. My favorite was a large wooden kitchen cupboard with lots of drawers and compartments. The drawers along the bottom of the cupboard were made of parallel bars of wood. I was amazed, and slightly grossed out, to learn that these drawers were intended to be cages for storing live chickens right inside your kitchen—even the bottom of the drawers was made of bars so the chicken poop could fall out of the cage and down onto the floor below! We liked the cabinet, and the story of its former use, so much that we ended up buying it and putting it in our living room—without any chickens, however!

So many different types and styles of furniture were on display. The antique dealers seemed to have something for everyone. By talking with them, we learned that European shoppers preferred to buy furniture in natural wood tones, while Americans went crazy for the bright colors of Tibetan styles. After seeing us so often, the antique store owners got to know us well and would telephone Felix whenever a new and promising shipment of merchandise arrived. We eventually bought quite a few items from these antique warehouses. One I remember with particular fondness was a lovely altar table, long and narrow in form but with some simple carving to give it an interesting shape. Although we used it as a side board in our dining room, it had probably come from some long-ago family's shrine. Felix put a lot of time and energy into buying pieces that he liked and found interesting. He was quite proud of his expanding collection and believed it would be worth a lot of money in Europe—if he could ever manage to get any of it back there to sell, that is.

One of the things Felix liked most about the antique shopping—and which I liked the least—was haggling. It became one of his favorite sports, so to speak. He just loved playing cat-and-mouse games with any merchant, but especially the antique dealers. He could keep the game going on and on, getting the shopkeeper to go lower and lower until finally the two of them would be shouting at each other, pretending to be insulted. I always stood off to one side, embarrassed and annoyed. Whenever Felix felt like the merchant wasn't giving him a rock-bottom price, his tactic was to walk away and, if possible, begin looking at another seller's merchandise. As often as not the first merchant would come running after him and accept Felix's "final" offer, usually with moans and wails of financial ruin.

By the time Felix had furnished several of the rooms in our apartment, he decided that the actual price that most merchants would accept was about one-fifth (20 percent) of the first price they quoted you. Felix's best French buddy, Michel, who had already lived in Shanghai for three years when we arrived, agreed with him on this. Even though I knew they were probably right, I just hated all the drama and pretense of the haggling game. However, I didn't want to fall victim to high prices either, so in time I developed my own system. I decided that I would pay a price for any item that was more or less what it would cost me back in Mexico. This cut the haggling way down, and when I was not in the mood for bargaining, which was most of the time, I would do my shopping at department stores, where the prices were fixed and there was no need to begin that awful cat-and-mouse routine.

Eventually I grew tired of traipsing through warehouse after warehouse every weekend—they were very cold in the winter and hot as a furnace in the summer. Felix seemed to have very little interest in visiting any shops I liked or even touring Shanghai's historic monuments or museums. I was hungering to get to know many parts of my new city better, but I didn't relish the idea of exploring all by myself. Then I got a really lucky break in the spring of 2004. Felix announced at dinner one night that he had invited the family of a business colleague to come and spend a week in our apartment. Normally I would not have been that enthusiastic about houseguests, but this time it was different. The fellow was named Kristophe, and he was a German who lived and worked in the distant city of Changchun. As was often the case with the Germans, his wife and son had remained behind and still lived in Germany. Now that his family was coming to visit him in China, he wanted to show them our beautiful city of Shanghai. It was a match made in heaven! I spoke German, our apartment had two extra bedrooms, and Kristophe and his family were happy to have me join them on their sightseeing trips all over town. I had a great time playing tourist with them and did not have to drag a grumpy Felix along with me.

I took them the first day for walks in two of my favorite spots, the historic Bund riverfront and the French Concession, to introduce them to our city. Then that evening Kristophe pulled out his guidebook to Shanghai, and like good Germans, he and his wife devised a well-organized list of the places they most wanted to see.

We spent two full days exploring the People's Square (Renmin Guangchang) in the center of Shanghai, a beautifully landscaped park with several impressive buildings housing some of the city's best museums. His wife especially wanted to tour the Shanghai Museum, which showcases five thousand years of Chinese art and artifacts. Its outside is as impressive as what's on display inside—three massive square stories are topped by a circular fourth story, symbolizing a round heaven above the square earth.

After several hours inside, Kristophe surprised me by leading us out of the museum and over to an old-fashioned building with a clock tower. He had done his research and explained to us that this building was all that remained of the People's Park original facilities. In the early twentieth century the park had been a horse-racing track and the center of ex-pat social life in our then-notorious city. This building had been the racetrack's elegant clubhouse. We went inside and found that it had been repurposed by the post-revolutionary government into an art museum. The Chinese paintings inside were nice, I suppose, but what really grabbed our attention was the building's lavish marble interior, which dated from the 1930s—Shanghai's glory years. Kristophe then led us back to the main entrance under the clock and up a flight of stairs that featured horses' heads worked into the design of the iron bannisters. On the top floor was a rooftop terrace with a restaurant-bar and a glorious view of People's Park below. It was such a pretty place to relax after visiting the museums. From that height, you could easily see the round shape of the park and imagine its former life as a racetrack. My dad would love this bar, I remember thinking, and I decided it would be a great place to bring him the next time he and my mother came to visit.

The Germans and I also saw Shanghai's famous Jade Buddha Temple. It had been closed for thirty years following the Communist revolution but now had reopened with about one hundred monks in residence. Another day we took a boat tour along the Huangpu River and got off in Pudong to see that side of town. I remember we all rode the elevator up the eighty-eight stories of the Jin Mao Tower, then the tallest in China. After that, at the request of Kristophe's son, we took a ride *under* the river from Pudong back to Puxi through the Bund Sightseeing Tunnel. Halfway between a subway trip and a carnival ride, the tunnel treats visitors to a neon-and-laser light show as they zip from one side of the river to the other. It even includes a musical soundtrack. Described by most people as psychedelic, kitschy, or just plain ridiculous, it is a very Shanghai experience, and something that everybody ought to experience at least once—so we did!

Funny thing about having German houseguests—they are just so casual about nudity, much more so than we are in Mexico. I remember walking into our kitchen the morning after they arrived. I was dressed only in my nightgown and barely awake as I stumbled into the room and found Kristophe pouring himself a cup of tea. He had just finished taking a shower and was completely nonchalant about the fact that he was wearing only tiniest of underpants, a bikini really.

As embarrassed as I was, I couldn't help but notice how much he looked like Daniel Craig, the actor who played James Bond. Oh my gosh! I was so startled that I could barely speak, and it took me three attempts to get out an appropriate greeting.

"*Buenos* . . . uh, good . . . uh, *guten morgen*," I finally managed to say, as I averted my eyes from the handsome, nearly nude guy in front of me.

"Ah, *guten morgen*, Adela!" he said with a pleasant, open smile, and then leaned over to give me a good-morning kiss. I almost fainted with shock, way too much for this conservative Mexican girl, and I beat a hasty retreat back to my room. Playing the tourist was only one of the pleasures of hosting the Germans that week! He was such a delight for my eyes, and I couldn't help but admire this Western version of male beauty, one that I had almost forgotten after so many months in Asia.

After about a year of shopping, when Felix had managed to decorate every possible space in our apartment, I breathed a sigh of relief. Thinking that we had finished with those interminable days of chasing furniture, I thought that the time had come when we could finally spend our weekends in a more relaxing, conventional manner. But no, his capricious imagination found another target. I did not even have time to savor a few weekends doing things I liked before his French spirit decided to dedicate itself to gourmet cooking.

Now every weekend he would bake pastries and cakes, which then inspired him to become a grill master, and of course, he had to buy all the equipment and cooking gadgets that baking and grilling would require. So off we went again on the weekends, searching through kitchen stores to buy equipment, then searching for a metalsmith who could build just the grill Felix himself had designed. He would scour the internet for barbecue recipes, and every weekend he would prepare one or two of them using various cuts of meat. To show his prowess as a chef, he usually invited someone, with or without their entire family, to dine with us at each of these feasts. It was a great day for him when we discovered a butcher shop that featured meat from Australia. They would prepare the meat in a style similar to what Americans use for cookouts, and not in the traditional Chinese style. All of this shopping and preparation was very time consuming. Eventually we found a supplier of meat who had come from Qingdao, a region of China renown for producing grain and therefore beef. His meat was as good as Australian beef, but not as expensive.

I was becoming very tired of always having to do what he liked, to do only what interested him. But being an optimist, I kept thinking these obsessions would eventually fade and he would become receptive to trying activities that were more to my liking. That did happen, but rarely. One special event does stand out in my mind. While touring the People's Park with Kristophe and his family, I saw posters advertising an upcoming performance of *Phantom of the Opera* at Shanghai's gorgeous and ultramodern opera house. Here was something that did appeal to my Frenchman, and with only a little campaigning on my part, we had a lovely night out at the theater, enjoying both the show and our inspection of this architectural masterpiece.

I was always hearing ideas about family outings from the *tai-tais*, and I did get him to try some of them. But you always had to be cautious in China because "anything can happen," and often did. Things were not always what they appeared to be to our Western eyes. The best example of this disconnect between West meets East happened to one of my *tai-tai* friends when she and her family visited the Shanghai Wild Animal Park.

My friend's name was Adriana. She and her family lived in another of the apartment buildings in our compound. Adriana was the interior decorator from Brazil I mentioned earlier—the one who so happily employed the *heihaizi*, or illegal child, as their male household helper. Adriana's neighbors across the hall were a family from India or Pakistan, I can't quite remember which. The wife and mother of this family was a pleasant and friendly woman who told Adriana that if she ever wanted to have a lovely family outing, she heartily recommended they visit this park. It was located on the opposite side of Shanghai on the Pudong side of the river, but it would be well worth the long drive, she assured them.

My friend had heard about these types of animal parks before. The animals are allowed to roam free while the human visitors drive through the park and watch them from inside a vehicle, usually the visitors' own car. It sounded like just the thing Adriana had been looking for. Her husband's parents were coming to visit them in Shanghai for a month, and she needed to find things to do that would be suitable for three generations. Adriana had two children ages twelve and three, plus she was eight months pregnant with her third child. Riding comfortably through the park while gazing at exotic animals would be interesting for the kids, she thought, but not too taxing for an older couple and a pregnant woman. It sounded perfect.

The first surprise upon arrival at the Wild Animal Park was the discovery that they could not ride through in their own car, a minivan that seated everyone comfortably. No, after buying their tickets they were told to wait for the park's bus, and when it arrived they could not believe their eyes. It was a jalopy of a bus, rickety, with big patches of rust showing through the peeling paint on its exterior. Once aboard the bus, they noticed that a number of the windows were stuck open or closed, and there was no way to move them. Her husband tried but could not get them to budge. The bus was rank with the smell of the driver's chain-smoked cigarettes, and many of the seats were stained with small globs of something reddish-brown and sticky. Sitting in the back of the bus, my friend braced herself for what she feared would be a bumpy ride. They had not chosen the seats in the rear, they had been relegated there by a group of Chinese tourists who arrived last, but had no qualms about pushing past the foreign family to board the bus first—remember, the Chinese do not follow the Western custom of lining up. Having lived in Shanghai for five years, my friends took this event calmly and boarded when they could.

The ride began in the field containing the herbivores. It was bumpy, but pleasant enough, even though the giraffes poked their heads halfway into the windows of the bus to reach the sweets offered to them by the Chinese passengers. Then the bus arrived at a big set of double gates, and that's when the real action began. As the bus came to a stop between the two gates, two park employees stepped up to the bus and tied several live chickens along each side of the bus. They hung them upside down about two feet below the passenger windows. When this happened the Chinese passengers started to get excited, although my friend and her family had no idea why. The employees opened the second gate, the driver floored the gas pedal, and the bus roared into the carnivore corral.

They knew it was the carnivore area because in no time a dozen or so thin, scrawny lions ran toward the bus and began leaping at the chickens tied along the outside. Intent on getting themselves a decent meal, the lions, clawing and growling, quickly dispatched every one of the chickens. Drops of their blood spattered around the inside and the outside of the bus, and chicken feathers flew in through the open windows. Adriana was frightened and shocked by the lions, and her poor kids were terrified and screaming. The Chinese passengers, however, were running from the windows on one side of the bus to the windows along the other side, hoping to get the best view as each lion made its "kill." This caused the rickety old bus to lean way over to one side and then to the other, and Adriana told me that had her husband and in-laws not moved quickly to counterbalance the lurching of the bus, she thought it might just have tumbled over sideways. The bus deposited its passengers back at the park's central plaza. More animals were on display here along a pedestrian trail, but Adriana and her family had had enough. They were all quite upset and just wanted to go home and try to forget about the dirty, dangerous bus ride and the macabre spectacle they had just witnessed.

As luck would have it, when they arrived back at their apartment they happened to meet their neighbor in the hall, the very woman who had recommended the Wild Animal Park to Adriana as a "lovely family experience." When she asked how the family had liked the park, Adriana told her they had decided to cut their visit short because they had found the lion experience just a little too intense.

"Oh, that's a shame," she said. "You missed the best part. In the lagoon at the center of the park the children could have bought live baby ducks to feed to the crocodiles."

Chapter 14
Weddings and Asian Beauty Secrets

Felix and I were invited to two weddings while we lived in China. The first was the wedding of my personal athletic trainer, Justin Wu, and the other was one of Felix's colleagues at work. I had seen plenty of old wedding portraits in the antique warehouses, so I knew that Shanghai's brides had been dressing up in fancy white bridal gowns for decades before the Communist revolution put wedding finery into disrepute. But I had done enough window-shopping in twenty-first-century Shanghai to know that splashy weddings were roaring back into fashion. So I was eager to attend Justin's wedding and see for myself how the young, modern Chinese were celebrating this major milestone in their lives.

One thing I learned right away was that creating formal and dramatic bridal portraits is perhaps the most important part of the wedding celebration for the Chinese. After all, the wedding lasts only a day, but a portrait is forever! At least, that seemed to be the prevailing opinion. In both of the weddings we attended, the couple had chosen a popular romantic movie for their wedding theme and had ordered personalized movie posters to be displayed at the wedding receptions—one poster at the door to the reception hall and another hung above the newlyweds' dinner table.

Justin and his wife had chosen the movie *Robin Hood*. On their wedding/movie poster the groom's face replaced that of Kevin Costner, and Maid Marion looked just like the bride. The other couple decided their theme would be *Top Gun*, so of course their movie posters featured Felix's friend and his bride as the courageous pilot and sexy flight instructor. Now, I just love movies, as you have probably figured out by now, but this seemed a bit strange and, well, too commercial even for me. Besides the fact that these movies were American and not Chinese, they were not exactly current. I suppose the Chinese were seeing them as classics and not just as "old" movies, but whatever the interpretation, it certainly speaks to the power of Hollywood—even on the opposite side of the world.

At the beginning of the reception, each bride wore an eye-catching white, Western-style wedding dress, but later on changed into another that looked more like a cocktail dress. At the end of Justin's wedding the bride changed yet again into a long, elegant *qipao*, the short-sleeve, high-neck fitted dress so fashionable in pre-revolutionary China. A tall mountain of champagne glasses was artfully stacked in front of the bridal table at each wedding. At the appropriate moment, waiters filled them all from the top glass on down with a bubbling cascade of wine and foam. They were quickly distributed to all the guests, and everyone raised their glass in a toast to the bridal couple.

At both weddings the guests were seated around circular tables, each of which had a centerpiece with several candles mounted in the center of a large "lazy Susan" turntable. During the course of the dinner the bridal couple was expected to visit each table and light the candles in the centerpiece using a long, metal wand with a lighted candle on the end. The guests then offered a toast to the couple with a very strong liquor, called *mao-tai*, which burns all the way down from your lips to your stomach. As a Mexican, I am used to our strong native tequila, but this *mao-tai* was something else again. Its taste is particularly shocking when you are expected to drink it down all at once, while everybody around you yells "*gan bei*," which is kind of like saying "cheers" but literally means "until the glass is empty!"

Then the food began to arrive . . . and arrive, and arrive. At Justin's wedding I counted twenty-five different dishes being served, one right after another. At times our table would have ten or so serving platters on its lazy Susan, which enabled all the guests to help themselves to whatever dish they wanted. As soon as we finished one platter of food, another would take its place. The variety of foods was tremendous—fish, shellfish, beef, pork, fowl, noodles, rice, soups, fruits, vegetables—with many of them quite exotic in their origin or preparation. Some of the ones I recognized were tongue of duck, jellyfish, and turtle cutlets arranged within the shell. There were also plenty of sea creatures I did not recognize, including some that looked more like extraterrestrials than fish. Whenever I asked my Chinese tablemates if they knew what a particular dish might be, they usually smiled and said something polite like, "I don't know exactly what it is either, but if they are serving it at Justin's wedding, it's sure to be delicious."

As I came in contact with more and more Chinese women—at parties, in our compound, or even on the streets—I became increasingly entranced by their grace and the perfection of their skin. Their complexions had many fewer spots or blemishes than those of women from Europe or the Americas, and their facial wrinkles seemed practically nonexistent. I remember one woman in particular, whom I judged to be maybe eighteen or twenty years old. She asked me politely about my children, then mentioned to my utter amazement that her daughter had just finished her studies at Oxford University! I just had to ask her age, which turned out to be forty-five. Okay, she was particularly impressive, but hardly alone in her youthful appearance. Did Chinese women possess some beauty secret that was as yet unknown in the West? Time and careful observation eventually taught me some important lessons, but did not yield all the answers I was seeking.

The first thing I noticed, and which Xiao Tian reinforced once we felt comfortable with one another, was that Chinese women stay out of the sun as much as possible. Almost every woman walking outside wore a hat—and not a small one, either, but a generous one designed to shield her face completely from the sun's rays. In cars, women drivers wore white cotton gloves to protect their hands from sun exposure whenever they were behind the wheel. Even the women I saw riding in those never-ending rivers of bicycles and motor scooters were wearing long sleeves, or they had put on sleeve extenders that could be removed when they reached their destinations.

Early on, I had realized that visitors to the swimming pool at the center of our compound nearly always sat in segregated groups—Westerners in the sunny spots and Chinese in the shade. I also noticed a funny distinction between East and West during exercise classes at the compound's sport center. My favorite class, after water aerobics, was one called Body Balance, which was a mixture of yoga and tai chi. The Western women who participated in this class were always having problems with their balance or equilibrium, and it was not unusual for one or more of us to fall over like a sack of potatoes at some point during the class. The Asian women who took the class with us, however, all seemed to handle the exercises with considerable grace and never seemed to lose their balance. But the tables were definitely turned during the step and aerobics classes. The Asians tried in vain to keep pace with us, but the Western women, like our famous Energizer bunny, could just keep on going and going!

The slow-motion exercises of tai chi were very widely practiced by people all over Shanghai. Large groups of people, especially senior citizens, could be seen performing these exercises early in the morning in parks all around the city. It is said to promote flexibility, balance, and a sense of well-being—which was easy to believe after watching the graceful, rhythmic patterns performed simultaneously by dozens and dozens of people exercising together. I doubt that even a handful of our Mexican or American senior citizens back home could do them half as well, even with considerable practice.

In addition to sun protection, Chinese women made great use of skin creams and lotions. The most popular one had as its main ingredient something I found quite strange—finely ground pearls. They could be freshwater or saltwater pearls, it did not seem to matter. Whether it was truly effective, or whether it was the lustrous look of fine, white pearls that made the lotion so popular, I don't know, but its use was very widespread. Another thing I learned was that Asian skin is much softer and more delicate than that of Europeans or Americans. Because of this, many international cosmetics companies make special versions of their products designed specifically for their Chinese and Asian customers. The same goes for hair products, especially hair dyes. All of these cosmetics are formulated to be milder and gentler to the skin so as to better suit Asian clients.

To discover whether the Chinese had some special beauty treatments that might work for me, I began to visit various salons for facials. Their technique surprised me. They would apply one lotion after another, always cleaning my face after each application, sometimes as much as seven times, but they would never work on my pores to clean them or extract blackheads. A facial treatment might last an hour and a half, and when I left the salon I would feel happy and relaxed, but my face still had the same spots and blackheads as before! My skin was definitely clean, though, polished and really, really clean, but I never got the results I was hoping for.

Another typical Chinese health and beauty practice was massage, and there were massage salons on practically every corner. Wonderful foot massage and body massages were available at very reasonable prices, and I indulged myself regularly. They were administered with considerable force, however, and at times it felt almost painful. But when they were over I always felt super relaxed, as if I were floating in the clouds. Certain salons employed blind people to give the massages, and these always seemed the best ones to me. You did not even have to pay or go into a salon to get your feet massaged! Many city parks had pathways paved with smooth river pebbles aligned vertically. Walking barefoot along these stone paths stimulates the acupressure points that we all have along the bottom of our feet. Well, of course I had to give it a try. Unaccustomed as I am to going barefoot, I found the walk unpleasant and painful, but I could see how someone who was not as tender-footed as I might find it quite stimulating.

A surprising thing about foot massage was that it was strongly recommended that pregnant women NOT get foot massages. The massage professionals said that stroking a certain area on the ankle stimulates the uterus and could cause a spontaneous abortion. True or not, my Danish friend and Mandarin-class partner, Hanna, was a big fan of foot massage. She considered these warnings to be nonsense and continued to get foot massages even after she became pregnant with her second child. Unfortunately, in about the fourth month of her pregnancy, she lost her baby. We were good friends by that time, and it was very sad. Were the foot massages to blame? There is no way to know for sure, but I paid a lot more attention to their warnings and advice after that.

Chapter 15
Thursdays with Mr. Wu

It was a great day for me when the company Felix worked for gave me a chauffeur! Felix's work contract included a car, but not a driver. However, my husband could be quite persuasive, and his tireless negotiations did finally result in getting me a driver in the spring of 2004. He would be all mine from 9:00 a.m. to 4:00 p.m. on Thursdays.

My first impression of my driver, Mr. Wu, was not a good one. During our first few shopping trips I found him mean looking and unresponsive. I was so glad to get regular transportation, however, that I just resigned myself to making the best of it. Grocery shopping in Shanghai was complicated and tiring, as I have mentioned before, and I believe it was the one thing we *tai-tais* struggled with the most, and enjoyed the least, among all our regular activities. So *any* help I could get to lighten my load was greatly appreciated, even if it came in the form of a grumpy, sullen Chinaman.

On grocery-shopping day I did not only go to the famous Carrefour, I also had to plan stops at several other stores in order to acquire the ingredients for our Western-style diet—actually, make that our French/Mexican/Asian diet. As much as we were learning to enjoy Chinese food, it was hard, really hard, to leave all our comfort foods behind. In order to complete my route, I tried to be ready and waiting for Mr. Wu at 9:00 a.m., and we usually did not get back home until the clock was striking four. In addition to getting the basics at Carrefour, I usually had to stop at an Australian supermarket called Pines to get red meat (especially for Felix's grilling), and then swing by another one called City Supermarket to get the French cheeses that were one of my husband's little pleasures in life. Before heading home, we would also stop at the Sheraton Hotel (Taiping Yang) to get decent bread at the German bakery located inside. We had had an unpleasant surprise the first time I tried buying bread from a Chinese bakery. The rolls were filled with a big dollop of sweet bean paste! Once again we had to remind ourselves of our survival mantra: "Remember, it's China, and anything can happen!"

One of the most peculiar things about grocery shopping in Shanghai was the sudden shortages of one product or another. Even something as basic as dishwashing powder might disappear for a while. Experienced *tai-tais* were always advising newcomers, "When you see something that is important for your family, buy as much of it as you can because you never know when or if you will see it again." That dishwashing-powder shortage was a particularly difficult one for the ex-pat *tai-tais*, but I also remember shortages from time to time of certain vegetables and many dairy products. Another drag on my shopping speed was the fact that Chinese shoppers were often very interested to explore and see for themselves just what the foreigner was buying. They would examine the items in my cart, and sometimes even help themselves to something I had selected. This happened in department stores as well. I remember once I was trying on shoes in the modern department store, Isetan. I was with my mother at the time, and she just could not believe it when a lady scooped up the pretty shoes I was in the process of removing from my feet and walked off with them. I know we have plenty of ill-mannered folks in Mexico, but I do believe our ill-mannered people are not nearly as bad as the ill-mannered people I encountered in China!

The longer I spent in China, of course, the better I was able to speak and understand Mandarin. I practiced as much as I could every day with Xiao Tian, and I was faithfully attending the twice-weekly classes in Mandarin with Hanna. Another chance to practice came when I started taking Julia to the park for fresh air and sunshine. I noticed that groups of *ayis* often gathered there while supervising their employers' children, so I decided to make an effort to interact with them and practice the words and phrases I was learning from Xiao Tian. I also did this partly to prove to Felix that my learning methods were going to work. He was very pessimistic about my progress, saying that even if I were able to communicate with Xiao Tian, she was probably the only one in China who would be able to understand me. Well, the *ayis* understood me! Not all that well at first, but our conversations improved each week! At first they didn't quite know what to think about this strange *tai-tai* who wanted to chat them up in their own language, but I kept on talking, especially about babies, and soon we were enjoying each other's company.

This made a tremendous difference in my relationship with my driver, Mr. Wu. As I began to speak to him in Mandarin phrases and make an honest attempt to communicate with him, his cold demeanor melted away. He began offering to carry the heavier items for me, and he would monitor how much the small merchants were charging me for this item or that to make sure I was not being overcharged just because I was a foreigner. As our relationship grew, he would even do me a great favor and extend the time he drove for me past four o'clock if we needed to finish up an important errand. He did not do this for any of his other *tai-tai* ladies, he once told me, because they were cold and unfriendly to him and the other Chinese drivers. (Most of them were Germans, famous in our ex-pat world for their chilly, reserved demeanor.)

With time, I began to truly enjoy our conversations, and since traffic was often snarled, I had plenty of time to talk with him. This eventually led to our regular Thursday lunch adventures. I would ask him to pick a different Chinese restaurant each week so we could eat together and I could learn more about his country. We went to some *v-e-r-y* interesting places, and I let Mr. Wu order whatever he wished for both of us. Each meal was like a banquet, and that is how I became a fan of dog meat. My favorite was actually dog-meat soup, which is a wintertime specialty in China. The Chinese believe that eating dog helps you stay warm in cold weather. True or not, I found it delicious. We dined at several restaurants famous for dog along the street Kaixuan Lu. These unfortunate dogs are raised on special farms specifically for their meat. Mr. Wu said they were enormous and looked like Great Danes.

If we were shopping in a part of town where Mr. Wu didn't know any good restaurants, he would often call other drivers on his cell phone and get advice on where to eat. He would also call them for tips on the best restaurant for dumplings or for won ton, if that's what he wanted me to try on a particular day. We had some fantastic lunches, and he would always remember to ask for silverware for me because, although I tried hard, I could never really get the hang of eating with chopsticks. He would also instruct the Chinese waiters to put all of my food together on one plate rather than bring numerous small dishes to the table. He knew that was the way Westerners usually eat their meals, and he wanted to make my dining experiences easy and fun.

I once read a great little book by an American university professor with many years' experience in China. He said that the Chinese have two standards of conduct in their relationships with other people—one for family and friends, and a completely different one for strangers. If you ever make the effort to truly make friends with a Chinese person, he explained, you will never know a truer friend. While I met many Chinese people in Shanghai, I only had the opportunity to truly make friends with two of them—Mr. Wu and Xiao Tian. Based on these two, I would have to say that the American professor was right. The better I got to know each of them, the more I cherished the relationship. It went way deeper that the typical employer-employee bond, and each one was so hard to let go when it eventually came time for us to leave China. But I'm getting ahead of myself. There are still plenty of stories to tell.

During my travels I have always tried to follow the advice that "when in Rome, do as the Romans do." In China that was a little harder to do than in other places I've been, but after so many lunches with Mr. Wu, I eventually decided I was ready to stop complicating my life and ruining my budget in an attempt to duplicate our Western cuisine every night. I let the cooking at our house gradually became more Asianized, and I encouraged Xiao Tian to buy what she liked in the markets and prepare it for Felix and me. After all, I had never seen a fat Chinese person.

As spring turned into summer 2004, I was beginning to feel a bit more "at home" in Shanghai. We had been here almost a year and were beginning to fall into a semicomfortable routine. But there was a surprise for us right around the corner. I had all but forgotten the intense heat that summer brought to our coastal city, and with it the massive invasion of mosquitoes. It was particularly bad in our neighborhood because the Shanghai Racquet Club and Apartments was bordered by large rice paddies. The grounds of our compound were also decorated with dozens and dozens of pots of floating flowers. These pots were a delight to the eyes, with their masses of pink or white blossoms floating in placid circles, but they were also a perfect breeding ground for mosquito larvae—as if the surrounding paddies didn't provide enough fresh water already!

Mosquito season began in June and did not let up until August. Even though our apartment had screens on the windows, the sheer numbers of mosquitoes were such that flotillas of the tiny bloodsuckers managed to swarm inside even when we made the quickest possible entrances and exits. We had not been in residence very long that first summer before we decided to buy mosquito netting to hang over our beds. My childhood dream of sleeping like a princess in a curtained, canopied bed actually came true in Shanghai, although not in quite the romantic way I had imagined.

We were already prepared with our bed nets for the invasion that second summer. The nets did allow us to get a decent night's sleep and gave our skin a respite from the irritation of insect repellent, but when we left our beds in the morning the problems began all over again. We felt we had to apply plenty of repellent due to the risk of contracting some tropical disease carried by mosquitoes, especially when we were outdoors. But this left us with a dilemma each time we left the apartment. Should we slather our exposed skin with repellent for the insects or with sunblock to prevent burning? It was a choice between being eaten alive by the mosquitoes or tanned to leather by the sun. There were no easy answers.

Never in my life have I been so badly mosquito bitten, and unfortunately the bite of these Asian mosquitoes provoked a particularly bad itch. Residents of our compound used to joke that the Chinese mosquitoes must prefer the novelty of foreign blood. At first I thought it was just an urban legend, but with time I came to believe it. Julia and I both have type-A+ blood, which is rare in China, and we were constantly under attack by the mosquitoes. Felix has type-O blood, much more common in Asia, and he did not seem to experience nearly the trouble with the mosquitoes that we did.

That first summer in Shanghai I discovered a battery-powered mosquito killer shaped like a small tennis racquet. It electrocuted any flying insect that came in contact with the netting. Nothing gave me more pleasure during those hot summer days than swinging the racquet around the rooms of our apartment and hearing the lovely little *zz-zz-tt* sound that accompanied the death of each tiny bloodsucker. When I began taking tennis lessons at the compound's Racquet Club, I would even practice my backhand and forehand swings as I worked my way from room to room battling the tiny opponents that infested our apartment each summer.

Of course, the *tai-tais* had plenty of advice to share about how to avoid mosquito bites. Some of it was dietary, such as don't eat bananas or avoid sugary food. Other advice included wearing light-colored clothing or burning citronella-oil candles, a highly touted "natural" repellent. Despite serious attempts to follow these tips, I noticed no difference in the frequency of our mosquito bites. I could not find any calamine lotion in the stores to alleviate our constant itching, but Xiao Tian introduced us to tea-tree oil, which worked fairly well, and sometimes we used Vicks VapoRub, too.

Our day of salvation came one morning when Xiao Tian showed up for work with a Chinese remedy for repelling mosquitoes that really did work. It was cheap and available at any pharmacy, and as best I can recall it was called *bao bao jie shui*. All we had to do was add a few drops of this magic elixir to our bathwater each day, and *poof!* The mosquitoes no longer found us appealing. It seemed to work by giving a slightly bitter smell to the bather's skin, although it was hardly apparent to humans. I was more than happy to give up my usual cologne for the bitter concoction that kept those horrible pests at bay. In fact, I came to regard it as blessed as holy water from any church in the world.

The mosquitoes had their way with the people of Shanghai only until the end of July each year. With the coming of August, vast clouds of dragonflies would arrive in the city and eat up nearly all the mosquitoes. We could see dark swarms of them flying between the tall buildings, and we knew (after that first year) that our relief was at hand. I guess it was all part of Mother Nature's plan.

Part 3

How Felix and I Found Each Other

Chapter 16
I Ace My Interview

Many of our new friends in China were curious about how Felix and I met and married. After all, how did a Mexican and a Frenchman ever find each other? The answer surprised everyone. We didn't meet at college, nor did we meet during visits to France or to Mexico. We met at Disney World.

From opposite sides of the Atlantic Ocean, Felix and I were both selected for positions as "cultural representatives" at the World Showcase, a section of Disney's Epcot Center. This wonderful program brought in young people from eleven countries to staff the small villages, or pavilions, as they are called, that comprise the World Showcase. Visitors to Disney World can get a taste of what traveling to each of these countries might be like by visiting the eleven pavilions, which are situated one after another around a large, circular lagoon. Felix's job was in the bakery at the French pavilion, and I sold handcrafts and souvenirs at shops in the Mexican pavilion. The year was 1996, and although neither of us knew it yet, it was a year that would change our lives in ways we could never have imagined—even in a "Magic Kingdom"!

I had not planned to seek work at Disney World. It came about suddenly and unexpectedly. The story of how Felix and I met has lots of twists and turns. This is how it happened.

I was in my second year at Universidad de las Americas, a private university in my hometown of Puebla. Back then the only plan I had for my life was to become an accountant. I thought perhaps I could help my dad in his accounting firm, or maybe I would work in the financial department of a large corporation. Dozens of international companies had branch offices in Puebla, and many, many more had offices in Mexico City.

One day I happened to notice a small sign in front of the exchange students office. It said, "Come to Work at Disney World's Epcot Center, sign up for interviews here!" I've always been a big fan of Disney. My dad took our entire family to Disney World several times when I was growing up, and we just loved it. So on the spur of the moment, I decided to apply. It would get me far away from an insipid little romance I wanted to nip in the bud, and it would be a great opportunity to spend some fun time in a place I already knew I loved. But it almost didn't happen. All of the one hundred interview slots were already taken, and I left the office thinking wistfully that it was too good to be true anyway.

I was walking down the hall to leave the building when the exchange students secretary came running out of her office looking frantically up and down the hall. Someone had just called to cancel their appointment, she called to me. Did I want to take their place? Of course I said yes.

The next week the director of my university's international affairs department interviewed all one hundred students and selected what he considered to be the top thirty candidates. These students (I had made the first cut) would be reinterviewed by the people from Disney two weeks later. I had never been in a job interview before, and I had no idea what to expect. It was handled by a team of two recruiters and would be conducted entirely in English.

I figured this would be an advantage for me. My parents do not speak English, but they made darn sure that my sister, brother, and I speak it well. My English lessons had begun in elementary school, plus I had sessions with private language tutors during the summer for six years. To make sure we got plenty of practice, my parents also sent us to summer camps in the United States, including twice to the Interlochen Music Camp in Michigan and once to a Catholic boarding school in Vermont. My parents love to travel, so we also visited many cities in the US and Canada on family vacations.

Yes, my dad was ahead of his time. Even way back then, in the 1980s, he had a global vision for his family and wanted his three kids to get plenty of international experience. He felt this would give us confidence and better prepare us to meet the challenges of the future. In addition to a firm grasp of English, he also decided that I should specialize in learning German while my sister Pilar concentrated on French. That way our family would be able to handle what he considered the three most important languages of Europe and the Americas. He also sent Pilar and me on summer trips to our special countries for practice when we were teenagers.

After the typical introductions, the Disney interviewer started off with a bold question. "Why should I choose you?" he asked me. "What makes you special? Sell yourself to me!"

That was a total surprise, those questions. Sell myself? Oh dear! I don't remember exactly what I said, but I think I started out saying how I enjoy being in a multicultural environment, and how I would like to share the wonders and the cultural riches of Mexico with others, blah, blah, blah.

What makes me special? I recall answering that my name, Adela, was as Mexican as a name could possibly be. And then I really got on a roll, explaining about the many Mexican women who played important roles during the Mexican Revolution, which started in 1910. They were called the *adelas*, or *adelitas* as a nickname. Some of these women accompanied their men into the battles of the revolution, others were kidnapped and forced to serve. They helped the soldiers carry munitions, acted as nurses, prepared food, brought comfort to the men, and sometimes bore them children. At times they even took the weapons into their own hands and fought alongside the soldiers. The *adelitas* have come to be recognized as national heroines, and there is even a famous folk song from the period that sings the praises of one particular *adelita*.

Later on in the interview, when asked what Disney character was my favorite, I said it was Belle, the young woman in *Beauty and the Beast*. Why?

Because I loved to read books just like her, and I felt the same feelings Belle expressed in her song at the beginning of the movie. She didn't want to be just somebody's wife. No sir, not her! She wanted more than just a provincial life. She wanted adventure in the world beyond her village, and she seemed a lot like me, I told him. Without really trying at all, I had the interviewer smiling and laughing (in a nice way) as he listened to my nervous chatter.

I also mentioned that I spoke German fluently as a third language and that I was currently taking my second year of French in college. The recruiter looked puzzled and asked why a Mexican girl without any family background in Germany or France would need to speak those languages. So I told him about my father and his global strategy for his kids. I told him I was studying French because my business major required that students take either Russian, Japanese, or French, and I chose French because I knew it would be the easiest.

At that point the recruiter came right out and offered me a job at one of Disney's luxury hotels. He figured that someone speaking four languages would be very useful in handling the many international tourists who come to Disney World. But I declined his offer, and told him that what I really wanted to do was work at Epcot. My reason, which I kept to myself, was that I wanted to be able to hang out with young people from all over the world. I knew I could do that at Epcot, but it wouldn't be as likely to happen at the resort hotels. Okay, he could arrange that, he said, and encouraged me to sign up for a one-year contract. Once again, I told him no. I couldn't do that, I said, because I needed to get back to the university and finish my degree. He agreed to a six-month contract. We smiled, shook hands, and the interview was over.

It was nice not having to wait and wonder if I had been accepted, like the other candidates did. I already knew the results, and as promised, my contract package arrived by mail at my home a month later. (Like all good Mexican young ladies, I still lived at home with my family.) On July 8, 1996, I boarded a flight out of Mexico City en route to Orlando. I had been to

Disney World before, but this time it would be different. This time I would become part of the show! I was twenty years old.

Felix's reason for pursuing a job at Disney World was totally different from mine. He planned to use his job at Epcot as a springboard to qualify for permanent residency in the United States. Unemployment rates were high in France in those days. His sister was married to an American guy, who had offered to be his sponsor and help him establish himself in the US. He was twenty-six years old.

Chapter 17
The Vista Way of Life

I was a bit surprised when I arrived at Disney World to find that a big group of other young people from all over the world had arrived along with me. We were told this group would be called our "fellow arrivals." We would be in training classes together, and we would live in an apartment community called Vista Way with all the other foreign nationals who worked at many different places throughout Disney World. I discovered I would be living in a three-bedroom apartment with five other girls. Disney always tried to put people from diverse nationalities together in these apartments, never two from the same place. So my roommates were an amazing international mix and came from China, France, Norway, Wales, and Austria. Just to make things as diverse as possible, the roommate assigned to me was, of course, the tall, blond Viking from Norway—*Could we be any more different?* I asked myself. It was a Vista Way tradition to throw a welcome party whenever another group of new arrivals appeared, so that night I got to meet many of my new neighbors at the Vista Way pool. There were drinks, lots of mingling, and it ended with many of the newcomers being thrown into the pool, another Vista Way tradition.

The next day my fellow arrivals and I began our training, which at Disney is called Traditions. Disney is well known for insisting that its employees adhere to the highest standards, both in dress and deportment, and I found their training to be interesting, very complete, and very motivating as well. To begin with, we were required to attend Traditions classes dressed in classic business attire, nothing sloppy or casual, and we sat at round tables, to foster teamwork they said, and not at desks. They instilled in everyone the importance of upholding the Disney philosophy, which included the Disney vocabulary, the Disney personality, and the Disney look.

We learned that the people who visit the Disney parks are our *guests*, not customers. We will be *cast members*, not employees, because we are all part of the show. And we don't wear uniforms, we wear *costumes* because we are not at work, we are *on stage*—or *backstage*, if we are someplace where we are not interacting directly with our guests.

They taught us to remember to greet each and every guest, which means to be polite, to smile, and to make eye contact. It was important to be *aggressively* friendly. That meant trying to make each guest feel special, letting them know that you were delighted to help them, and to even try to *anticipate* their needs whenever possible. We were also taught how to give directions by pointing with two fingers, instead of just one, because in some parts of the world pointing with one finger is considered terribly rude.

They also talked about the Disney look, which delineates exactly how cast members must appear while on stage. Hair color and makeup must be natural looking and subtle. Haircuts for men and women must be in a traditional, conservative style, and jewelry must be kept to a minimum—small earrings (no hoops for safety), one ring, one watch, and no necklaces. Absolutely no visible tattoos and no facial hair for the men. They also included lessons in personal hygiene and encouraged cast members to take a shower every day and to wear deodorant. I laughed when I heard that, but later on I realized they put in these guidelines specifically for the French and German cast members. In the past, a number of them were found to be not that fond of showering and deodorant, which was offensive to Disney's American guests, especially in the heat of Florida. That was not a problem among the Mexican cast members, I can assure you! As cast members, we were all supposed to look perfectly neat and tidy at all times. I must say that every person who had been selected for the World Showcase was already a pretty good-looking example of their national type, and with the rules imposed by the Disney look, we presented an outstanding example of the wholesome, clean-cut youth of the world! Which is exactly what the Disney folks were going for.

I have to confess that the Disney look and the Disney personality have stuck with me, even now. It was such effective training that I still smile, look people in the eye, and do my best to treat my coworkers and acquaintances in a positive, friendly manner, even if I'm not in a good mood or don't especially like them. I still dress with the best care and style that I can manage, no matter what the occasion. Once a cast member, always a cast member, I suppose.

After two full days in Traditions, we were taken on a tour of the Magic Kingdom and Epcot that completely blew my mind. First of all, the park that our guests see is actually the second story of a massive underground city. So many of the things that keep Disney World going are located underground. That way the guests never have to see the thousands of operations and employees at work day and night keeping everything fresh and fantastic "on stage." The wardrobe areas included what seemed like acres of costumes hanging from racks, and cast members had only to ask to pick up a fresh costume whenever needed. There were also big changing rooms with lockers nearby, and cafeterias and break rooms for times when we would be "backstage." Tunnels crisscrossed the underground areas, and they were full of people dressed in the most amazing variety of costumes walking to and from their work areas. These tunnels are why guests never see a cast member that seems out of place. Someone in costume for Adventureland, for example, never walks through Tomorrowland on his way to going on stage—he or she exits the tunnel system right into the appropriate spot.

The only part of the underground tour that wasn't pleasant was seeing so many costumed Disney characters eating lunch, hanging out together, or smoking while on break. That forced me to admit to myself once and for all that the characters aren't actually real—no, they were human beings just like me or you! I couldn't help but be slightly disillusioned somehow. But then I reminded myself that something wonderful was about to happen. Soon, very soon, I would be in their shoes—going on stage and becoming part of that magic myself! I was thrilled to be there and be part of it all.

After our Traditions training we were divided into groups and given specialized training for the specific jobs to which we were assigned. On my employment application I had stated that my first choice of jobs would be in Merchandise. I thought working in a shop selling Mexican crafts and souvenirs would be easy and fun. My second choice was Attractions, which meant working on a ride or special activity, and my last choice was Food and Beverage. But that did not seem to matter once I arrived. In the Mexican pavilion, *everybody* started out working in our pavilion's attraction, El Rio del Tiempo, or in English, The River of Time. It was an indoor boat ride that carried visitors past elaborate scenes from Mexico's mythology and history. It lasted eight minutes and featured lots of animatronic puppets singing and dancing to upbeat Mexican folk music. There were even scenes from a typical Mexican market. One of the merchants actually talks directly to the guests floating by, bargaining with them and imploring them to buy his wonderful wares.

To enhance the drama of El Rio del Tiempo, the interior of the building was kept quite dark. While this made for great theater, it also made it a cold, dark, and damp place to work. So much so that among ourselves, the Mexican cast members referred to it as The Time Swamp. Our costumes were especially colorful, probably to make us easily visible in all that darkness. Mine consisted of a parrot-green skirt and a ruffled yellow blouse, topped by a striped poncho that, while colorful, made my skin itch. I felt like a giant walking piñata, or maybe a colorful tropical bird. I was eager to please and wanted to enhance our show, so I usually braided my hair and wound it up and across the top of my head into a classic Mexican hairstyle. You have probably seen it before. It was made famous by our great female painter, Frida Kahlo, who braided her hair this way in most of her self-portraits. Our guests loved it, and I got lots of comments and compliments on it.

Although I had visited Disney World several times before, I had no idea just how hard the cast members have to work to keep those attractions running smoothly. Our job at El Rio del Tiempo had three parts. First came the queue line, which requires you to welcome each guest and encourage them to line up in an orderly fashion. Second came the loading zone, where you must quickly, clearly, and of course, very politely ask the guests, "Hi there! How many in your party?" Then, depending on the number of guests and their physical size, you had to think fast and assign them to the proper boarding lane to insure an even distribution of weight. A mistake in boarding could cause the boat to get stuck "up river," and then you'd have a traffic jam with boats bumping into each other—not good! It was a real challenge to work in the loading zone because you had to get sixteen people seated in less than one minute, and you had to say *each and every time*, "Step in please, and watch your step!" Plus, you always had to accommodate guests with special requests. Some people wanted to sit only in the front or the back, and others had limited mobility or special needs. After repeating the same phrases over and over each day for a week, my Norwegian roommate started complaining that I must be loading riverboats in my dreams because I would repeat the boarding phrases over and over in my sleep! The third part of the process was handling the control console and dispatching the boats in a timely manner. Needless to say, the loader and the dispatcher had to work in careful coordination.

One of the best things about being assigned to the Swamp, I mean, the River of Time, was that I got to know Agustin. He was a friendly fellow, one of the nicest guys working in the Mexican pavilion. In fact, he was the only Mexican cast member who was pleasant to me when I first arrived. I couldn't understand what was going on; the other Mexicans were treating me like a pariah. I tried to be friendly and nice, but got the cold shoulder from everyone. After a few days I gave up. I did my job as best I could, but spent all my free time getting to know the cast members from other countries. I made some great friends, went on lots of dates, and had a wonderful time. I wasn't going to mope around just because the Mexicans were acting like jerks! Agustin even introduced me to his German roommate, Mark, and we went out for a while. He was a nice guy, and I really enjoyed the opportunity to practice my German with him. Unfortunately, Mark was still hung up on a girl he had recently broken up with, so after a couple of weeks my German practice came to an end.

One thing Mark told me before we broke up was that my good buddy Agustin was giving him the creeps. Why? Because Agustin was a practitioner of *santeria cubana*. This African-inspired religious cult from Cuba involved talking to spirits and consulting with your guardian angel, which is something everyone has (according to Agustin) if you just know how to contact him (or her). Poor Mark was freaked out by this crazy Mexican who slept in his room and talked to spirits. He told me that he made certain he drank enough beer each night to ensure he slept through whatever visitations or conversations Agustin might be having with the spirit world. But this didn't bother me, and I kept up my friendship with my one and only Mexican friend. Was he crazy, as Mark believed? Well, maybe it was fate, maybe dumb luck, or maybe it was true *santeria* prophecy—I don't pretend to know—but two weeks before I met Felix, Agustin made a formal prediction that I was about the meet the man I would marry. But I'm getting ahead of myself. I met Felix during my fourth month at Disney World, so let's get back to my earlier days there.

The apartment community on Vista Way, where all the foreign workers at Disney lived, had both two-bedroom and three-bedroom units. I felt fortunate to be assigned to a three-bedroom one because that gave me more opportunities to make friends. As usual in these cases, I got to know some of my roommates better than others. The Chinese girl worked as a sales clerk in the Chinese pavilion at Epcot. She hardly ever spoke and pretty much kept to herself, except on the few occasions when she hung out with her fellow Chinese cast members. Later on, we found out that her government strongly discouraged her from socializing with foreigners. What a lost opportunity for her, and for me, too! Had I known that in just seven years I would be living in Shanghai, I would have spent a lot more time asking her questions about her homeland.

The French girl worked at the reception desk in one of the Disney hotels. She was the oldest one of us and behaved more maturely as well. The girl from Wales was a lifeguard at Disney's Typhoon Lagoon water park. She spent long hours in the heat under the strong Florida sun, so when she got home she was usually exhausted and would go to bed early. Sometimes she even had to go to work at 5:00 a.m. for special training in safety or lifeguarding procedures. Her costume resembled a *Baywatch* bathing suit, and she looked just like one of the girls on the TV program, too.

The girl from Austria worked in the Christmas shop at Disney's downtown Orlando marketplace, not within the park itself. She was younger, twenty years old, just like me. We both lamented the fact that the laws in the United States prohibited us from buying alcoholic drinks, so we put our heads together to solve that little problem. She had her mom send her two blank driver's license cards from home. We typed in our names and faked the other information, then stamped them in an official-looking manner with an Austrian coin covered in red Magic Marker ink. It worked! Whenever a bartender questioned us, saying sarcastically that I sure didn't look Austrian, I told him my mother was from Vienna and started speaking in German. No problem!

I shared my bedroom with the girl from Norway. It was a strange experience because we were opposites in every possible way. She was a tall, platinum blond, and very pretty. She received great tips in her job as a waitress in the Norwegian pavilion's restaurant, so she made considerably more money than the rest of us. She was very proud of this and could afford to do a lot more shopping and traveling than we could. She turned the air conditioning on so strong every night that I believe the Sea World penguins could have happily frolicked in our room, and then—she slept completely naked, saying that her skin needed to breathe! It was so damn cold that I wore a sweatshirt over my winter pajamas every night, and I was still freezing. It was unbelievably awkward, but it made me the envy of every guy living in Vista Way! They would all joke around and say how they would just *love* to swap rooms with me. After a while she began bringing her Italian boyfriend home to spend the night with her, and to put it nicely, I soon realized that the three of us had become roommates. She was very liberal and open minded, as the Scandinavians are famous for, and I realized that perhaps I wasn't as open minded as I thought. My father would have been totally shocked had I told him this, but of course I didn't.

Our apartment was furnished, but still stark and undecorated when I arrived. So I quickly set about to decorate the common areas, like the kitchen and living room. I brought in some flowers, throw pillows, and a Mexican rug. To foster a bit of bonding with my fellow residents, I suggested that we have a dinner party once a week. We could take turns cooking a meal that would feature traditional foods from our part of the world and share a little bit about our lives with each other. That idea went over well, and when it was my turn I made chicken consommé and *chilaquiles* with green salsa, which proved to be quite a success. I still remember the menus from several of those dinners. The girl from Austria made schnitzel with potatoes, and the Chinese girl made fried rice. Best of all, however, was the French girl's *coq au vin*. It was fantastic.

When Disney guests arrive at the gate to the World Showcase, the Mexican pavilion is the first one on the left, and for some reason I never figured out, the Norwegian pavilion is located right next to ours. So we got to know our Viking neighbors quite well, if for no other reason than proximity. We met each other frequently at the employee cafeteria located just behind our two pavilions, and our two groups seemed to get along better than most, in spite of our obvious physical differences. Lots of Mexican-Norwegian couples formed (and re-formed), and there were even some marriages between the two. But what really brought us together, the one thing we truly had in common, was our love of drinking.

I remember we had lots of Mexico versus Norway drinking challenges to see which group could better hold their liquor. Unfortunately, our proud tequila drinkers managed to lose every single match. Whatever those Vikings drink to keep themselves warm in the winter must have a much higher alcohol content than Mexican tequila, because my Aztec team would end up passed out on the couches after every party, while the Vikings still managed somehow to walk, or crawl, their way back home. I found myself attracted to several Norwegian guys and did go out with them a couple of times, but the attraction never lasted. They were nice and funny, but were just not polite to women in the ways that we Mexican girls have learned to expect. They would walk right through a door and never think about holding it open for their date. I had grown up expecting this, and the first time my Norwegian fellow let the door slam back into my face, it hit my nose and actually caused it to bleed. They also expected to start a sexual relationship right away, and since I was raised in conservative Catholic Mexico, that just wasn't going to happen.

After putting in four months at El Rio del Tiempo, a.k.a. The Swamp, I was allowed to move up into a merchandise position at one of the small shops in the Mexican pavilion. Life became easier and much more pleasant. As a salesperson, I also got to wear a different costume, thank goodness. It was a long, white dress with a red sash, very pretty, and flattering to every girl's figure. The boys had a shirt-and-pants outfit in matching colors. I spent the rest of my contract working in the various arts-and-crafts shops within our pavilion. My favorite was the one just outside the main building, called El Rancherito, because it faced the lagoon at the center of the World Showcase. From this shop you could enjoy the mariachi band that performed several times a day, and best of all, you were on stage *outside* the pavilion. Working inside our pavilion got to be kind of depressing because day after day we worked in the dark. The interior was set up like a typical Mexican village during an evening of fiesta. While charming and romantic, the eternal evening seemed to mess with our biological clocks and left us feeling like a colony of bats or other nocturnal animals. After a while we all started looking kind of pale, which was definitely odd for a group of young Mexicans.

Once I completed the training sessions to qualify for the merchandise position, I was able to request overtime jobs on my days off. This was great for two reasons. First, I was able to earn double-time pay, which was about twelve dollars per hour in 1996, and second, I could now work in shops all over Disney World. Since I did not have a car, it was hard to go anywhere on my days off. So, like most of the foreign cast members, I enjoyed earning those "big bucks" and accepted work in totally different shops whenever I could. I remember it was a lot of fun to dress up like a pirate and sell souvenirs at the Pirates of the Caribbean shop or put on an American granny dress and work at the Emporium on Main Street USA.

Then some of the American workers began to protest that the foreign workers' J-1 visas only entitled us to work in venues at the World Showcase, so that put a stop to our working anywhere else. I have to admit that it got pretty funny sometimes watching a Chinese person dressed up to work with the Norwegians on her day off, or a blond German trying to fit in with the bronzed Mexicans in our pavilion. The only place where overtime positions were never available was the Japanese pavilion. Those hard-working people seemed never to slow down, and you hardly ever saw a non-Japanese cast member filling in there.

When we finished our shift on stage, the workers from the World Showcase pavilions would take Disney shuttle buses back to the apartments on Vista Way. I was always tired and the buses were always crowded, but I didn't mind. I usually ended up sitting on the lap of some handsome Norwegian guy or crowding close to a hot-looking German. I must say, they were the nicest and happiest bus rides I've ever taken! There were parties along Vista Way almost every night, and many bars and restaurants in the towns nearby offered special discounts to Disney employees. It was almost impossible to get to bed before 2:00 a.m. Since I was hired through a university, my contract included mandatory classes at Disney University every Wednesday morning. They included topics in business and resort management, and they were actually quite interesting. But most Wednesday mornings I was so exhausted from the party the night before and the "Vista Way of Life" that I could barely stay awake. Sadly, these classes were a total waste for me. I don't remember much about them at all.

Chapter 18
A Prophecy Come True

As the months went by, I was gradually and grudgingly accepted by the other cast members at the Mexican pavilion, thanks to my special buddy Agustin. He got to know me well as we worked side by side at The Swamp, and he convinced the others that I was okay and they should give me a chance. He told me they had been put off by the fact that I came from the city of Puebla, something my Disney name tag told them at first glance. So based on nothing more than that, they decided I must be a snob. I don't know why, but this is a prejudice that lots of other Mexicans have about *poblanos* (residents of Puebla). I guess my coworkers figured it was better to snub first before you yourself get snubbed! I just wish they had taken a few moments to get to know me before they rushed to judgment. Anyway, their attitude softened and eventually we all became friends.

So I was grateful to Agustin and happy to continue our friendship, even though his *santeria* ways could get a little weird at times. Whenever he was off work, Agustin dressed completely in white, for purification he said. He claimed to have regular contact with his guardian angel, named Miguel, who had been either a pirate or a slave (I don't remember which) during Cuba's colonial era. One night I was at a party with Agustin, and we were both drinking beer. He suddenly gave me a very intense look and announced, "Adela, I have just had a vision—a vision of your guardian angel!"

I just laughed and asked him to describe this so-called angel. I stopped laughing as he gave me a pretty good description of my great-grandmother Carmen, who had died shortly after I was born. According to what family members have told me, she was very elegant and loved all things French.

But the weirdest coincidence was that I knew Carmen had been fascinated by spiritualism and organized séances in her home with friends. He said Carmen was trying to get in touch with me. I almost flipped out. How could a guy who had never met my family know all this? I put down my can of beer and walked home in total shock.

I was in my apartment a few weeks later when I got a sudden craving for ice cream. There wasn't any in our freezer, but I figured Agustin would probably have some, so I paid him a visit. While I was there eating my ice cream, he offered me a peek into my future. This involved going into a trance and communicating with the spirits. Well, who could resist such an offer?

I remember watching Augustin sink into his trance and, after a few minutes, take a handful of small seashells and throw them like dice onto a red cloth. This was supposed to facilitate his communication with the spirits. During his trance the spirits told him that I was about to meet the great love of my life and that we would marry. He even described just what this wonderful man would look like. He went on to say that Great-Grandmother Carmen, my guardian angel, was the power bringing us together. It was spooky fun and an entertaining way to spend an evening, but I didn't take this "message" from my great-grandmother very seriously at the time. Much later, however, I would be struck by the incredible coincidence that Carmen had had a lifelong fascination with spiritualism and with France. One of her grandmothers had even emigrated to Mexico from somewhere near Paris.

Did my Francophile great-grandmother really send Felix to me? I'll never know for sure, but there were times in my life when I thought it must be true.

The day I met Felix, I wasn't working. I was enjoying some free time, walking around Epcot, and exploring several of the pavilions on the far side of the lake. It started to rain, so I ducked into the French pavilion, which I had always found attractive. All the buildings were designed to recall La Belle Époque of French history, the late 1800s, and the restaurant here was among Disney World's most popular. I decided to buy a snack at the French bakery while I waited for the rain to let up. Felix should not have been working at the bakery counter that day. He was filling in for the regular person who was ill, and he only did that once, on that one afternoon.

With my first glance up at Felix, I was literally struck dumb. I could not move, or even speak, as he looked down at me with his lovely blue-gray eyes and soft smile. His first words to me were anything but romantic, however. He simply said, "That will be four dollars and fifty cents, madame." But even that sounded *so-o-o* sweet and sexy in his gorgeous French accent. When I failed to respond, he repeated the price and gave me an even sweeter smile. I continued to stare at him, but finally managed to speak.

"Do you live on Vista Way?" I blurted.

"Yes, I do," he said with surprise. "What about you?" That afternoon I was not wearing my Disney costume, so I looked like just another tourist.

"Me too," I managed to say. He asked where I was from, and I said only that I was from Mexico. I paid for my chocolate eclair, then turned around and left the shop, thinking what a gorgeous guy he was. I never expected to see him again.

Five days later he came to see me at the Mexican pavilion. He did not know my name and had only seen me once. He just asked for the girl with the green eyes, and with only that bit of information, he found me.

The rest, as they say, is history. We fell quickly and deeply in love. He was the classic Frenchman—tall and strong, with light-brown hair, fair skin, and the most delicious French accent. He was fun loving and lived each day to the fullest, and his smile—the smile that lit up his face could be so tender and sweet! I, on the other hand, was very Mexican—vivacious and energetic, with black hair and, of course, green eyes. Even though I had traveled widely for my age, I was still very young and quite naïve, in the way that only a good Catholic girl from provincial Mexico could be. We could not have been more different, yet destiny (or was it my great-grandmother?) had somehow brought us together. We celebrated my twenty-first birthday together, and we became inseparable. When we were out together people often thought that we were honeymooners because we were so obviously crazy for each other. I was very surprised to learn that Felix lived in the same apartment as Fabio, the boyfriend of my Norwegian roommate, but we had never met before. Strange how things like that happen sometimes.

Felix had the manners, the voice, and that *je ne sais quoi* that none of my other international dates even came close to. He was loving, passionate, handsome, and—perfect! And like most things that seem perfect, perhaps too good to be true. But that bit of wisdom didn't even occur to me. I was young and totally in love.

In January 1997, I extended my contract with Disney three more months so I could spend extra time with Felix. But time passed quickly, and I returned to Mexico in April, feeling extremely sad and depressed about our separation. But not for long! Soon after, Felix changed his mind about pursuing permanent residency in the United States. He resigned from Disney early, before his contract ended, and came to Mexico in August to seek his fortune and be with me. Everyone thought it was terribly bold and romantic, but at that time I could only think of it as an act of passionate love—he gave up everything so that we could be together!

Felix spoke only a few words of Spanish, but that didn't worry him. He enrolled in intensive language classes, and in six months he spoke Spanish well enough to get a decent job. I continued to live at home with my family while Felix rented a room with one of my tender-hearted aunts. No way could we have lived together, as Felix had expected. Puebla society is conservative, and my family very traditional—not at all like the freethinkers he grew up with back in Europe. Skeptical at first, my family soon became very fond of Felix, which wasn't hard. He could be so charming, and I was so much in love with him. My father, of course, had his suspicions and kept his eye on Felix from the start. Why do you think he was offered a room with my aunt? It wasn't purely kindness on the part of my family!

After assessing the situation in Puebla, Felix realized that the only way we could truly be together would be to get married. It all seemed rather quaint to him, but if that's what was required, then that's what he would do. Things went well, and within a few months we became engaged.

On August 19, 1998, we were married in the beautiful chapel of Nuestra Señora de la Candelaria y Guadalupe, a fashionable setting for weddings in the Xonaca neighborhood of Puebla. The photograph that ran in *El Sol de Puebla*, our hometown newspaper, shows Felix and me standing in front of a golden baroque altar adorned with paintings of two saints and, of course, Mexico's beloved patroness, the Virgin of Guadalupe.

Felix's parents and his delightful, elderly Uncle Serge flew in from France for the occasion, as did his sister and her American husband. Almost all my family members still lived in Puebla, so that was easy, but Felix and I especially welcomed my father's brother and his American wife of twenty years, who joined us from North Carolina—see, Dad, international marriages can be successful! A dozen or so of our friends from Disney World also came to celebrate with us. The wedding reception was held at the golf club where my family has a membership. Felix suggested to my father that we decorate the main wall of the reception hall with two huge flags, one French and one Mexican, their poles crossed to make an X to symbolize the union of two nations and two people. My father, however, said that was a bit much.

I was insanely happy, and we danced the night away surrounded by family and friends. For me, it was a dream come true. I felt incredibly lucky to find such a deep love so early in my life. I rejoiced at having avoided all the broken hearts, tears, and headaches that so many other women endure on the road to true love—if they ever even find it. I have always loved ice cream, and with Felix I told myself I had found my Häagen-Dazs of men on the very first try.

I was twenty-two years old. Thanks to my family's assistance, I finished at the university, graduated, and found a good job at one of Puebla's best employers. Life was so good!

Chapter 19
More Mexicans Arrive

When we first came to live at the Shanghai Racquet Club, I was the only Mexican for miles around, and I did not encounter another for almost a year. Then one day a *tai-tai* from Singapore, named Christine, called me on the phone. She was very excited and told me that she had just discovered that her new neighbors were a family from Mexico.

Christine lived in Forest Manor. This compound was located adjacent to ours, but it was much ritzier. Many houses there were truly mansions and rented for six thousand to ten thousand dollars a month. They were lovely, but built in a hodgepodge of styles. Some houses looked like they came right out of a storybook, such as *Gone with the Wind* or even *Heidi*. Others had lakes with impressive fountains that reminded me of Versailles. It kind of blew my mind to see this panorama, so foreign, bordering the rice paddies and rickety, overcrowded apartments that ringed the perimeter of Forest Manor. I sincerely hoped that the Mexican family moving in, and especially the wife, would not be as snobby as some of those houses suggested.

My friend made the arrangements and soon introduced me to Judy, who had been living with her husband and kids in Shanghai for ten years—an eon in ex-pat time! The family had moved from the newer Pudong area of Shanghai to our side of town, Puxi, and to our local district of Gubei so that her children could attend the American school located nearby.

I shouldn't have worried—I liked Judy immediately, and we became good friends. She came from Ciudad Juárez in northern Mexico and had twin boys and a younger girl. Her husband worked for an American company, and she had her own business exporting Chinese furniture. With ten years' experience living in China, Judy was an expert at ex-pat living and became something of a mentor to me. She knew much more than just where to shop for different foods and medicines. Years of experience had taught her how to get things done in China and how to accomplish things in the easiest, fastest way. This wonderful woman knew not only how to survive in China, but how to thrive in our complex metropolis. She was a treasure trove of information for a novice ex-pat like me, and she was happy to share her knowledge and her stories of the early days when Westerners were just beginning to arrive.

She told me that when she first came in Shanghai in the early 1990s, her husband's company allowed them three expenses-paid trips to Hong Kong each year. Wow, three vacations a year? I asked her. No, no, she explained. These were intended for shopping, not relaxation. On each trip they were allowed to send back one shipping container of purchases. What did she buy? Her answers surprised me. Primarily household necessities, she said, that were not yet available in China, such as toilet paper, tissues, medicines, and sanitary products. She said I should thank God that I had arrived at a time when life in China was much more modern and Western friendly. *My gosh*, I thought to myself, *if this is Western friendly, I don't even want to imagine what the "good old days" were like!*

With her years of experience, Judy had become an expert at the extreme sport of supermarket shopping, something that tried the patience of all ex-pat homemakers. One time, I remember, we had a long conversation about how to successfully navigate a supermarket in Shanghai, and we came up with a list of the skills a shopper must develop in order to manage a family home and not succumb to either panic or rage. It gave us a good laugh, but there was still an undercurrent of resentment at how the Chinese could turn such a normal errand into such a trial.

As best I remember, the skills required included:

1. Avoiding collisions with other shoppers. Residents of Shanghai drive bicycles, cars, and shopping carts with equal exuberance.

2. Enduring the ramming of your shopping cart by others without losing your temper.
3. Avoiding being swept along by the river of shoppers that takes you away from your intended route and wastes your time.
4. Holding tightly to the product in your hands so the ever-curious Chinese shopper won't snatch it away from you.
5. Guarding the items in your cart to avoid lazy or inquisitive shoppers helping themselves to your stuff instead of finding their own.
6. Designing a shopping route that will take you to all the different places you need to go in the shortest time possible. Congestion in the shopping aisles can be just as daunting as it is on the streets.
7. Adapting to the frequent and seemingly illogical changes in the layout of the stores, which happened constantly.
8. Remaining always alert to counteract accusations by other shoppers that you are stealing, as happened to me. (But that's a story for later on.)
9. Keeping your sense of humor, and remembering—in China anything can happen!

After her years in Shanghai, Judy had reached the most advanced level in the extreme sport of grocery shopping, and she was adept at all the skills mentioned above. To keep herself amused and her temper in check, Judy told me that she would often keep a count of how many times she encountered a shopper breaking any of the rules in the list above. I never reached her level of expertise at this sport, but I would have liked to.

Judy was kind enough to invite my mom and dad to have brunch at her house one time when they were visiting us in Shanghai, and none of us will ever forget what happened that morning. She was going to serve *machaca con huevo*, a Mexican breakfast specialty, and we were all looking forward to some yummy food prepared *a la Mexicana*. When we arrived at her house, she opened the door and began to apologize profusely, saying brunch would not be ready for a while yet. Her *ayi* had phoned early that morning to say that she could not come to work that day. As Judy explained it, the *ayi* had received an official summons from her local government precinct. She had been told to report that morning to a stadium to witness an execution. Some people had been convicted of crimes, condemned to death, and were to be shot in front of a live audience, she said.

My parents and I just stood there with our mouths gaping open as she explained all this to us. Brutal? Yes, it was. But then I recalled how safe I felt on the streets of Shanghai because their crime rate is so very low, unlike the crime rate in my homeland. I felt uneasy for the rest of the day, my thoughts swinging from one side of that dilemma to the other.

Another thing I remember discussing with Judy, when I got to know her better, was her belief that her family was being spied on by the Chinese government. Felix and I had heard the same thing from other ex-pat families. They said that the government hired foreign-language students to monitor phone conversations and e-mails to keep track of what we foreigners were doing. At first, I doubted this. There were so many of us, and most of the foreign families' conversation would be just daily chitchat. The enormity of the task made it seem unlikely. Even so, Felix suspected that it might be true and said it would be a good idea to be careful about what we say during phone calls and in our e-mails.

Eventually, however, Felix found pretty good evidence that such surveillance was real. He went to work one morning very early, about 5:00 a.m., because he had some work to catch up on. When he opened the e-mail on his computer, he was very surprised to find that all the e-mail messages that had arrived overnight had already been marked as "read." Then, as he was staring at them in confusion, they all suddenly changed to be marked as "unread," and he had not touched a thing on his computer! After that experience, we were much more careful about anything we said on the phone or wrote on our computers, and I began to give Judy's comments on spying more credence. She said that Chinese neighbors and acquaintances she did not know very well seemed to know just too many details about her and her family—things she had not discussed with them. Judy was a very reserved person and did not engage in idle chitchat with just anybody. She eventually began to suspect that there were even hidden cameras in her house because people kept surprising her with their knowledge of her private family matters.

One of Judy's observations about ex-pat life in China struck me harder than any other. In her experience, families going through the rigors of life in a foreign land seemed to follow one of two paths. Either the families united and became stronger, or they were torn apart by the pressures of living abroad. There was no middle ground, she said, and she explained it like this—when you have no extended family members or good friends to turn to, a successful family will learn to work together to solve the many issues that they must confront on a daily basis. The husband and wife must develop a truly confident and interdependent relationship, which strengthens the marital bond. If for whatever reason the couple cannot achieve this level of cooperation, the marriage will disintegrate as they separately encounter stress after stress. They will lose faith in each other, and the family will rupture. Unfortunately, according to Judy, more families fail than succeed at this task, and over the years she had seen a parade of families from Europe and the Americas arrive in China full of excitement, only to leave in distress after just a year or two. I had never thought this could be a possibility in my life, and I remember worrying about it for some time. *Could Felix and I ever become one of those sad statistics?* I asked myself. *Surely not!*

To my surprise and delight, shortly after Judy and her family moved into Forest Manor, the company her husband worked for transferred three more Mexican families to Shanghai, and another one arrived a few months later. What tremendous luck! I was so happy to meet all of them. Like Judy, they were all from the northern part of Mexico—Ciudad Juárez, Durango,

El Paso, and Reynosa. Now I had some girlfriends that I could really enjoy and feel "at home" with!

We would go out to lunch together from time to time, have playdates with our children, and we even got together occasionally to cook Mexican food. It was difficult to get this right because the true ingredients were hard to find, but each of us would bring whatever seasonings we had in our own kitchen. We would then experiment with various Asian ingredients to try and make the dishes taste right, and it usually worked. Well, it worked more or less, and half the fun was in the experimentation! We did find some Chinese peppers that, if you used a bit of imagination, did have a flavor similar to the poblano chiles that I love and dearly missed.

I remember one time during my regular grocery run to Carrefour I came upon a big supply of green tomatillos. I couldn't believe my luck—I had never seen them for sale in China before! Tomatillos are an essential ingredient in making that exquisite Mexican topping, *salsa verde*, and I bought every one they had in stock that day, about eight kilos. That's about eighteen pounds! I divided them up among my Mexican friends, and each one of us made several liters of *salsa verde*, which we stored in any container we could find to fill up our freezers, because who knows when we might encounter tomatillos again! (Actually, I never saw them in China again.) Only much later did we learn that Selma, the quiet one in our group, had been growing tomatillos in secret in pots on her terrace. She had been keeping them hidden from us, and even from her best friend Ana, as if we were going to steal them away. Well, they were precious—maybe Selma was right to take precautions!

As much as I loved hanging out with my new Mexican friends, I found myself keeping a secret from them as well. There was something about myself that I could not share with them, at least not right away, and I went to considerable lengths to keep it hidden.

I had learned the hard way that other Mexicans generally do not think kindly about *poblanos*, that is, people from my city of Puebla in central Mexico. We apparently have a reputation for being conceited and haughty.

How Felix and I Found Each Other

This had become painfully obvious when I began working at the Mexican pavilion in Epcot Center at Disney World. I was really hurt when the other Mexicans rejected me, and I certainly did not want a repeat of that situation, especially now that I was so very far from home. I decided I'd better not say anything to my new friends about where in Mexico I came from.

It wasn't easy. Whenever the topic of hometowns came up, I tried to be evasive and then changed the subject as quickly as I could. They knew I wasn't from northern Mexico like they were, but they never guessed that they were in the presence of a *poblana*! I think I managed to avoid their suspicions, at least in part, thanks to my mother. Even though she has lived most of her life in Puebla, her family comes from Monterrey in the north. Because of that, none of the three kids in my family speak with the sing-song accent that immediately announces one's Puebla origins.

My unveiling came about at Bianca's house. We had gathered there one morning to wax away our leg hair. I figured that such an intimate gathering might provide me the best chance of keeping their trust as I revealed my origins. I remember being very nervous and worried that morning. I started the conversation by saying, "Girls, I have something I need to confess to you." They looked at me with expressions of caring and empathy, which gave me the courage to continue.

"There is something I've been keeping secret about my background," I continued. That caught their attention, and they looked up at me in surprise and began to ask questions.

Was I a lesbian?
Had I been born a man?
Did I have a lover I needed to hide from my husband?
Perhaps I had been involved in prostitution before I married?

No, no, no, and no! They were all laughing now, and Bianca, sensing I needed some help to continue, got up and served us all a quick shot of tequila to loosen my tongue. "No, girls," I finally managed to say. "I am none of the things you have said. I am . . . I am a *poblana*!"

Hearing this, their eyebrows all shot up, but they didn't utter a word. They had actually had a *poblana* living among them for some time now, and nobody had noticed—shocking! In spite of my confession, my Mexican friends kept me in their circle and nothing bad happened, except for a few jokes every now and then about being the only southern girl in the group.

I could now relax. Thank goodness I had gotten that off my chest!

A few months later Felix came home with the news that the company we had both worked for in Mexico, and for whom Felix still worked, had sent a second Mexican to work at the office in Shanghai. Well, technically, this new fellow was the *first* Mexican sent to work here because Felix is French, but anyway—a Mexican with his wife and family arrived in Shanghai to work in Felix's office in late 2004. I was very glad to hear that another *paisano*, or fellow countryman, was coming to join our ex-pat community. The more, the merrier was my feeling on expanding our circle of Mexican friends. But this time, things did not go so well, and it had nothing at all to do with being *poblano*.

The couple was much older than us. Their oldest son, who was at university back in Mexico, traveled back and forth to China. He was a bright young man who would buy interesting items while visiting his family, and then take them home in his suitcase to sell later on campus. Their middle child, a girl, dedicated herself to learning Mandarin while living here with her family. Their youngest son, Fernando, attended the American school in Gubei, near our compound. The father had a good ex-pat employment contract with Felix's company, so I don't really understand why Fernando decided to cause trouble one day—big trouble, as it turned out—but he did.

One fine morning while riding his motorbike to school, fifteen-year-old Fernando decided to grab the purse of a young Chinese lady who was walking along the sidewalk. He kept her wallet, but made the grave mistake of selling her cell phone on the street for quick cash. He got about twenty dollars for it, telling its purchaser that he was selling his phone because he was about to return to his own country. Meanwhile, the young Chinese woman went immediately to the nearest police station and reported the theft of her purse and phone, setting in motion the Chinese criminal justice system. Within a matter of hours, as Fernando and his family were sitting down to their evening meal, the doorbell rang. It was the Chinese police coming to arrest Fernando. They took him off to jail immediately, to the utter horror of his parents. In a city with millions of people and thousands of ex-pats, the Chinese authorities had quickly and accurately determined precisely who was responsible for the theft and where that person could be found—an accomplishment that was as amazing as it was frightening!

Fernando's father had the good sense to call the human resources department of our company for help and legal advice. The company lawyers must have done a terrific job because Fernando only had to spend one night in jail. But he was deported immediately and barred from ever entering China again. Felix said his father was very lucky not to lose his job, and he stayed to complete his three-year work contract. Fernando, meanwhile, had to live with relatives back in Mexico until his family returned. In most cases, if a family member were deemed to be guilty of a crime (for example, possession of an illegal drug), the accused was taken to jail, the father would lose his job, and the entire family would be deported from China as soon as possible.

This episode caused quite a scandal among the entire ex-pat community, and I was really ashamed that someone from my own country had done something so immoral and stupid. After that, every time I told someone proudly that I came from Mexico, their next question would always be, Are you the one whose son robbed a Chinese lady on the street? How embarrassing.

Part 4

Storm Clouds Gather over Shanghai

Chapter 20
Felix's Love/Hate Relationship with China

One of the easiest things to like about China was drinking tea. It's everywhere. Most restaurants serve tea at some point during every meal, and many Chinese people carry their own tea concoctions around with them in thermos bottles, just as Americans carry around bottled water. There were many varieties of tea, but the most popular seemed to be a type of green tea, called *lu cha*. (I could easily remember the name because I have an Aunt Lucha in Puebla.) It was very tasty and rich in antioxidants, which were said to help keep your skin healthy. Maybe this has something to do with the youthful look I couldn't help but notice in many Chinese ladies. I don't know that for sure, but Xiao Tian drank lots and lots of green tea, but only until early afternoon. After that, she said, it would interfere with her sleep. An unfortunate side effect of green tea, which I also couldn't help but notice, was that it left an ugly greenish-brown stain on the teeth of the drinker. It took a really dedicated tooth brusher to keep these stains under control, and many Chinese just did not seem to be that dedicated.

At some point during our first year in China Felix decided that he too should bring a thermos of tea to work. Whether he truly liked the taste or whether he just wanted to fit in with his colleagues at work, I'm not really sure, but every three or four days we would prepare his brew at home, boiling three different types of roots and some small seeds that the Chinese called "wolf eyes." Felix had one of his friends at work write down the recipe for this tea in Chinese characters so that I could buy the proper ingredients. They were not sold at Carrefour, he cautioned Felix, we would have to get them from a traditional Chinese pharmacy. But it would be worth it, he said, because this tea would help alleviate fatigue and boost the immune system, plus the seeds would help keep his eyes healthy.

We had noticed several of these pharmacies in the neighborhood around our compound, and they turned out to be fascinating places to explore. Inside each one was shelf after shelf of bottles and bowls containing all kinds of strange and mysterious ingredients—roots, seeds, flowers, herbs, minerals, animal parts, and who knows what else. Many of them looked like something an evil witch might use to create a malevolent potion. I did recognize a few items from time to time, and once I even found red Jamaica flowers for sale! They are widely used in Mexico to make a delicious red drink, kind of like punch. I was so pleased to find that little taste of home!

All of these pharmacies used the famous Chinese medicine cabinets with their dozens of small, square drawers for storing and organizing their wares. Antique medicine cabinets had become a popular purchase for many ex-pat families because they were decorative as well as useful, but I knew I didn't want one—remembering what one had hidden away in all those little drawers would have been just too confusing, if you ask me. With time I learned to identify some of the pharmacies' most common ingredients, like a popular herb called "bird nest" because it looked just like one. Sadly, it wasn't that unusual to come across rather notorious ingredients for sale in these shops, like powdered tiger bone or shark fins. Secretly, I hoped the tiger powder was fake, because tigers are endangered and need to keep their bones for themselves. One of the uses for shark fins was to make a famous and expensive gourmet soup. It is very thick, with thin strips of meat floating in the broth, but to me there was nothing special about its flavor. Later on, I learned that when these sharks are caught, the fishermen simply cut off the shark's top and side fins, then toss the animal right back into the sea. This practice is particularly cruel because the mutilated shark can no longer swim properly and will die slowly of asphyxiation. To me it was amazing to learn what a tremendous variety of foods, drinks, or "medicines" the Chinese will consume in their pursuit of nutrition or better health.

One thing the Chinese disdain but Westerners love dearly is sugary drinks, like our soda pop. Several people I met warned me about drinking lots of sugar. They said it causes premature wrinkles because sugar breaks down the collagen in our skins. (Another factor in the youthful look of Chinese women?!) I discovered another health and beauty tip inadvertently when I tried, repeatedly and in vain, to order a glass of cool water to drink with my meals in restaurants. They always brought me hot boiled water, just as if I'd ordered tea, even in the middle of summer! When I was finally able to ask a Chinese person (actually I think it was Mr. Wu) why this happened, he explained that "everyone knows" it is healthier to drink your water hot. Drinking hot water, he said, helps digest the fat in foods and eliminate it from the body to minimize weight gain. Well, I thought to myself, here's one more reason why they all look so thin!

For me, the longer I lived in China, the more I found myself adopting aspects of Chinese culture. I was falling in love with certain styles of Chinese clothing and fashions, and I was making a sincere and somewhat successful effort to learn to speak Mandarin. As the months went by, and with the help of Xiao Tian, I was also incorporating more and more Asian food to our family diet. Every day in China was a fascinating, although at times frustrating, exploration into a new world—ancient and modern at the same time. I loved living here, venturing out to learn more about the Chinese culture swirling around me, then retreating back into my "golden cage" of Western culture (our compound) when I'd had enough.

As for Felix, he would loudly proclaim "when in Rome, do as the Romans do." Well, that is what he said, but in reality he was very selective about what parts of Chinese culture he would make his own. We certainly did "shop 'til we dropped" during our first year in Shanghai, and he filled our apartment with Chinese furniture and art. He also declared that we must all now remove our shoes whenever we entered our apartment to avoid bringing in dirt from the streets, which is also typically Chinese, and of course there was all that tea he drank. But he never dropped his attitude of superiority toward the Chinese in their table manners, and he loudly criticized any errors or confusion on the part of employees in restaurants or shops—something I found very embarrassing.

Okay, it was true that the service in restaurants featuring Western-style food could be chaotic at times. I remember one "Italian restaurant" where they served us the meal backward, starting with the dessert before moving on to the entrée and then the soup. In other restaurants we often got our entire meal—soup, entrée, and dessert—piled on the table all at once. But to be fair, that's the way typical Chinese restaurants operate. All the dishes are presented at once, so you can choose exactly what you want to eat and when you want to eat it.

And yes, it is true that the Chinese typically burp loudly at the end of a meal, and they slurp their soups and other liquids. But this is not considered ill mannered in their society. One particular surprise was finding that the Chinese frequently eat fruit at the end of a meal, especially watermelon, and think nothing of spitting the seeds out in every direction like a machine gun. This is just their way, but Felix would often react to things like this with bold and obvious disgust and make loud, sarcastic remarks. This would really stress me out. After all, we were the ones who were guests in their country. We were the foreigners, not them. They had invited us here to help them build a modern economy and reenter the world markets. In my opinion, we were lucky to get this opportunity. It was obvious even in 2004 that they wouldn't need the ex-pats' help for too many more years, and maybe they wouldn't always be as willing to put up with us and our intrusions into their daily lives.

After some time in Shanghai, I began to wonder if Felix's impatience with the Chinese and their customs was a result of the stresses and frustrations he experienced as he struggled to work alongside them. This was not an easy thing to do. Like most foreign businesses in China, the company Felix worked for operated as a "joint venture." This meant that each ex-pat worker had a Chinese counterpart with whom he must share and carry out his job. In theory, this sounds as if it would be very useful while working in a foreign country, but my husband often complained how difficult it was to actually get anything done this way. Making joint decisions was not easy, especially since Westerners and Chinese organize things and assign priorities in very different ways. Hierarchies were extremely important. When the boss made a decision, even if it seemed crazy and all the subordinates realized it was crazy, the Chinese employees would never question it, much less offer any contradictory advice. The boss was the boss, and that's all there was to it. Of course, you find this attitude in many Western businesses as well, but the Chinese carried it to extremes. Felix often felt as if he were simply going through the motions of working, doing things that he knew would not matter in the long run, rather than using his time at work to accomplish tasks he knew were more vital to the success of a particular project.

And that "time at work" was another big problem. It seemed to last so much longer than necessary. The Chinese businessmen worked very long hours, primarily, Felix decided, because it was the accepted custom to do so. Even when they did not have anything left to do, they all continued to hang out at work. It was like a contest, Felix complained over and over, to see who could spend the most time at the office—the first one to leave was the loser! On more than one occasion a young woman who worked with Felix told me that she did indeed prefer to stay late at the office rather than leave early and go home. By staying at the office, she could enjoy the air conditioning. During the summer months, she said, the temperature inside her home made it almost uninhabitable in the evening. In addition to working long hours, the companies often planned official dinners, which extended the work day well into the evening. There were rarely any wives at these dinners. The Chinese felt that a wife's place was in the home, and the Germans, of which there were many in Felix's company, usually left their wives living comfortably back in Europe. So even though I had easy access to a babysitter (Xiao Tian), these dinners were no way for Felix and I to spend any extra time with each other.

Felix also told me that one of his greatest frustrations was never knowing what to expect from his Chinese partners and coworkers. At meetings he (and the other Western employees) would reach certain agreements with the Chinese, and they would even put them in writing and everyone would sign them. They would all appear happy and satisfied with the agreement. But when it came time to implement whatever was agreed upon, the Chinese would ignore the agreement and do whatever they wanted, turning their back on what had been decided with the foreigners. This lead to a lot of insecurity and anger on the part of the Western businessmen, leaving them nervous and uncertain in any mutual projects they undertook with the Chinese.

All of this was just part of what a typical China Day might bring. While life wasn't always easy for me and the other *tai-tais*, I think it was much harder for the husbands since they had to deal with the (to us) unpredictable Chinese manners and customs every hour of the work week. In fact, after a year or so in Shanghai, I began to realize that husband after husband was succumbing to what I began to call the "Presidential Syndrome." They would all begin their new jobs in China with genuine enthusiasm and in good condition, both mentally and physically. But sooner or later, each man began to show a slow but steady decline, not unlike what one sees in the men who reach the presidency in either Mexico or the United States. It could even begin to appear after just a few months, when the stress and strain of having to endure just too many China Days began to wear down even a well-prepared and optimistic husband. They seemed to lose their hair faster, and they would gain or lose more weight than was healthy for them. Their skin would deteriorate as well, becoming dry and pale after the long hours our husbands spent working in their artificially lighted and air-conditioned offices. In addition, most of them did not speak any Mandarin Chinese, which only served to heighten their stress. Our "presidential" husbands looked tired all the time. This was especially true if they had to drive themselves back and forth to work each day in Shanghai's heavy, snarled traffic, as Felix did.

Soon after arriving in Shanghai, we realized that most ex-pat families got chauffeurs as a perk of the husband's employment. This totally made sense—huge amounts of stress and strain could be avoided if Westerners were driven to and from work each day. Not only could they rest or catch up on work during the drive, which always took at least an hour, they could avoid being held responsible for any traffic accidents. In China, the foreigner was *always* held responsible, no matter what the circumstances of the accident nor how major or minor it might be.

I felt bad for my husband (and me) at first to be missing such a valuable service. After several months, however, I learned from other *tai-tais* that the cost of hiring a chauffeur for a five-day work week was $150 to $170 a month. That's only about $40 a week! The driver could take Felix to work, come back for me in the middle of the day (to do a little shopping or whatever), then return to pick up Felix in the evening. It would alleviate so much stress! However, when I proposed this, Felix was adamantly against hiring a chauffeur. He said we shouldn't waste money on things that weren't absolutely necessary, but to me it would have been money well spent. After a while he did manage to get Mr. Wu for me, and I was always grateful to have my friendly driver for our Thursday expeditions. But in this case Felix's penny pinching hurt more than just his own health and wellness. It seriously affected our family dynamic.

He was always tired, always stressed out. Any errand I couldn't complete on Thursdays had to be done on weekends, which robbed Felix of his opportunity to rest or pursue his own activities. He became increasingly short tempered, which made our evenings and weekends together tense instead of relaxing. I'm sure that a chauffeur would have made all our lives easier, but Felix wouldn't hear of it. It wasn't like we were short on money, either. Felix's employer paid so many of our bills as part of his employment contract that we had plenty of money to spend as well as save for the future. But he was still determined to hold on to as much money as he could.

Due to his constant fatigue he jealously guarded his sleeping time and became very grouchy if awakened before he was ready—especially by a crying baby. Unfortunately, Julia woke up hungry and howling each morning about five o'clock. So to keep the peace in our family, I began taking her out each morning for an early walk. As soon as Julia woke up, I'd give her a quick bottle of milk, and out the door we'd go to speed walk around our compound. It was peaceful and beautiful to be out as the new day dawned. Eventually Julia and I even began to explore beyond our compound and into the neighborhoods nearby. Felix's "presidential" fatigue turned this early-bird walk into something of a personal tradition for me, and I kept it up for years. If it wasn't raining or absolutely freezing, Julia and I were up and out each day to greet the sun.

By the fall of 2004 we had been in Shanghai for over a year, and Felix had taken the family on several trips to exotic locations both inside and outside China. We'd had fun, sure, but I was ready to visit some places that had a special appeal for me. Felix had been very busy at work that autumn, so I decided to take the bull by the horns and make the travel arrangements myself for our upcoming Christmas holidays. Thinking it over, I remembered how much I had loved the movie *The Beach* starring Leonardo DiCaprio. Being from Mexico, I have had the pleasure of visiting our beautiful Caribbean beaches in Cancun and Playa del Carmen, but the beach in that movie was something else again! Now that I was living in Asia, I knew I had what was probably my one and only chance to see that beach in person. By talking to several people in our compound, I learned that "my beach" was located on the Phi Phi Islands in Thailand. So I organized a trip to Thailand for our family.

We would first fly to Bangkok, then take a connecting flight to Phuket where we would stay at a seaside resort from December 23 to 30. From Phuket we could surely take a day trip to my special beach! I made all the necessary reservations, imagining the whole time how much fun we would have and how happy Felix would be to find such a nice vacation all planned out for him. He wouldn't have to do anything, just relax and enjoy the trip!

But that is not what happened. When I told Felix about my plans for the trip to Phuket, he got very upset. He angrily told me that we had done enough traveling that year, and he made me recall all the places I had been, such as Beijing with my parents, Bali, and the limestone karst mountains of Guilin. He scolded me and reminded me what the primary goal for our family should be—and it was not traveling! He said that we should be saving money to build our dream house in Mexico when our time in China was over. He definitely did not want to spend more money on travel, and his answer to my plans was a final and nonnegotiable *No*. So with a heavy heart, I cancelled all the arrangements for my dream trip.

That evening our actual fight lasted only about thirty minutes, but his real punishment was just beginning. He ignored me and barely spoke to me for the next three days. He acted as if I had done something truly awful and saved all his attention for Julia, talking only to her in silly French baby talk. He would only acknowledge me by muttering "thank you" when I served him his meals or "pass me the salt" (or whatever) every now and then. This seemed to go on for an eternity, so for the sake of family peace, I finally decided I'd better apologize for not involving him in the decision to spend Christmas vacation in Thailand.

That brought an immediate smile to his face. He began kissing me and acting all lovey dovey again. After a session of passionate lovemaking, we managed to reestablish a fragile truce between us. But it wasn't a true reconciliation. At least it felt artificial to me, because I was troubled by his lack of respect for me and my interests, for my likes and dislikes. Things seemed to be always about him and his needs these days. Only his opinions mattered. Not for the first time, I found myself beginning to resent my role in our family. My new position as the stay-at-home wife and mother was beginning to wear thin, very thin.

In addition to his cruel rejection of my plans for the vacation, I knew perfectly well that money was not the real issue. When Felix signed his work contract with the company here in Shanghai, one of the perks was an annual travel budget for our entire family. It stipulated that the company would pay for us to fly *in business class* to our home country once each year. It was a generous sum of money and a typical perk for ex-pat employees in those days. Right after we arrived, Felix went to speak to the personnel manager for foreign employees. He asked her if we could we use the money in this travel budget to pay for vacation travel instead of using it just to fly back and forth to Mexico. She said yes, so it was the company who paid for our airline tickets and resort hotels that year, not us. The only money to come out of our pockets on "my" trip would have been for food and any extra activities at the resort.

He had actually managed to get a really good deal for our family, of that I have no doubt. My husband could really turn on the charm when he wanted to. As we say in Mexico, Felix could "even convince the devil to move hell someplace closer to heaven." When he told me about this conversation with the personnel manager, I could totally picture the episode in my mind. I had watched Felix win people over to his way of thinking many times. He would approach his target with a sweet, shy smile, look directly into their eyes, and talk to them in his beautiful French accent as if nobody else in the world mattered, only them. He always assumed an attitude of "excuse me, I don't want to bother you, but . . ." People found him irresistible, especially women. His manners were impeccable, and his eyes a tender blue. Felix wasn't the most intelligent person I've ever met, but he more than made up for it with his personality. Oh, that charm! After years of being seduced, I was finally beginning to realize just how dangerous it could be.

So our second Christmas in Shanghai arrived with little fanfare, and with it came the cold, gray weather of December. We stayed at home, and Felix and I kept to our usual routines, the bitter feelings over my cancelled trip diminished but not forgotten. Then came Boxing Day, December 26, and we learned with horror of the terrible tsunami in the eastern Indian Ocean. Entire communities had been swept away by waves topping twenty feet, and the death toll eventually climbed to 230,000 people in fourteen countries. It was one of the deadliest natural disasters in recorded history, and everyone in our compound knew someone who had gone to Southeast Asia for the holidays, or knew someone who *might* have gone. It was a time of great fear and stress for us all, not knowing who might have perished or been injured, who might not be coming home to Shanghai.

As friends and neighbors made their way home after the disaster, the stories they told were frightening and heartbreaking. We knew that Jimmy, a young fellow who lived down the hall from us, had gone somewhere in Thailand for the holidays. When we did not hear from him after a week or so, we feared the worst. Luckily, on the day of the tsunami, he had left the coast early in the morning to go on a tour of the mountains, so he was saved. It had taken extra days for him to make his way home to Shanghai, and he arrived shocked and traumatized by what he saw.

Another couple I knew from the gym in our compound were physical education teachers at the nearby Shanghai American school. They were both in great shape and looked as if they had just stepped off the cover of a fitness magazine. They had taken their two children, ages six and three, on vacation to one of the beaches hardest hit by the tsunami, and all four of them were on the beach that morning. As I heard her describe it later, they were combing the beach and looking at all the little marine animals trapped in tidal pools as the ocean receded. They thought it was just low tide. Then they heard a roar, looked up, and saw the water rushing toward them. They screamed at each other to grab a kid, and then ran as fast as they could to a rocky cliff nearby, scrambling up it as quickly as humanly possible. All four of them escaped the water, but arrived home covered with cuts and bruises.

The most dramatic story I heard came from a Venezuelan friend, who was traveling with her husband and teenage sons. They were staying at a resort located on high ground overlooking the beach. She said that her youngest son, about twelve, had felt the tremor of the earthquake that preceded the tsunami and noticed the water was pulling back from the beach. The family was just sitting down to breakfast on their terrace, and the boy told his parents that he had just learned in school that whenever there is an earth tremor and the ocean recedes, a dangerously big wave would soon come roaring back. This is called a tsunami, he told them. The rest of the family chuckled and did not take the youngster seriously. Like many people, they thought the wide stretch of beach was simply due to the tide being at low ebb. They were in for a horrible surprise only a few minutes later when they heard and then saw the huge wave coming in. Looking down on the beach, they witnessed the violence of the wave as it slammed the people on the beach into trees or buildings along the shore and then sucked them back out to sea again. Very few people were fast enough to escape the tons of rushing water. At first my friends stood frozen in horror on their terrace above the beach, but then recovered their wits and went down to help pull people from the water.

Several residents of our compound never made it back from their fatal holiday. None of them were my special *tai-tai* friends, but everybody knew someone who had perished. It was a terrible time for all of us, but for me it was a special nightmare because—IT COULD HAVE BEEN ME TRAPPED BY THAT WAVE!

The dream vacation that I had so joyously planned and that Felix had emphatically vetoed would have put us precisely in the path of the tsunami. I had arranged for us to stay in Phuket, one of the most heavily damaged resort towns in the area, and knowing me, I would have been down exploring the beach with Julia while Felix slept the morning away back in the hotel. Had we followed my plans, I would not be here now to tell my story.

Hearing about the destruction caused by the tsunami, I didn't know whether to be happy or sad, angry or grateful. But in this case I thanked God for Felix's stubborn attitude that somehow saved our lives. I can only say that I guess I just wasn't meant to be there.

Chapter 21
Raising a Global Child

My daughter Julia arrived in China when she was four months old. With a French father and a Mexican mother, she was destined to become bilingual. This is something Felix and I were proud of and hoped to encourage throughout her upbringing. But we were not quite prepared for the mélange of language skills she developed as a child growing up in Shanghai.

In addition to hearing both French and Spanish, Julia spent a lot of time around Xiao Tian, our bright and loving housekeeper. Xiao Tian naturally spoke to her in Mandarin, so it really wasn't too surprising that Julia's first words were in that language, especially since her bewildered mother was working so hard to communicate with her *ayi* in that language. I have a vivid memory of carrying Julia in my arms as she pointed up to the sky and said, "Look, Mommy, look! Airplane!" Except what she actually said was "*Kan, mam. Kan, feiji!*"

In addition to this trio of languages, we were socializing with people from many different countries in our compound. Groups of ex-pats generally spoke to each other in English unless everyone happened to be from the same country. This gave Julia plenty of exposure to English as well. That meant four languages!

We should have seen it coming, but we didn't. We knew that she had grasped the concept that one thing could have multiple names. For example—fish/poisson/yu/pez/Nemo. But we were totally blown away when Julia finally connected the words floating around in her head to make her first complete sentence—*Wo yao yellow yfu, por favor, mami, merci.* The poor

147

child had managed to put all four languages together to tell me one morning that she wanted to wear her yellow dress!

It is truly incredible how children can capture and synthesize so much information in their tiny brains. Actually, I doubt any other person besides me could have understood that sentence, but when I heard it I was both impressed and horrified. What had we done?! Is it even possible for a child to learn four languages at once? To grow up to be not bilingual, but quadrilingual?

Well, we were destined to find out one way or another. Felix insisted that he be able to talk to his daughter in French, and I wasn't going to stop speaking to her in Spanish, since I expected our family to return to Mexico one day. Plus, Chinese and English permeated the atmosphere both in our home and everywhere we went.

"You'll see, *ma cherie*. It will all work out for the best," Felix said with confidence. Our daughter would become one of those lucky kids who is at home in both the East and the West, he predicted with pride. She would become a true "global child."

That was one of the buzzwords being thrown around in modern Shanghai and other cities where multinational corporations were bringing Asian and Western business leaders together. Global children would be brought up in both worlds and be comfortable in both cultures. It was widely believed they would become the first "world citizens" and be instrumental in bridging the gap between East and West. They would bring the people of the world closer together!

Felix adopted this idea enthusiastically, at least on the surface. He would go on and on about what this represented for Julia's future—to be coming of age in such a crossroads of history. But living with a global child wasn't always what he expected. I remember one time was when Julia was almost three years old. Felix was correcting her manners—in French, of course—when he told her, "*Julia, il faut dire merci a Papa!*" (Julia, you must say thank you to Daddy!) Without missing a beat, our daughter sang out in her high, clear voice, "*Xie xie ahh, Papa, xie xie ahh!*" She even managed to emphasize the *ahh*, which is typical of the Shanghai way to say thank you!

Well, this was just too much globalization for our proud Frenchman. Instead of praising his daughter for being so adaptable, he got angry and blamed *me* for letting her spend too much time with the housekeeper! Well, it would have been hard to keep them apart. Julia and Xiao Tian were very fond of each other, and the three of us spent many hours together each day. In addition to teaching her words, Xiao Tian was also making sure Julia learned to love rice and to eat it with chopsticks. She even brought Julia a pair designed specifically for children. They were joined at the top to make them kind of like miniature tongs.

Of course, what Felix did not yet know was that the Chinese words were coming not just from Xiao Tian, but from me as well. I was working hard to expand my grasp of Mandarin. I knew it was absolutely necessary if I wanted to truly experience life outside our compound—and there was so much life out there to experience! After a year or so I had progressed to the point where I could chat with the Chinese nannies I met in the park or tell shopkeepers what it was I wanted to buy from them. It was so gratifying to know that other Chinese people could understand my conversation, not just Xiao Tian, who was, as I have said, exceptionally bright and clever.

Felix never believed my attempts to learn Chinese would be successful, so I didn't bother to keep him informed of my progress. Imagine his surprise when he realized during our second year in Shanghai that I was becoming the official translator on all our family outings! We might be out shopping or riding in a taxi, and all it took was for me to say a few words or phrases in Mandarin to the merchant or driver. From that point on, that person would direct the rest of the conversation to me, saying "Xiaojie (señorita), tell your husband this . . ." or "Xiaojie, what is your husband trying to say?" It was a sweet moment indeed.

I never did learn to read or write in Mandarin, not at all. People told me that it typically takes about ten years to be able to do that. After I met Xiao Tian's daughter, Chi Moon, who was eleven years old, I tried to teach her English, but it didn't work out. Very few Chinese are able to understand our alphabet, and I found it impossible to teach her without it, although God knows I tried.

Julia, who learned Chinese by ear listening to Xiao Tian (and me), seemed to catch on pretty quickly, probably due to her tender age. What surprised me most, however, was her preference. Of her four languages, Julia definitely preferred Chinese. People with experience told me that small children seemed to gravitate to Chinese because it sounds very musical to them.

True, Chinese is characterized as a tonal language by linguists. That means that the tone with which one speaks any word in Chinese determines its meaning. We use different tones when speaking words in English, too. But in English, the tone we use changes only the feeling or emotion behind the word; it doesn't change the definition of the word, as it does in Chinese. To learn Chinese, one has to first learn to hear the four tones implicit in the language, and then to produce them vocally. I got pretty good at it eventually, but Chinese never did sound very musical to me. I found it rather harsh and noisy—and definitely not romantic and sexy, like French. I was just thankful that the Chinese I needed to learn was Mandarin and not Cantonese, the version of Chinese used in the southern regions of China. In that case I would have had to deal with six tones, instead of just four!

As Julia got older, I was impressed to see that she could even tell which language to use with all the different people she encountered. In those days it wasn't usual for Chinese pedestrians to approach us on the street and try to take a photograph of the little foreigner with curly, blond hair. But Julia hated having her picture taken—remember our modeling fiasco? She would usually run and hide between my legs yelling *"Bu yao, bu yao!"* which means "I don't want to!" That left little doubt in the minds of the well-meaning pedestrians what she thought about photography. Felix may have been known far and wide for his charming personality, but his daughter, at age three, still had a ways to go.

☼

Throughout our ex-pat community, everybody seemed to agree that Shanghai was the ideal place to raise children. It was easy to get domestic help, and they also felt that the facilities at the Racquet Club and the nearby American and French schools were great for families. Felix proposed the idea of having a second child after we had lived in Shanghai for about a year. I didn't feel ready for a second time on the baby merry-go-round, but Felix campaigned hard. He felt that Julia deserved a companion and stressed that this birth would be free of cost with his company's excellent medical insurance. Besides, he said, our family situation couldn't be better! Well, I felt our family situation could have been a little more tranquil, but eventually he won me over. I guess I gave in because his arguments seemed valid, and they were echoed by everyone around me.

I passed the first three months of my pregnancy nearly underground, it seems. I felt nauseous almost all the time, and so I rarely left the apartment. Every time I went out, it seemed, I was assaulted by the odor of frying food. It seemed to hang in the air everywhere, and I was especially nauseated by strong smells.

That awful first trimester of pregnancy was just coming to an end when my French father-in-law and his girlfriend arrived for a visit in May 2005. Prior their arrival, his dad had mentioned a desire to visit Phuket, and suddenly Felix decided it would be perfectly fine for all five of us to go to the beach in Thailand—not one word about saving up money to build that dream home back in Mexico! This time Felix organized the whole thing. I was feeling too tired and nauseous to argue or discuss the family holiday.

Once in Phuket, I was amazed to find that just five months after the tsunami tragedy everything was beautiful again. It looked as if nothing of such magnitude had ever happened. Only small pockets of debris or damaged areas remained, and they were generally hidden behind fences. Everywhere we went, the Thai people were extremely kind and polite. They thanked us over and over for coming back to Thailand. My heart almost broke every time I thought about what these people had been through.

We stayed at a great resort right on the beach. Every night we went to lovely candlelit restaurants by the sea, where we dined on delicious curries and my new favorite Thai dishes, pad thai noodles and *tom yum goong* soup. The soup reminded me of the tasty seafood soups we have in Mexico, but with far more exotic seasonings. The restaurants usually featured performances by troupes of traditional Thai dancers. Their movements and shiny, sparkling costumes managed to catch and hold the attention of all the diners, even two-year-old Julia.

I was particularly captivated by the artistic fruit carvings that accompanied all our meals. They were so pretty and appealing that I felt a little guilty eating such beautifully prepared food. Our hotel offered classes in the art of fruit carving, and I made sure I signed up to attend. We got to observe as a chef carved watermelons, cantaloupes, and papayas into all kinds of fantastic shapes. Then our instructor gave us special carving knives and showed the class how to cut simple shapes on the easiest of the fruits to carve—tomatoes, lemons, and zucchini.

One morning at breakfast my father-in-law commented how happy he was with the resort Felix had chosen. My husband smiled and replied with pride, "Yes, and it is *so-o-o* cheap!" The entire week, including airfare and the hotel with breakfast, cost only seven hundred US dollars. Even transportation to and from the airport was included.

Then he turned to me, and I will never forget what he said next. "You see, *ma cherie*, we just need to wait for the next world tragedy to occur so we can go on another great, cheap vacation. Imagine the high holiday prices we would have paid had we come last December when you got that idea in your head."

I couldn't believe my ears. I felt so angry at him, both for what he said and the sarcastic tone in which he said it. I honestly thought I was going to throw up—partly due to the pregnancy, of course, but also due to the sickening cynicism of my husband's words. What happened in Thailand was a human tragedy on a tremendous scale, and he thought of it as just a great opportunity to save some money. What kind of person had I married?

I couldn't tell whether his comment was serious or in jest, but either way it seemed awful. I excused myself and went straight to the ladies' room, to be alone and to regain control of my temper.

Later that week, I investigated how to arrange a visit to "my beach" on the Phi Phi Islands, but my dream would remain unfulfilled. The only way to get there was by speedboat, and they strongly warned female tourists not to take this kind of transport if they were pregnant. I was so disappointed, but I couldn't very well hide the fact that I was pregnant. I still looked kind of green in the face most of the time, and I was still vomiting unexpectedly every now and then.

As an alternative, we were advised to take a sail on a big junk boat to an island made famous many years ago in the James Bond movie *The Man with the Golden Gun*, starring Roger Moore. Thanks to my dad I have always been a Bond fan, so the visit was a pretty good consolation prize. In that big old junk, we sailed on calm seas past steep, jungle-covered mountains that plunged right down into the sea. The aqua-green water was just mesmerizing and contrasted so beautifully with the deep-green mountains and blue sky. It was fantastic, unlike anything else I have ever seen.

Before we went home, we all went for a ride on the beach. I have always had a fantasy that one day I would ride horseback along a gorgeous beach. Well, this beach was plenty gorgeous, but our steed wasn't quite so romantic. It was an elephant, but so much fun! I still remember it years later as a highlight of my time in Thailand.

Chapter 22
Deeper Problems with Felix

Once back in Shanghai my pregnancy seemed to fly by. I was feeling much better now, and I was once again able to enjoy the company of my wonderful women friends. The *tai-tais* were such a great source of compassion and so helpful to a young mother, and my newer Mexican friends provided a comforting link back to my homeland and the people I knew and loved. To be honest, my women friends were much more helpful to me during those months of pregnancy than my own husband. I would make excuses for him because he worked so hard at his office, but as time went on I had to acknowledge a darker reason for his distant attitude.

I will never forget one particular shopping trip and Felix's reaction to what was for me a very traumatic episode. I was at Carrefour with my Mexican friend, Gaby. She was the one with the chauffeur named Cruise, who always appeared with the haircut and aviator sunglasses of his hero, Tom. I needed to buy just a few things, including some newborn-size diapers in preparation for the upcoming birth. Gaby agreed to go with me since she had several small items to purchase as well. We got into separate lines at the cash registers as we were getting ready to leave. In line behind Gaby was an elderly Chinese couple in drab clothes that seemed almost like a uniform. He was in gray and she was in blue, and they may have even been the clothes the couple would have worn several decades earlier during the Maoist years. Anyway, Gaby grew quite annoyed with them because they were being very pushy and bumping her with their shopping cart. So in passive-aggressive retaliation, Gaby decided to go as slowly as possible through the checkout procedure and make it last as long as possible. I got finished first, and I waited for her just beyond the cashier stations. Watching Gaby was sort of like watching a film in slow motion, and I knew she was doing it just to upset the rude folks behind her.

When she was finally done, we gathered our bags and began to walk out of Carrefour. Suddenly the people around us began shouting, especially the elderly Chinese couple who had been just behind Gaby in line. We were trying to figure out what in the world was going on when two policemen came up to us, followed by two security guards dressed in the green uniforms that one saw everywhere in those days, and they began to yell, too—at us! That's when we realized that *we* were the focus of all this anger. Thank goodness I had lived in China long enough by that time to eventually understand that the crowd was accusing me of stealing the package of newborn diapers. All that shouting scared me to death. I began to tremble—in fear, but also in anger—and my mind kept flashing back to images I remembered of the actor Richard Gere, when he was locked up in a Chinese jail in the movie *Red Corner*.

It probably had something to do with all the pregnancy hormones coursing through my body, but suddenly I became so enraged that I began to shout back at the gathering mob with the strongest words I knew. At top volume, I shouted that I had most certainly paid for the diapers, that the package was too big to fit into one of the store's official plastic shopping bags, and if they would just back off a moment I would find my receipt. All this time the cashier who had handled my purchase did not say a word. She just looked on passively and did absolutely nothing to help me. I fished the receipt out of my purse, handed it to the guards, and they quickly said that everything was all right. But I was so furious I couldn't let things end there. I turned toward that rude Chinese couple who had started the whole thing, reached back into my purse for a big wad of paper money, and shook it in their faces snarling, "*Waiguoren, you qian, ni kan dau ma!*" which meant "We foreigners have money!"

Gaby was trying to calm me down and probably thought that I was about to burst a blood vessel from sheer anger. Fortunately, that did not happen, but I'm still surprised that my son wasn't born right then and there on the floor at Carrefour. Just then two store managers arrived on the scene, and I have never been so happy to see a couple of Frenchmen in my life. Since Felix is French, I was able to explain to them exactly what had just happened. They apologized and told me that incidents like mine were not uncommon. Gaby took me to a nearby Starbucks so I could sit down and recover. It took an hour and a green-tea Frappuccino before I felt like myself again and we could go home.

That night when I told Felix what had happened, he was not sympathetic at all. In fact, he said it was all my fault because in my eighth month of pregnancy I ought to be resting at home and not out running around with my Mexican friends. I had expected at least a hug or a few words of sympathy from him, but I got nothing. I remember becoming quite angry. I wasn't out running around, I told him. I was buying diapers at the supermarket, for Pete's sake!

For some time, Felix had been getting more and more upset whenever I went out with my friends. Here we were in a fascinating city halfway around the world, and he wanted me to just stay home all the time—what a waste of a great opportunity that would have been! His rationale was that it was unhealthy for Julia to be exposed to the pollution and the turbulent streets of Shanghai, so she should remain inside the sanctuary of our compound as much as possible, *and* since Julia should always be at her mother's side and not tended by *ayi*, I should stay home, too.

It eventually reached the point that whenever I wanted to go beyond our compound for a change of scenery, perhaps to go shopping with friends or attend a luncheon of the Shanghai Expatriate Association, I would have to deal with an angry husband when he got home from work. He acted as if I were doing something sinful or reckless. It would often take him several days to "forgive" me, and he wouldn't speak to me, except when absolutely necessary, until he did. It was his way to punish me for doing anything or going anywhere without his approval. He even went so far as to tell me the only time I should leave our compound was on my shopping day with Mr. Wu.

Thank goodness for Thursdays and Mr. Wu! We were continuing to have a good time with our shopping and lunch adventures. I don't think Felix ever understood what a good friend he had become, or maybe he was jealous, but I will never forget the evening Felix came home from work and told me the wife of one of his colleagues was not getting along with her chauffeur. He actually expected me to simply switch chauffeurs with this woman, as if the relationship I had built with Mr. Wu mattered not at all! Felix would do things like this frequently as a way to ingratiate himself with friends and colleagues. It was one aspect of the "charming personality" he cultivated, but this time I categorically refused. I wasn't going to give up one of the best parts of my life in Shanghai so Felix could earn brownie points at the office. Felix was becoming, as we say in Mexico, "light in the street, but dark at home." He really seemed to care much more about pleasing other people than he did about taking good care of members of his own family.

Of course, whenever friends or relatives of Felix came to visit us in Shanghai, these stay-at-home rules did not apply. It was then A-okay for me to forsake our mother-daughter bond, leave Julia behind with Xiao Tian, and escort his visitors all over town. He got totally carried away with the idea of protecting Julia from the "dangers" outside our compound. When I told him one morning that I was going to take Julia with me and my parents (Julia's loving and capable grandparents!) as we went out to tour the historic parts of Shanghai, he practically threatened me, saying that if anything happened to his daughter, it would be my fault.

During our early days in Shanghai he had begun calling me during the day "just to say hello," but before long he was calling me at least twice a day to see where I was or who I was with. If he did not get me on our house phone, he would call on my cell phone, always saying that he missed me, that he wanted to say how much he loved me, or that he was longing to spend more time with me if only he could. Yet when the weekend arrived, he usually claimed to be exhausted and needed to catch up on extra sleep, or he would become engrossed in his cooking or shopping projects and practically ignore Julia and me.

At first I tried not to let his periods of giving me the cold shoulder bother me too much. Thank goodness I had lots of women friends close-by and we did lots of things together, often inside the compound—visiting each other at home or meeting at the sports club, where lots of activities were scheduled. Being with the *tai-tais* helped me feel less isolated. With them, I felt appreciated and understood, and I could survive the days when I was a *persona non grata* in the eyes of my husband. I tried the best I could to live a reasonable life under the strict rules Felix laid down. With time I came to realize that he was actually very insecure and was afraid that I would betray him somehow, so he disguised his fears as concern for me. I concentrated on his good qualities and tried not to think too much about his irritating ones.

Then my new Mexican friends arrived, and I began to realize how confining my marriage was becoming. They helped open my eyes to Felix's growing inflexibility in a way my "foreign" *tai-tai* friends could not—or perhaps would not. I guess as fellow countrymen (or women), they felt more comfortable talking with me about intimate, personal matters. After hanging out with my Mexican girlfriends for several months, I became bold enough to not answer my cell phone when we were out together and caller ID told me it was Felix on the other end. That did not work for long, however. Felix soon began calling them on their cell phones to track me down. I had been living in a state of denial about the problems in our marriage, but my Mexican friends recognized them and made me take notice.

I'm sure Felix was aware of their effect on me. He would show his displeasure when any of them dropped by unexpectedly, and he could be quite rude about it. I recall one time when Gaby came by to bring me some *mole*, a thick and delicious Mexican sauce served with meat. He answered the door, opening it just a bit to say, "Adela's busy," even though I wasn't. Hearing the reason for her visit, he opened the door just a little wider, reached out to take the dish of *mole*, and then closed the door in her face. I was so embarrassed.

I finally had to acknowledge that Felix had become a control freak. He wanted to be in charge of everything—friends, activities, money— even when he wasn't actually present. It was a hard, sad thing to admit. But how does a woman with one small child and another on the way stand up to an overbearing husband? By our second year in Shanghai he was insisting that he alone should handle our family finances. He said I lost the privilege to participate in these decisions because I wasn't earning money anymore.

I didn't know what to do or how to make changes when Felix felt no inclination to change. Sometimes I actually felt a sense of relief that he worked such long hours. He often said that I should be glad that I wasn't a working mother, that my life was so easy compared to his because I could stay home and take a nap whenever I wanted to. But I didn't give up a promising career in Mexico by choice! I gave it up to support him and his dream job in Shanghai, not to live confined to the inside of compound.

A golden cage is still a cage if you can't let yourself out.

Another reason I was feeling ever more frustration with Felix was his circle of French friends and the French ex-pat community in general. Maybe being an ex-pat in a country far from home made them all remember things back in France with more affection, but I got mighty tired of hearing them constantly sing the praises of French life and culture. To keep the peace in my marriage and to avoid spoiling my relationship with Felix's friends, I decided to keep my mouth shut, but I was reminded during almost every encounter with French nationals about the greatness of France and how they had the most beautiful capital city, the best food, the best wines, best fashions, best art, best cheeses, best writers, best perfumes, best poets, best desserts, best designers, best makeup brands, best . . . you name it and France had the very best, every time!

The more I got to know my first friend in Shanghai—Agnes—and her husband, the harder I found it to enjoy spending time with them. Well, not Agnes herself—she was awfully nice for a French person—but I could not stand her husband. He was constantly trying to flirt with me, and the way he would look at me, slowly running his eyes up and down my body, made me feel very uncomfortable. What bothered me the most was that Agnes never seemed to notice—ever!

Looking back on it now, I think she just pretended not to notice. As I met more and more French ex-pats, I realized that the French always choose to ignore an awkward situation and smile as if nothing unusual is going on—and they certainly never talk about it. My theory is that either they do not have blood in their veins, or their self-control is far beyond what other Europeans and Latin Americans can manage. Even though by this time I had a French passport (by marriage to Felix) and dual Mexican-French citizenship, I knew I would never be able to acquire that cool French *savoir faire*. For better or worse, in my heart and soul I would always and forever be proudly *mexicaine*.

Then there was the huge issue of Felix's boyhood friend, Michel, who had been so helpful to us when we first arrived in Shanghai. He was always friendly and polite to me, but he confided way too much about his love life when the three of us got together, and it left me distressed and disturbed. He blamed everything on his American wife. He told us that after their son was born six years ago, his wife stopped having sex with him, so his multiple affairs were a result of his deep loneliness. Well, his wife was something of a witch, but I would bet that she considered her anger justified because she felt forced into marrying him. Her strict Italian Catholic family insisted on this when she and Michel admitted to them she was pregnant. Her weight ballooned, and she couldn't manage to lose either the fat or her anger. To keep Michel out of her bed, he told us, she actually breastfed the boy until he was four! Michel told us how embarrassing it was for him to go out in public with a child who would literally pull up his mother's shirt and howl "I want tits, tits, tits!"

I was shocked to hear such graphic details about his sad home life, but I was totally unprepared for what came next. One day he announced he had joined an internet site called Adult FriendFinder. Men and women from Shanghai and many other cities around the world posted their photos and personal details in order to arrange dates for sex with each other. Michel loved this site and said he was able to find dates in most of the Asian cities he visited on business. This was great, according to him, because it was so easy to hide these "dates" from his wife. Whenever he felt the need to "find a friend" in Shanghai, he would arrange to meet the women during his lunch hour. He thought that Russian women, who had migrated to Shanghai in droves to work as prostitutes, were the most beautiful women in the world, but his particular favorites were the Japanese women who came to Shanghai on business trips.

He described how exciting it was to meet these women from Japan. They were all very classy. They showed up wearing beautifully tailored suits and carrying expensive designer accessories. According to him, these businesswomen were in no hurry to get married and settle down back in Japan. The men were very controlling, they told him, and they did not relish the idea of losing their freedom too soon. He found them very attractive and, best of all, great in bed. He loved how their skin was so much softer than the Europeans' and that they had so much less body hair. They would usually meet him in very posh places in Xintiandi, a hub of boutiques, chic bars, art galleries, and expensive restaurants located near the historic French Concession. Well, even I could see how Xintiandi would be the ideal spot for a tryst. To me, this part of Shanghai always brought to mind the Montmartre district of Paris and what I imagined it would have been like during its heyday in the 1890s.

I couldn't help but be embarrassed whenever he brought this topic up, which was often. Even though he was a great storyteller and described his adventures with great verve and humor, I just did not know what to do or what to think about all this. He had been so helpful and friendly to us, and I remember feeling sorry for him when he described how he loved his wife and had tried to make her happy. I guess we will never know the truth about that marriage. But in those days, I still believed strongly in love and had not yet realized how cynical French men could be.

Even more troubling, this Don Juan was Felix's best friend, his buddy from childhood. What did that say about my husband? Would he develop the wandering eye that Michel boasted of so openly? Was he secretly jealous of Michel's adventures? The whole thing made me nervous and upset.

It all came to a head one day late in the spring of 2005 when I got an unexpected phone call from Michel. I could barely understand him because he was crying and his English had such a heavy French accent. "For the love of God," I remember him saying, "please bring some medical supplies and come meet me at [such-and-such] hotel. Alexis [his wife] beat me up. I need your help."

At first I thought this was just a prank, and I told him, "Listen, Michel, I am feeling really morning sick right now, and if this is a joke I am going to beat you up myself."

But he sounded truly desperate, so I took some antiseptic and bandages and went to the hotel, half expecting this to be a total waste of my time. But when he opened the door and I saw his face, I had to stifle a scream. It was swollen, and he had bleeding cuts all over his face, neck, and chest. He told me they had had a terrible fight. His wife had indeed beaten him up, and he had fled the house to get help.

I treated his wounds as best I could and called Felix for advice. We ended up bringing Michel home to stay with us while he healed. He looked so bad that he decided to postpone an upcoming business meeting in Beijing until the following month. He attempted to call his wife a few days after the incident, but she didn't answer their home phone or her cell phone. It turns out she wasn't even living in their apartment any longer. She had vanished. Friends told him she had taken their son and gone back to the US.

He stayed with us a few weeks until he felt and looked better, then flew to the US to look for them.

We did not see Michel again for two years, and by that time he was a changed man. But that is part of a later story.

Chapter 23
The Real Reason We Moved to China

It is said that French men make excellent lovers, but terrible husbands. I did not encounter this saying until it was way too late to turn back. When I hear it now, I always think of the song by The Black Eyed Peas that goes, "if I only knew then all the things I know now." But back in the early days of my courtship and marriage, I had never heard those words. And even if I had, I doubt I would ever have believed they could apply to me or my life.

When Felix popped the question of our moving to Shanghai, we had been married for just over four years. I felt a great love and passion for him, and I was confident that finding my wonderful husband at such an early age proved our bond was deep and true. And then there was my great-grandmother Carmen. The remarkable coincidences that brought Felix and me together certainly made it seem like she had sent him to me, or so I liked to tell myself. I had never been attracted to the men of Mexico, and even less to those of my hometown, Puebla. To me they seemed just a little too macho and full of themselves, and I felt there was little interesting or novel to learn from them. Maybe the foreign travel and languages I learned early in life set me up for a love of the exotic. My mother even had premonitions about all of this. She told me she remembers that when she was bathing me as an infant, she would often daydream about my future sweetheart, who had surely been born already and was waiting for me in some other part of the world.

A few months before China grabbed his attention, Felix had experienced a great blow to his career hopes. Our employer had a policy that required all its junior executives to take an extensive exam. Felix spent months preparing for it, but when it came time to take the exam in the latter part of 2002, he did not pass. This meant he would not be eligible for significant promotions in the future. He was just crushed, and remained upset for weeks afterward. He became disillusioned with his career and distant in his relationships, with me and everyone else in his life. My heart ached to see him like this.

Felix had been talking for several years about how anxious he was to have children. Each year of our marriage the pressure he put on me increased, and he would complain to friends and even acquaintances how frustrating it was to be married to the *only* woman in Mexico who did *not* want to be a mother. It was true. I was not keen on childbirth and motherhood, at least not in the early years of our marriage. I was just reaching my middle twenties, and I loved my job, my life, and my freedom!

For four years I had given him every excuse I could think of to postpone motherhood. First, I needed to finish college, I told him, and then I needed to get my career off to a good start, which was in truth something very important to me, even if it did provide yet another reason to delay having children. He kept repeating that all he would ever need in life to be completely happy was to have a job, a house, a car, and a baby. He even carried his campaign to my mother, telling her with tears flowing down his cheeks how he so desperately yearned to be a father. There is no doubt that he won her over. I remember well my mother and father admonishing me to "remember, daughter, all the obstacles he has overcome just to be with you." Naturally this brought a lot of tension into our marriage, lots of anxiety and arguments, with every fight ultimately resolving itself in the bedroom.

Finally, Felix delivered his *coup de grace*. He announced he would divorce me if I didn't become pregnant, and soon! I should have recognized this ultimatum was a blatant attempt to exert control over me, but I didn't. I was young, and I loved him in such a blind and unexperienced way. Plus, I was totally shocked that he would even use the D-word with me. It felt like he had thrown a bucket of ice water in my face. In Puebla society, divorce was still considered a huge personal failure, a disastrous and immoral thing to do. For women especially, it affected not only your personal reputation, but cast a pall on the social standing of the entire family. I could not even imagine putting myself and my family into such disgrace. It was unthinkable.

So I allowed myself to become pregnant because everyone else in my family, except my uncle's American wife, thought it was the right thing to do. My ob-gyn told me that it typically takes a healthy couple about a year to conceive. Not me. After taking birth-control pills for nearly six years, I got pregnant the very first month I quit taking them! Felix took all the credit, of course. He boasted to everyone about his manhood. "You see, I got her pregnant on the first try," he would say, "because where I put my eye, I put my bullet." I just wanted to slap him because I felt so damn bad when I was pregnant. Even today, when I'm feeling fine, I still do. But then came the exam failure, and I thought perhaps the pregnancy was a good thing after all. Surely the coming of his first child would help lift his spirits.

But, of course, Felix found another way to get over the blues, a change so enormous that his impending fatherhood paled in comparison. I never actively opposed his plan to move to China. It seemed like a long shot at best, and the truth is that I never really expected he would pull it off. Only later did I learn how hard he campaigned to achieve this transfer. He vigorously sought the support of his former boss, who had already moved back to Europe, and he conferred with and courted another executive already in Shanghai to push his plan along. But then, as 2002 rolled over into 2003 and I realized everything was falling into place, I got really scared. My God! He was actually going to get what he wanted! What I had considered just a daydream for my disappointed husband had rapidly turned into a nightmare for me. Once again, I realized later on, I had underestimated my husband's charm and the lengths to which he would go to get what he wanted.

Fast-forward to 2005. Once again I fell under his spell (and that of everyone else in Shanghai's ex-pat community, it seemed) and agreed to have a second child. I guess that I forgot, or perhaps suppressed, the memories of Julia's birth. During the entire nine months of my pregnancy in Mexico, I had stifled my doubts. I tried hard to believe my mother and aunts, who kept telling me that as soon as I held my sweet babe in my arms I would be overcome with joy and happiness.

Well, not quite.

The sight of my flabby postpartum body with its hairy-caterpillar Cesarean scar upset me so much that I had a panic attack and fainted in my bathroom at the hospital. I hated the idea of breastfeeding, and only attempted it to please Felix, once again ignoring my own instincts. It was so painful, however, that I gave it up after two weeks. Staying home and dealing with the care of a newborn seemed like hell on earth to me, but looking back on it now I think some of that anxiety was probably due to the stress of our looming move to China and the specter of a SARS epidemic.

So I was actually relieved when my maternity leave was over, and I gladly went back to work I actually enjoyed—but only for about two months. Then the time arrived to say goodbye to my job, my colleagues, and my family and follow my Frenchman across the Pacific Ocean to China.

Chapter 24
Birth of Sebastian

Hoping to create some pleasant memories surrounding the birth of our second child, I made lots of inquiries about the options for giving birth in China. None of them looked good. Several *tai-tais* even warned me away from Shanghai's maternity hospitals with personal accounts of unsanitary delivery rooms, crude treatment by the medical professionals, and even the botched stitching of a Cesarean incision. None of this helped to calm my already jittery nerves. Then I heard from two other friends about their wonderful experiences at the Matilda International Hospital in Hong Kong. The maternity ward looked like a luxury hotel, they said, and the medical staff all spoke perfect English, and with a British accent, no less! Plus, Felix and I had even visited the Matilda Hospital before. In February 2005, Felix had the ligaments of his knee repaired there by an Australian specialist. I remember the surgeon had a gorgeous office with a beautiful view of the city, and his walls were adorned with autographed posters of world-famous rugby stars who had been his patients.

I would have *loved* to have my second child in that hospital. However, there was one major complication. The airline rules would only allow women to fly up until the beginning of their seventh month of pregnancy, so maternity patients from abroad had to arrive two months ahead of their due date. If they wished, patients could spend that time in the hospital's apartment complex, which even had shuttle buses to drop the women off in the city center for shopping or lunch. I remember thinking how great that sounded—a restful prenatal vacation in one of Asia's most cultured and Westernized cities! I could relax and await the birth without anxiety or fear.

Felix didn't go for that idea at all. He claimed he couldn't possibly be abandoned and left alone in Shanghai—alone, with an experienced housekeeper to take care of both him and Julia! Yeah, right. But instead of just saying no, Felix once again turned on his charm machine. With his tender eyes and soft smile, he explained to me over and over that he just couldn't stand to be home alone, that he would miss me too much and would be constantly worried about me. The best thing for our family, he whispered in his seductive French accent, would be for us to remain always together and to never be parted. I realize now that I simply lacked the courage to stand up for myself, especially at this critical moment in my life. The cold truth was that he preferred I stay in Shanghai because he absolutely did not want to be left alone with Julia, our strong-willed toddler, even with the capable Xiao Tian on hand every day. My sister, Pilar, also volunteered to come to Shanghai and stay in our home to help us for a few months. But no, even that would not satisfy him.

So I had to keep looking for a solution to my birth anxieties in Shanghai. Funny, now that I think about it—Felix never even considered having his knee operation in China. Knee surgery requires surgical expertise, he told me when I challenged him about this. Having a baby? That is just an everyday event.

Imagine my relief when Felix and I learned that a brand-new hospital had opened in Shanghai. It was built specifically for foreigners and was supposed to practice medicine along more Western lines. Felix and I even visited this new hospital, and I had to admit that everything looked pretty nice. So I calmed down for a few months—until I heard what happened to an American friend of mine there just one week before my due date. Two weeks after her Cesarean birth she developed a fever and began to bleed again. It turned out that she had developed an infection because a gauze pad was left inside her body after the surgery. They had to operate on her again to remove it! At that point there was nothing I could do except scold myself over and over. I should have gone to Hong Kong, I lamented. I should have insisted on going to a real hospital where they practiced modern, Western medicine. But it was way too late for that.

Another reason I felt nervous throughout this pregnancy was that I had never been able to meet the doctor who would be handling the birth, even though I had asked many times to do so. This was so different from my first pregnancy in Mexico. I had gone to the same ob-gyn for several years. He supervised my pregnancy and was a comforting presence throughout the entire birth process. In China, my pregnancy had been monitored not by a doctor or nurse, but by another type of healthcare worker, whom they called a midwife. Whether she had the same type of training given to nurse-midwives in the US was unclear. She handled my prenatal appointments, took the ultrasounds, and did everything else that was required as well. She spoke good English and had worked in San Francisco, California, for several years. She seemed trustworthy, and I did not doubt she knew what she was doing. But she was emphatic that everything in my pregnancy was going well, and I would only need to see a doctor if a problem arose.

The date of my scheduled Cesarean arrived. It was October 14, 2005, and I will never forget that night as long as I live. Every year on my son's birthday, after his party, I fix myself a good, strong drink and congratulate myself for having survived it. Sebastian himself seemed to have agreed with the date because I had already begun to feel some contractions early that morning. I was assigned to a very nice birthing suite. The bedroom area had a Jacuzzi and a large plasma television, and the sitting area included a small dining table with chairs. My sister Pilar, whom I had invited to visit us anyway, arrived shortly after Felix and I did. When she saw the suite she joked that we might as well organize a party since we certainly had the space for one! *Maybe this is going to be all right after all*, I remember thinking. The hospital's modern and luxurious setting was beginning to put my mind at ease.

It was only a few minutes before the Cesarean began that I finally got to meet my obstetrician. Dr. Chen was a short, compact fellow, but what I remember most was that when he flashed his big, toothy smile, his eyes would completely disappear—not very comforting. He wasted no time on introductions but started speaking to me in what I thought was an overly familiar manner and *in Chinese*, so I had a hard time understanding him, much less responding to him. So much for the advantages of a hospital for foreigners!

The next thing I knew Felix and I were in the operating room. In spite of the anesthesia I could hear every sound around me, including the chattering of the operating staff. They were all talking very loud in that special dialect spoken around Shanghai, and I swear I felt like I was lying in the middle of a Chinese market. At that point I would have given anything to be back with my Mexican ob-gyn in whom I had so much faith, but that was obviously not going to happen. The only thing I could do was to put myself into the sweet hands of the blessed Virgin of Guadalupe and pray.

The surgical team brought Sebastian into the world without delay, which was a considerable relief, but they just could not stop with their personal conversations. The general topic now turned to the baby and how he just did not look like the baby of a foreigner. No, they decided after much discussion, he looked much more like a Chinese baby! That was the very last thing I wanted to hear out of their mouths—questioning the parentage of my newborn. My husband looked at me with a startled expression, and then took a good, long look at the baby. Had I been able, I would have screamed at the doctor and his team to stop with their ridiculous speculations, but under the influence of the anesthesia I could do nothing of the kind.

At that point an alarm sounded, and the mood of the room abruptly changed. Everyone except the surgeon and the anesthesiologist left the room at a run. They put Sebastian in a baby bed with wheels and took him away with them, or at least that's what we thought. What they actually did was wheel him out into the corridor and leave him there, unwashed and bundled in a blanket.

I know this because Pilar was waiting outside the operating room and walked over to see what was in the little rolling bed. She was surprised to find they had left a baby alone and unsupervised in the hall, and she was even more surprised to find that the baby was her nephew! She was able to read our name on his little identity bracelet. She took a few photos of Sebastian and waited anxiously by his bed, not wanting to leave him until someone showed up to take care of him. After at least twenty-five minutes (she timed it), a nurse returned to take Sebastian to the baby nursery. Okay, so there had been an emergency elsewhere in the maternity ward, I understand that, but my child had been completely ignored during the first few vital minutes after his birth! Shortly after everyone ran from the room, the anesthesiologist gave me a shot "to help me rest," and I spent the remainder of the day in a weird state of dreaminess, knowing nothing of my baby boy out in the corridor.

As I regained consciousness early that evening, I found myself back in my hospital suite. My arm was hurting from an IV saline drip line. It could not be removed for twenty-four hours, they told me. The next thing I noticed was that the bed felt very wet between my legs. With all the cords and cables attached to me, I could barely reach down to explore the situation. When I got my hand back out from under the blanket, I almost gagged. My fingers were covered with blood! They had not put any type of feminine napkin or pad between my legs. I was just bleeding freely onto what looked like a flattened-out Pampers diaper. When I asked the Chinese nurses for a sanitary napkin between my legs, they replied, "Cannot do that. Wait until doctor comes tomorrow morning. You must ask Western doctor if it is allowed or not."

When they left, I immediately asked Felix to please get me one of the pads I had brought myself to the hospital. I couldn't stand it another minute. But he would not disobey the nurses and bring me one. They were in my suitcase just across the room, but I had to lie there in a puddle of my own blood all night long because they would only change that diaper thing every six hours or so.

It was horrible and disgusting, but that wasn't all. The nurses insisted that I begin to breastfeed Sebastian that very evening. I told them that I hated breastfeeding, that I was exhausted, that I just wasn't up to it, and to please give him some formula. But they would have none of it. "We give formula only to baby when mother is dying, or mother very sick," they announced. "You okay! You be patriotic mother! You feed baby, or baby dies hungry."

That was just too much. I cared less than nothing about being a patriotic mother, and in my very uncomfortable condition, I begged my husband to please order these nurses to let me sleep and to bottle-feed the baby that night. To my utter dismay, he suddenly turned into a dedicated member of La Leche League and joined the nurses in their campaign to have me begin breastfeeding immediately. Since I could barely move, much less fight back, the nurses brought Sebastian to my breast every couple of hours throughout that hellish night and urged him on with a kindly but very Chinglish chorus of "Suck, baby, suck. You good baby. Suck, baby, suck. Good baby."

It was a surreal nightmare. With all the blood, the IV tubes, the pain, my bare breasts, the chanting nurses, and the anger I felt toward my husband, I didn't know whether to cry, laugh, or howl with indignation. And it was so hot! The parts of my body that weren't covered with blood were soaking in sweat. When I asked Felix to put on the air conditioning, he said that he felt cold and didn't want to risk getting sick. So I just had to continue to sweat.

The next morning the shift changed, and a new pair of nurses came into my room. I was so relieved to get rid of the night nurses that I consented right away to their request to see my Cesarean incision. Surely, I thought, life with these two would have to be better. How foolish I was! The moment one of them opened my hospital gown she began a vigorous massage of my entire abdomen, even right along my incision line! I screamed, and she explained that this was "to make sure everything gets back into place" and continued the massage over my protests and tears of pain. I grabbed the bars on the side of the bed and yelled in my best Mandarin that this is absolutely not what is done postpartum in Mexico, but she ignored me and kept going. When she finally quit, I slumped back on my pillow in relief, only to have the second, and younger, nurse step up and start the massage all over again. Apparently she was in training, and I was her patient to practice on! I was crying and could not even see them through my tears when the first nurse said, "Good! We come back and do this three times a day."

I was horrified and begged my husband one more time to intervene and forbid this regimen of torture, and I will never forget, or forgive, his response. "The nurses know their job, and they know how to do it," he said calmly. "We are in their country, so we must be adaptable and do what they say is good for you. We mustn't be close minded."

I couldn't believe it—*We* must not be close minded! My God! He was not enduring this torture, I was! At that moment I was sure that I hated him, hated him intensely. These people were hurting me, really hurting me, and doing something I knew wasn't necessary for a postpartum recovery. I felt completely impotent, and he wasn't going to do a thing to help me.

As promised, the massages continued three times a day for my entire five-day hospital stay. I don't think I could have survived without the secret precautions I had decided to take weeks before. Several of my wonderful *tai-tai* friends had warned me that the only pain reliever allowed by the Chinese hospitals for post-Cesarean pain was Tylenol (acetaminophen). I was pretty sure I would need something stronger than that, so I arranged with my sister to bring some Vicodin tablets (hydrocodone) from Mexico with her to the hospital. When nobody was watching, I would take my magic pills. I felt like a naughty child who was sneaking pieces of candy, but I swear it saved my life!

The nurses, and their accomplice Felix, never caught on, although the nurses made several comments on my serene and stoic manner. "You very strong woman, you never in pain," they would say to me. "You never ask for painkillers. Your race very resistant!" This time it was *my* turn to ignore *them*.

With the help of my magic pills, the remaining days of my hospital stay weren't too bad. The food was really good—it was catered by a well-known French restaurant nearby—and several *tai-tai* friends came by to visit. On my last night there, the hospital staff brought in an elegantly set round table, and Felix and I were treated to a romantic, candlelit dinner with champagne. It was such a stark contrast to that first night of horror. But as we dined together, I couldn't help thinking that I would have gladly traded the entire dinner for just a little bit of flexibility on the part of the doctors and nurses. It was just one more example of the topsy-turvy life of an ex-pat in China. Anything goes! Anything can happen, and you must always be prepared for the unexpected!

The Chinese medical staff never did stop giving me their opinions concerning Sebastian's appearance. Every single person who entered my room to check on him had to make some sort of comment about how he looked much more like a Chinese baby than a Western one. They would even ask me if Felix was the father of the baby, or perhaps the adoptive father. It was so rude and upsetting. Sebastian was experiencing jaundice, which gave his skin a yellow tone, but this is a fairly common condition in newborns, and you would think the staff would be familiar with this and not be so callous.

No mother of a newborn wants to hear such comments or experience the doubtful expression of her husband! The irony of all this is that within a year, everyone would be telling me how much my son looked like his father. Truly, they are practically clones of each other, with the same fair skin and sandy hair. Actually, neither one of my children looks at all like me. When they were small and we would go out together in public, strangers would often mistake me for their nanny!

At last it was time to leave the hospital and return home. Felix left to go pick up Julia and Xiao Tian so they could come and greet the new member of the family. I stayed behind to pack and complete the checkout process, making sure that I got a proper copy of Sebastian's birth certificate. This important document would be required to register his birth at both the Mexican and French embassies later on.

Before we left, the public relations manager of the hospital came to take a photo of the new baby and his family. He proudly announced that

Sebastian was baby number 101 to be born there, and he told us the photo would become part of the hospital archive and put on display in the lobby. He had us pose together. I held up the baby and managed what was probably a very weak smile, then turned and headed thankfully out the door toward home.

In Mexico it is customary for new mothers to take forty days to rest and recuperate at home after the birth of a baby. Translated directly from Spanish, it would be called in English a postpartum quarantine or *cuarentena*, which literally means forty of something, just like a dozen means twelve. Many women also wear a heavy girdle that stretches from just under the breasts to below the hips. It is supposed to "help things get back into place" in your abdomen, and it is a much more humane way to go about it than those torturous massages given to me by the nurses in the hospital. I wasn't thrilled at the idea of staying home for almost six weeks, but my *cuarentena* was made so much more enjoyable by the awesome help of my *tai-tai* friends. I didn't have to worry about cooking dinner or grocery shopping for over a month after I brought Sebastian home. These wonderful women cooked us dinner every night! Felix and I feasted on home-cooked meals from an amazing variety of cuisines, including Italian, American, German, Danish, Japanese, Mexican, French, and Singaporean, to name just a few. It was a stay-at-home gourmet adventure, and I was so thankful for all their love and help.

By the time I completed my *cuarentena* it was already late November, and I was more than ready to rejoin the outside world. In fact, I was so happy to be able to leave the apartment that I did not even mind that my first outing was just to take the baby for his first immunizations. It was Thursday and Mr. Wu was waiting for us on the street below. By that time Mr. Wu and I had become good friends, and I greeted him with a big smile and gave him the address of the hospital.

However, it was obvious that Mr. Wu was not at all happy to see either me or Sebastian that morning. He was quite upset, and said that I shouldn't even be leaving my apartment at all until Sebastian was three months old. It was dangerous and unhealthy, he said to me as his brow furrowed in concern, and he wanted me to turn around and go back inside.

It was very kind of him to be worried about me, and I appreciated his concern, but I had been dreaming of this day for five weeks, and I would not be deterred! I politely but firmly explained to him that (1) in Mexico, we only expect the postpartum confinement to last forty days, (2) this is how I handled myself after the birth of Julia, (3) I was sure everything was going to be all right, and (4) I would take full responsibility for this trip to get these "crucial" immunizations done.

After thinking it over very carefully, he reluctantly agreed to drive us to the hospital. On the way there, he told me all about the postpartum customs in China. After she gives birth, he explained, a Chinese woman expects to remain at home for three full months. She is attended by the entire family and is fed a special type of chicken soup that is supposed to aid in lactation. (*Isn't it amazing*, I remember thinking, *how chicken soup is universally valued for its healing properties!*) During these three months of rest, the new mother is not even supposed to take a bath because it is believed that her body is in a weakened state and bathing might cause illness. She is only allowed sponge baths. *Well*, I thought, *that explains why my nurses at the hospital insisted that I not take a bath until authorized by the doctor!* Some new mothers even refrain from brushing their teeth, he told me.

The end of this three-month period brings about two important events. The baby gets its first haircut (sometimes they even shave the baby's head), and its hair is made into a little brush or amulet, which is kept and displayed somewhere special in the family home. The family also gives a party to present the baby to friends and extended family. *And*, I said to myself, *I'll bet the new mother is also celebrating the end of a* cuarentena *even longer than my own!*

When we arrived at the hospital, I noticed the lobby now had a big new display of photos showing all the babies who had been born in the new hospital. A long, colorful mural showcased dozens of photos of smiling parents and their newborns. Finally, I spotted our picture. There we were, way over in a corner of the display—our famous little 101, fast asleep in the arms of his not-so-patriotic mother, his non-Chinese father standing to one side, and his indignant big sister scowling up at the camera. It certainly wasn't the most charming photo in the group, but hey! I felt like it was a testament to my survival, and I promised myself right then and there I would *never* put myself in that position ever again—and I never have.

A month or so later Felix and I went downtown to the Mexican embassy to register Sebastian as a new citizen of Mexico. One requirement was that you had to bring another Mexican with you to sign as a witness. Lucky for us, we had recently met another Mexican couple in Shanghai, and their new baby was born in October, too. So we did each other the favor of acting as witnesses when the time came. Their names were Rosaura and Esteban, and I was looking forward to the pleasure of having another couple of Mexican friends in Shanghai.

Unfortunately, our budding relationship was cut shorter than I could ever have imagined. I didn't know it yet, but Felix was getting ready to change our destiny all over again. With Christmas coming and a new baby at home, I was busy and blissfully oblivious to any clues coming from my husband. Pilar was thoroughly enjoying her time in Shanghai and was still occupying one of our two guest rooms. My parents would be flying in from Mexico to meet their new grandson, and we would all spend Christmas and New Year's together.

My parents still have photos from that Christmas 2005, our third and last in China. My favorites show Julia, who was then almost three years old, with some of her playgroup friends. They were all dressed as angels and sang carols at a Christmas party held in our compound's clubhouse. They made quite a multicultural choir. Baby Sebastian was dressed in soft, brown reindeer pajamas that had "antlers" sewn onto the hood—so cute. They were a gift from my parents, who also brought Julia a Mexican skirt and embroidered blouse. She looked like a miniature version of *La China Poblana*, and I knew very well it was more than just a gift. In his own not-too-subtle way, my father was reminding me not to forget my homeland.

On Christmas Day we all went for brunch at the club in the center of our compound, but for New Year's Eve we did something really special. My father insisted on taking us to dine at one of the fabulous restaurants along Shanghai's historic Bund waterfront. The food was delicious, but the glowing skyline of Pudong across the river was the real showstopper that evening. It was so beautiful, and I realized that I had grown to love this incredible, impossible city. With my growing command of Mandarin and my extended "family" of *tai-tai* friends, I was finally beginning to feel at home.

Chapter 25
Leaving Shanghai Behind

Baby Sebastian had just turned three months old when Felix gave me the news that wonderful new opportunities awaited our family in Kuala Lumpur, the capital city of Malaysia. He found out through the company grapevine that one of the executives he had worked for back in Mexico had recently been sent to Asia and put in charge of the company's brand-new Singapore and Malaysia division. Felix had gotten in touch with his former boss and convinced him to hire him straight away.

I couldn't believe it when he told me what he had in mind for us. Just a few weeks before, Felix and I had discussed whether or not he should renew his three-year work contract, which would be coming to an end soon. He told me *just a few weeks ago* that he would like to stay in Shanghai for another three years, this time working for a sister company of his employer. I had happily agreed. I was getting fluent enough in Mandarin to feel comfortable (more or less), and I now had a great group of friends with the *tai-tais* and other members of the ex-pat community, especially my Mexican girlfriends.

Felix suddenly flipped the cards in the game of our life all over again. He now said he wanted to leave Shanghai more than anything in the world. He was sick and tired of dealing with the horrible traffic, he said, as well as the enigmatic Chinese, the pollution, and the lack of family time. He also said how interesting and valuable to his career it would be for him to get in on the ground floor of a whole new division of the company. He could see that I was not at all eager to move. So once again he began to ooze charm, emphasizing how this would be an excellent move, not just for his career but for our family as well. His commute time, which would be so much shorter in Malaysia, could now become extra time to spend together as a family. In addition, he continued, as he played his ace card, if we lived in an economy that was more developed and more capitalist, our family's shopping and medical options would be so much better.

And so Felix managed to win me over one more time. The winter of 2005–2006 was the coldest we had experienced in Shanghai. We even saw snow for the first time. "It will be so much warmer in Malaysia," Felix reminded me, "and the lower levels of pollution will be so much better for our kids."

Well, I had to admit he had a good point there. Julia had been suffering from asthma attacks and allergies since she was tiny, and they seemed to get so much worse during the cold winter months. She had terrible bouts of coughing and spent much of the winter miserably sick. I often had to get up at night to ease her breathing with an inhaler or even a nebulizer. I particularly remember one time when my father-in-law was visiting with his girlfriend. It was March, and I was up in the middle of the night with Julia, who was suffering through one of her never-ending colds. He got up and came into Julia's room. He did not seem at all concerned about her health, nor did he ask if there was anything he could do to help us. He just complained that he was having trouble sleeping and demanded, "Can't you do something about that cough?" Felix was angry when he found out I had suggested his father could go stay at the Hilton, but I told him it was simply a reasonable reply to a rude question.

With Felix's campaign in high gear, he persuaded me that Malaysia might be an interesting place to live after all, and I agreed to take a four-day "look and see" trip to Kuala Lumpur. The company paid for everything, including our stay at the beautiful Shangri-La Hotel downtown. We had visited Malaysia twice before on vacations, but this time I would be looking at everything with a keener eye. We visited several houses and condominiums with a local real estate agent, checked out the medical services available, and made a quick search of the school choices available for Julia. Since she was just turning three, we left her at home with Xiao Tian. I would have my hands full carrying Sebastian and all his baby gear, plus Julia was already a dynamic child, high spirited and full of energy.

By the end of the trip, Felix and I agreed that we would make the move. We both loved the apartment we found in the Bangsar area. It was a lovely penthouse with a large terrace overlooking downtown Kuala Lumpur and its famous Petronas Towers, the twin skyscrapers that are among the tallest buildings in the world. We told ourselves that our family would make Kuala Lumpur our home for three years, but this would be our last ex-pat adventure. After our Malaysian experience, we would go back to Mexico.

Having to make so many important decisions on such short notice made the trip very nerve-wracking. I remember how amazed I was to discover I had lost seven kilos (fifteen pounds) during the week of our "look and see" trip, especially since I recalled sampling lots of the local food and eating plenty of chocolate. I have always dealt with stressful situations by adding chocolate to my life, and this time was no exception. When I got back to Shanghai everyone in the compound asked me what on earth I had done to lose so much weight from one week to the next. I simply shrugged and said with a smile, "Stress, my dears, stress." And then I had to tell them that we were moving.

As soon as we got back to Shanghai, Felix hit the ground running to prepare for his new assignment. Right after the Chinese New Year (mid-February), he left for Malaysia to sign his new contract and prepare for our arrival. The kids and I continued to live in our same compound for about a month, but in a smaller service apartment until our new place was ready in Kuala Lumpur, or K-L, as everyone called it for short. The drama that I had lived through three years ago when I moved to China began to repeat itself. Except this time, I handled all the packing and shipping of the cargo container with one kid in my arms and another running around my knees. Thank God I had Xiao Tian to help me and keep me going.

☼

It was so hard to say goodbye to everyone in Shanghai, so hard. My *tai-tai* friends organized a lovely farewell luncheon for me at the compound's clubhouse. I remember the date, February 16, 2006, and that there were four tables with eight ladies seated around each one. The centerpieces were bouquets of tulips, my favorite flower, and the colorful icing on the chocolate cake spelled out "Goodbye" in English, French, Spanish, and Mandarin. It was so touching. Everyone took turns standing up and recalling a Shanghai moment or a memory that was special to them because it was something we did together. I felt my heart breaking, and such a sense of loss took hold of me. We had been so much more than friends. We were like a family, supporting each other. Despite our many nationalities, we cared for each other in good times and in bad. When you were sick or home with a new baby, it was such a wonderful relief to know that you could count on your friends to watch your kids, go grocery shopping for you, or cook dinner for your family. I hugged everyone and thanked them for being a part of my life in Shanghai.

Saying goodbye to Mr. Wu, my driver, was not easy either. We had shared so many shopping trips together, and so many interesting lunches! He was such a kind man and so much more than just a chauffeur—he was my friend. During my recent pregnancy he had found and escorted me to one of the only restaurants serving the out-of-season food I seemed to be craving—dog-meat soup! Then after my *cuarentena* was over, Mr. Wu would wait in the car and watch Sebastian while I did my shopping. If the baby woke up and was ready to eat, Mr. Wu would call my cell phone and let me know. On our last drive together, he told me it had truly been a pleasure driving around Shanghai with me, unlike his usual clients, the cold and unexpressive German ladies. As we said farewell, I almost cried when he told me "*Moxigeren tai-tai zui hao le.*" It means "The Mexican lady is the best." He gave me his business card, and I told him I would call him again if I ever returned to Shanghai.

Leaving Xiao Tian behind was the hardest of all. We had learned so much from each other. I worried about many things during those last tumultuous weeks in Shanghai, but Xiao Tian's future employment prospects was not one of them. As soon as people heard we were leaving, she began to get job offers from my friends, who recognized what an extraordinary *ayi* she was. In those days the typical pay for an *ayi* was $90–120 dollars per month for a six-day work week. Some people, particularly the Europeans, said that Felix and I spoiled the pay scale for *ayis* because we paid Xiao Tian about $180 dollars a month. But she was so worth it! Her cooking was great. She could prepare a wide variety of dishes from Chinese, Mexican, and French cuisines, plus she was wonderful with kids. In the end I gave her my cell phone, our rice cooker, and three months' wages to thank her for all the love and care she gave to us during our two and a half years in Shanghai.

Two weeks before our departure date, little Sebastian suddenly became ill. He had a high fever and a nonstop cough that interfered with his breathing. I was very worried because, after all, he was only five months old. So I took him to the hospital and, wouldn't you know, had to endure yet another misadventure with the Chinese healthcare system. It was as if Shanghai could not let us leave without experiencing one more China Day. The doctor who examined Sebastian told me, "Your son is very sick, he has pneumonia. We have medicine A, medicine B, and medicine C, but none of these is what your baby needs. But if you want, you can choose one of them and we'll see if it helps." I almost fainted with shock and the absurdity of it all!

I decided to phone Felix, explain what the emergency was, and leave for Malaysia as soon as possible in order to get the appropriate medicine. That meant Julia and I had to rush to get vaccinated against Japanese encephalitis before leaving. We had been warned about this tropical disease, which is carried by mosquitoes. It was endemic in Malaysia and could be fatal or cause permanent brain damage. The shot was extremely painful. Julia and I both cried, even though we got the vaccine that was imported from Hong Kong and not the local one, which my *tai-tai* friends said caused more adverse reactions.

So after three days of intensified preparations, my children and I fled China for our next ex-pat home in Malaysia. We were leaving a city I had grown to love, "the city close to the sea," which is the meaning of Shanghai in Chinese, and were heading for "the muddy estuary," which is the translation of Kuala Lumpur in Malay. I should have seen that as an omen, but at the time I did not.

I was truly sorry that our hasty retreat did not allow me time to say farewell to Shanghai as I had always imagined I would. I had always known this day would come, just not so soon. I had imagined myself having a drink, all alone, at the iconic Peace Hotel overlooking the downtown Bund riverfront. I would thank Shanghai for all the beautiful and challenging moments she had added to my life. From the beginning I had always thought of this city as a grand lady. She was cosmopolitan, always changing, and simply amazing—complicated, but with a charm all her own. As our plane lifted off the airport runway, I tried to comfort myself by repeating one of my favorite quotations. Paraphrasing the Colombian writer, Gabriel Garcia Marquez, I reminded myself not to cry because something wonderful has come to an end. Smile, because it happened!

Part 5

Life in Malaysia

Chapter 26
Hasty Arrival in Kuala Lumpur

Leaving the airport in Kuala Lumpur, Felix and I didn't waste any time looking around the city but drove straight to our new apartment in the Bangsar neighborhood. The weather was very hot (this city is practically on the equator), and we had to get out of our winter clothes and into something cooler as soon as possible. At the apartment, I took a few minutes to get reacquainted with Gaby, the young Filipino woman who would be our new maid. We inherited her, literally, from the British family who had recently vacated the apartment. They recommended we hire her, and it seemed the easiest thing to do at the time, although I wasn't particularly impressed by her. We then jumped back into the car to get Sebastian to a doctor. Thank goodness there were a couple of Malaysians among my *taitai* friends in Shanghai. Before we left, I had asked them for the name of a good hospital in the Bangsar area, and that is where we were headed.

At the hospital reception desk, I asked to see a pediatrician and got my first lesson in how Malaysian society operates. The receptionist asked me, in that very particular Malaysian-accented English, "Madam, do you wish to see a doctor who is Chinese, Malay, or Indian?"

I was completely floored by her question and finally responded that it did not matter to me what race the person was as long as he or she was a properly licensed pediatrician and could see my five-month-old child ASAP!

We were assigned to a female Malay doctor whose long Muslim name was honestly impossible for me to remember. The only part I recognized was "Noor," probably due to the former Queen Noor of Jordan. So I simply referred to her as Dr. Noor for the rest our time at the hospital, and that seemed to work for everybody.

She had very expressive eyes, which was good, because her hands and eyes were the only parts of her that I could see. Her nose and mouth were always covered by a medical mask, her hair was completely covered by a *chador* (scarf), and she wore the traditional Malay Muslim outfit for women, called an *abaya*. It cloaked her body completely. It was very colorful though, and her scarf was held in place by a fancy, decorative pin. I would soon learn that Malay women are considered the most open minded in Asia because their *abayas* and *chadors* don't have to be black, like in Saudi Arabia, but could be in any color, even lively batik prints.

But still—as a Western woman, I was surprised and nervous not to be able to at least see the face of the doctor who would be treating my child. I remember concentrating on her eyes and looking deeply into them—not in that Disney way that has forever stayed with me, but with the anxious and desperate look of a mother. I did my best to describe my son's condition and our accelerated journey out of Shanghai to get help for him.

Dr. Noor examined Sebastian and immediately admitted him to the hospital—which brought up a new problem. I would be able to stay here with him, but of course, Julia could not. She would have to stay alone at the apartment with Gaby, a total stranger to her, since Felix had to report to work the next day. Our apartment was full of boxes from our shipping container, and there wasn't a single thing to eat there yet, but I was so worried and stressed out about Sebastian that I forgot to give Felix any instructions about what to do in my absence. I assumed that between the two of them, he and Gaby could handle things at home.

Sebastian was immediately put on a heavy regimen of antibiotics and scheduled to start percussion treatments the next day. Percussion treatments? That sounded more like something I would have expected at Interlochen Music Camp than here at a hospital, and I thought I must have misunderstood what Dr. Noor was saying through her mask. But I had not. Early the next morning a nurse arrived to take Sebastian down to the respiratory clinic for the first of his percussion treatments. The therapist wrapped him up tightly in a white sheet, laid him head down on an inclined surface, and began to pat him firmly on the back with her hand. She kept it up for about ten minutes, with him crying the whole time and me feeling so bad for him that I wanted to cry, too. But the worst was yet to come.

Another therapist showed up with a plastic bag. One end of the bag had a long, thin tube connected to it. The other end was connected to small pumping machine. Together, the two nurses inserted the long tube down Sebastian's nose and turned on the pump to suck the loosened mucus and phlegm out of his lungs. It was horrifying to watch. I could clearly see the milky fluids, and some blood as well, filling up the bag. We, and I do mean *we*, survived five of these early-morning percussion treatments. I think it was almost as painful for me to watch as it was for Sebastian to experience. But it worked, and after five days I was able to take him home.

I arrived at the apartment to find poor little Julia cranky and painfully constipated because she had been fed only white rice and meat—typical Filipino food that Gaby had *borrowed* from her friend, the Filipino maid to the Chinese couple living above us. It had been five days, and neither Felix nor Gaby had thought to buy groceries! Of course, there was nothing with which to cook any groceries because the same unpacked boxes that were lying on our floor five days ago were still there, untouched. Neither Felix nor Gaby had thought to unpack any boxes while I was gone either.

Now I began to realize just how much I was going to miss Xiao Tian, my partner and soulmate in housekeeping for almost three years! Life at home in Malaysia was not going to be nearly as pleasant as it had been in Shanghai with my wonderful Xiao Tian. We had tried so hard to bring her with us to Malaysia, but the laws of both countries made that impossible. It was clear that my new maid wasn't going to be as proactive or as hard a worker as Xiao Tian. Well, I would just have to make the best of it, I told myself.

I quickly unpacked a few boxes, ones I knew to contain kitchen items, and then questioned Gaby about the location of the nearest supermarket.

Then all four of us—kids, Gaby, and me—took the elevator to the ground floor, and I hailed a taxi to take us to Cold Storage supermarket in a nearby shopping center.

As I moved up and down the aisles of the supermarket, rapidly selecting foods I knew my kids and husband would actually eat, Gaby became more and more agitated. Each time I reached for an item, just like a robot my Filipino would announce, "Ma'am, that is *halal*," or "Ma'am, that is not *halal*."

I couldn't figure out what in the world she was talking about. What is this *halal*/non-*halal* thing, and should I be concerned about it? To my Mexican self, my selections looked like proper ham, beef, or chicken. I didn't have time to investigate what she was going on and on about. I just needed to grab the essentials to feed my family for a few days, and that is what I did. I finished the shopping and was able to get us all back home rather quickly, but I could tell from her facial expressions that Gaby was worried about just what kind of woman she was now working for.

Shortly afterward, I did some research into the *halal*/non-*halal* designation. *Halal* refers to foods that Muslims are permitted to eat according to Sharia law and is usually applied to meat and other animal products. Pork is never permitted and is always non-*halal*; other animal products may or may not be *halal*, depending on their source and how the animal was killed or processed. Certain sections of many supermarkets in Malaysia were devoted exclusively to *halal* products. No wonder Gaby was so concerned; I might as well have been a heretic in her eyes.

My first week in Kuala Lumpur was certainly an eye-opener—exhausting and chaotic, but full of hope that life here was going to get better for all four of us. It just had to, right? Welcome to your new life, Adelita!

Chapter 27
Getting Acquainted with K-L

I sincerely hoped that life here would be easier and more pleasant than the daily struggle of life in Shanghai. For one thing, I was very happy with our new apartment. We were on the fourteenth floor of a building on the top of a steep hill, and the view was magnificent! The famous Petronas Twin Towers, until 2004 the tallest buildings in the world, dominated the skyline, and we could see many of Kuala Lumpur's other skyscrapers from our long balcony, which had a 180-degree view. As in Shanghai, many of the buildings were illuminated at night with soft, lovely colors.

The first morning at home in our apartment started with a bang—or rather a shout. At dawn in a Muslim country the faithful are called to prayer by the loud, singing voice of the *muezzin*, or priest, who usually performs this duty from the top of the mosque's minaret tower. When I say loud, I'm not exaggerating. His voice was amplified by powerful loudspeakers. That first morning I was caught completely unaware and awoke with a start. I didn't know what happening—was there an emergency in our new neighborhood? A fire, perhaps? Within a few minutes, however, I figured it out. It soon became part of my daily routine, a sort of lullaby telling me that I would have to wake up soon but could still relax in bed for a few minutes before beginning my day.

The view from our windows was indeed lovely, but that was not the only reason we chose a sky-high residence. During our "look and see" trip to Kuala Lumpur, Felix's company had given us a booklet called "Living and Working in K-L." It had lots of helpful information in it, and I devoured the book during our short visit. I wanted to learn everything I could about the city before I made the decision to move here. One paragraph in particular grabbed my attention. It advised new residents who rented houses to be sure to spread sulfur powder around the perimeter of the house and yard to discourage the cobra snakes from visiting. Well, that settled it. We would not be renting a house! Instead, I searched for an apartment as high off the ground as possible. I could never have put my kids to sleep at night with a tranquil mind knowing there might be cobras lurking about! Luckily, Felix liked the idea of an apartment in the sky. He had visions of himself barbecuing on the terrace every weekend, just as he had done in Shanghai during the warm-weather months. So he readily agreed with my proposal.

Our apartment building sat on a hill called Bukit Jara, and it immediately reminded me of the La Paz hill in my hometown of Puebla back in Mexico. La Paz had been the new and fashionable neighborhood when I was a child in the 1980s, just as Bukit Jara was now the place for posh houses and apartments in K-L, the nickname everyone used for Kuala Lumpur. Our new address was on a street called Jalan Kapas. I could tell from many road signs that *jalan* meant street, and I figured out that *kapas* must mean cotton. I had noticed that word on the clothing tags of any new garment I bought that felt like it was made of cotton material.

We shared the fourteenth floor with only one other apartment. A single penthouse apartment occupied the entire top floor above us. We heard about its full-time occupant, Mr. Chang, and its occasional occupant, Mrs. Chang, long before we met them. Their Filipino maid, Edna, and my new maid, Gaby, were good friends. Thank goodness Gaby had someone from whom she could borrow food during my five-day stay in the hospital with Sebastian! Without Edna to rely on, I hate to imagine what Gaby might have tried to feed my poor Julia. The more days I spent with Gaby, the less enthusiastic I was about having her as part of our family. She was sullen and seemed to have very little interest in doing her job well. I could already tell it was going to take some significant effort on my part to train her before I would feel comfortable leaving her to run the household without close supervision. I was missing Xiao Tian more than I ever imagined possible.

Since Julia was now three years old and a very energetic child, Felix and I decided she was ready for more interaction with kids her own age. Unfortunately, we didn't know any other families in K-L yet, but I remembered that the family who lived in our apartment before us had had a small child. I asked Gaby about it, and she said the child had attended a kindergarten nearby. So we set out the next morning to investigate this for Julia. This *tadika* (kindergarten in Malaysian) was run by a very nice Malay woman and was located just ten blocks from our house, which was important because Felix drove our only car to work every day.

Only one other Western family had children attending this *tadika*. However, touring the *tadika* gave me a very good feeling about its staff and students, so I decided to enroll Julia immediately—and that's when I discovered the true ups and downs that would come with life on our lovely hill. Every morning I'd walk *down*hill with Julia in her stroller to the *tadika*, which was generally a very pleasant way to get some early morning exercise. The trip back up the hill at one o'clock, however, was just the opposite. The afternoon heat was intense, as was the energy required to push that stroller back up the hill. After three years of working out with Justin Wu at the Shanghai Racquet Club, I thought my body would be in great shape, but no. The heat and the hill combined to sap all my energy, and I was barely able make the climb back up each afternoon.

I talked with Felix about getting another car or having me drop him off at work, but he flatly refused. I had been driving for years in the busy traffic of Puebla, but Felix was adamant that I couldn't possibly manage in K-L because they drive on the left side of the street, a legacy of their days as a British colony. I felt certain this was a skill I could master—after all, he had succeeded in mastering this "difficult" task. But he wouldn't listen, and so to avoid another long and bitter argument I gave in—but temporarily, I told myself. Without a car I had to either walk or take a taxi whenever I needed to leave home, not unlike my time in Shanghai.

Julia loved attending the *tadika*. She came home each day happy, sweaty from the heat, and tired enough to take a two-hour nap. So despite the grueling climb, she and I continued our daily treks up and down the hill. It certainly helped keep me physically fit and gave me an additional two-hour break from Julia's high-spirited antics. So in the long run I felt it was worth the effort.

The *tadika* teachers spoke mainly in English with their little students, which Julia knew slightly from interacting with all the ex-pats in Shanghai. Julia was not a child who talked a lot back in those days. Probably her little brain was still trying to make sense of all the conversations thrown at her in Spanish, French, English, Chinese, and now that very special form of Malay-accented English. I often wondered if she ever asked herself what had happened to Mandarin. Why she never heard anyone speak to her in Mandarin ever again. It was practically her mother tongue, but I guess that's something I'll never be able to answer.

Here in K-L she was immersed in English for several hours each day, and eventually she began to show a preference for English over all the other languages she had used, although she continued to understand Spanish very well, I could tell. I was happy with her choice because speaking English had opened so many doors for me in my life. So I did my best to encourage her. I remember I had to be vigilant in those days to make sure she learned the proper pronunciation of English words and didn't lapse into that very special way of speaking English found only in Malaysia. But I am proud to say that to this very day she continues to be a fine speaker of English, even though we returned to live in Mexico almost ten years ago.

During our first visit to K-L I was quite surprised to learn that English is actually one of Malaysia's two official languages. *Fantastic*, I thought to myself, *now I'll be able to talk with everyone!* Malaysia was a British colony for about two hundred years, gaining its independence after World War II. The people still keep many British traditions like afternoon teatime and driving on the left. In fact, many upper-class Malaysians still send their sons and daughters for university degrees in Oxford, Cambridge, or Edinburg. The widespread use of English allowed Felix and me to move about in K-L much more easily than we were able to do in China. Almost everyone in K-L with a reasonable level of education spoke decent English, and many people spoke it very well. The other official language is Bahasa Melayu, which is the original Malay language and closely related to one of the languages of Indonesia. It is spoken by the people native to Malaysia, no matter what their level of education. Lucky for us, Bahasa Melayu is written using our Roman alphabet, unlike Mandarin with its thousands of Chinese characters. I found it easy to read and pronounce, and I didn't have any trouble memorizing the key words or phrases I would need to use in daily life, such as the words for food items or place-names, or even how to ask for directions. For my first few months in Malaysia this seemed like a dream come true, although I did find that there were still plenty of other things to surprise us in our new home.

One day shortly after moving to K-L, I decided to take the kids and explore a beautiful park not far from our apartment. Even though it was in the middle of the city, the park backed up to mountains that were covered by tropical forest, and a clear, cold stream carried water down from the mountain slopes through the center of the park. The day we were there children were catching fish with nets along the stream. It was a lovely, tranquil scene. We walked around the park and then stopped for a picnic near the children's playground. Julia ran over to the swings while I spread my cloth on the ground and brought out some plastic containers of fruit for us to snack on. It did not take long before I began to hear a variety of hoots and strange cries. The treetops near us began to shake, and from them descended a troop of wild monkeys. Big ones, small ones, and plenty of middle-size ones came barreling straight toward us, whooping and hollering as they ran. I totally freaked out and managed to grab only my son and my camera before I ran terrified in the opposite direction. Bringing the fruit had been a big mistake! In their frantic grab for our food, the monkeys tossed our belongings all around and even overturned Sebastian's stroller. Thank heavens Julia was a dozen or so yards away from us, over at the playground, but she watched in horror as her mother and brother fled for their lives. We quickly realized the monkeys were not interested in us, only our food, but by the time Julia reached me and climbed into my arms, we were both in tears.

That night I thanked God that we returned home safe and sound. Our only loss was one of my plastic containers. Even so, I couldn't help but spend the evening longing for home, where you could take your family to the park and not be attacked by wild animals. As it turned out, that was only the first of many encounters I would have with monkeys in Malaysia. These meetings always left me feeling a bit uneasy—maybe because their faces are so eerily human. Monkeys would come climbing out of garbage cans while I waited on the street for a taxi, and they often appeared in the trees near our bus stop. My most unnerving encounter with Malaysia's urban fauna, however, did not involve monkeys. I was standing outside our apartment building one day when I heard something hit the sidewalk right behind me. I checked my clothes and purse to see if I had dropped anything. Then I turned all the way around and saw that a green-and-yellow snake had fallen out of the tree right above me. Had I been standing twelve inches closer to the tree, it would have landed on my head! I never learned what kind of snake it was, but it scared the living daylights out of me. Thank goodness the doorman was standing nearby and helped me calm down.

Chapter 28
Too Much Change, Much Too Fast

The stress of moving our family (and sick infant) abruptly from one country into another completely different one finally hit me about two months after our arrival in Kuala Lumpur. I had been steadily losing weight, and one afternoon I just began vomiting for no apparent reason. At first I thought I must have eaten something bad, but the vomiting continued through the night.

The next morning, I took a taxi to a Japanese clinic down the hill where the doctor told me I needed a biopsy because I might have stomach cancer. That was not the kind of diagnosis I wanted to hear, so I went back home and tried to cope with the nausea using some Mexican over-the-counter medicines I had saved from my parents' visit last Christmas. After another miserable night, when I couldn't even keep down a spoonful of water, I decided I was too weak to recover on my own and took myself to Pantai Hospital by taxi. Felix had left at the crack of dawn to catch a plane for a three-day work assignment in Singapore.

At the hospital I had the incredible good luck to be assigned to a well-known Indian doctor named Mahendra Rash. He was kind and listened carefully to everything I had to say. I began to feel a bit better just by talking with this wonderful, sympathetic man. As I described how I felt, he gave me a compassionate look and said, "My dear, I would like to admit you to the hospital. You look dehydrated and not well at all. And since you haven't eaten anything recently, I strongly recommend that you stay overnight so we can help you to get better." He went on to say that I really should have a biopsy because it was possible that I might actually have stomach cancer.

Well, that was the second time in two days someone had mentioned the C-word, so I decided to stay for a laparoscopic exam and biopsy. After I woke up from the anesthesia, Dr. Rash came into my room. "My dear," he said to me, "I don't see anything that worries me, but let's wait for the biopsy results just to be sure, okay?" Then he pulled a chair up next to my bed and looked at me with the kindest expression on his face, one that made me feel safe, understood, and comforted in a way that I had not felt in quite some time, and he said, "My dear, if you don't mind, can you tell me—how has your life been recently?" And so I told him all about our abrupt move from Shanghai, Sebastian's pneumonia, my husband's frequent business trips and long hours, my not having a car, having to unpack and set up a new home for my family, being a newcomer in K-L, and finally my problems with a moody and uncooperative Filipino maid.

Dr. Rash listened to all of this, then remained quiet for a few moments after I had finished. "My dear," he said, "you have certainly been through a lot lately. My diagnosis is that you are stressed out and are having a nervous crisis. I recommend that you stay with us overnight. We will put in an intravenous line to get you rehydrated, and we will add an antivomiting medicine so you can start keeping down fluids and, soon, food."

I felt so weak and sick that I knew I had better do what he said. So I called Gaby to give her some instructions regarding the kids, and I asked if she could stay overnight. She didn't sound too happy about that. So I offered to pay her overtime, and she felt better about it. I slept like a baby that night and felt like a new person the next morning.

Before discharging me from the hospital, Dr. Rash came by to see me one more time. "My little Mexican, I was thinking about you last evening after I left the hospital. You are so far from home, child, and I feel as though I must give you some advice before you leave. I hope you don't mind, but I think you must either take yoga classes to help you handle the stress in your life, or—or you should change husbands."

"Ha-ha-ha," I laughed out loud at that one, and Dr. Rash gave me one of his beautiful smiles. Obviously I had to go for the less radical option, and I joined a yoga class as soon as I could. It met three times a week in the Bangsar Village area, which was within walking distance, about three kilometers downhill from our apartment.

Pretty soon I was back on track healthwise and working to adapt to my new surroundings. As the weeks went by, however, I began to realize that I had been wrong to think that the widespread use of English would make our lives better. In the short run, it did make some things easier. But with Kuala Lumpur's long history of Western contacts and pervasive use of English, ex-pats here just didn't need each other very much. In China, things were so foreign and so hard for Westerners to comprehend that ex-pats naturally banded together in order to survive and feel some sense of comfort. There was no counterpart to the *tai-tais* in K-L, nor any neighborhoods dedicated to foreigners like our Shanghai Racquet Club. The ex-pats pretty much did their own thing—every family for itself.

It was hard to comprehend at first, but the ease of living in K-L actually made life harder for me, socially speaking. It was so ironic! And it's not like I didn't try. I visited every ex-pat group I could find but couldn't seem to fit in anywhere. Mexicans in Malaysia were practically nonexistent. Most of the ex-pats were British, and I guess I paid the price for their history with the French. As soon as they heard my husband was French, they lost all interest in furthering their acquaintance with *me*. After many attempts with British groups, I tried joining the group of Latin American ladies. I was invited to one meeting, but all of them were so old, mostly ambassadors' wives. They were nice, but their activities centered around knitting, cooking, and praying the rosary, so I lost heart and never went back.

Chapter 29
Felix at Work in Malaysia

The biggest lure that Felix used to entice me to leave Shanghai—that he would have more time for the family because his commute would be so much shorter—went by the wayside very quickly. His new boss, a German fellow we had both known from our jobs back in Puebla, demanded long hours from his employees. This time, he and Felix were the only foreigners in the office. Everyone else was local, a mix of all three ethnic groups. That meant there were no lonely ex-pats for us to befriend at his office, and all the locals already had plenty of family and friends nearby. The one advantage here in K-L was the actual building where he worked. The offices and showroom were modern and stylish; in fact, they were quite impressive. In Shanghai, Felix's office had been ugly, with dark-blue windows and mismatched décor, plus it sat next to a busy market on Caoyang Lu. Felix loved his swanky new work environment. It bolstered his ego and gave him the feeling that, as far as his career was concerned, he had definitely *arrived*.

Felix's boss, Bernd, was someone I encountered regularly back in Mexico when I had worked as a technical translator and assistant to one of the managers of our company. Bernd had worked near me, but in another department, and I remembered him well. He was strong tempered and impatient about almost everything. I also recalled that he had liked me a little too much back in those days. He knew I was hard-working and had a good sense of humor, so he frequently came around to flirt, even though he knew I was married to his subordinate. He tried more than once to convince me to come and work as his assistant, but I knew enough about him by then to say thanks, but no thanks. I really liked the boss I had, and I enjoyed the work I did with him.

Now that we were in Malaysia, the biggest problem with Bernd was not his temperament—it was the fact that he had left his wife comfortably back in Germany, as so many of the German men did. Without his family nearby, Bernd really had nothing better to do than work—and when Bernd worked, he expected everyone else to be at work, too. Felix typically arrived at his office by 8:00 a.m. and did not get home until at least 7:00 p.m., but usually closer to 9:00 or 10:00 p.m. Since Bernd didn't have his wife close-by, he liked to party after work, and Felix was frequently expected to accompany him to various bars and nightclubs. Needless to say, I was not enthusiastic about these nocturnal adventures. As if that weren't enough, the company often organized workshops or sales seminars on the weekends. These corporate weekends were usually held at nearby beach resorts, and families were *not* encouraged to attend. Once or twice I managed to convince Felix to bring us along, promising that we wouldn't interfere with his work activities, but I didn't get lucky very often. Felix also had regular business trips back to the company's headquarters in Europe, or more frequently, to Singapore.

My husband and I did not spend more time together after we moved to Malaysia; we spent less. I do remember a few occasions when the company held a weekend event for families. They were organized by a woman named Mandy from the human resources department. She was married with two little daughters, so she was more keen than Bernd to plan family activities. The most memorable of these was our trip to a deer farm and the Kuala Gandah Elephant Sanctuary in Pahang, about two hours by car from K-L. I have always been fond of elephants, so I made sure I got Felix to sign us up for this one.

Our visit to the deer farm was quick and not all that interesting, although Julia did enjoy hand-feeding a (friendly!) macaque monkey, and Felix really surprised everyone when he volunteered to handle a big, green snake. Most of our time was spent with the elephants. We watched them being fed and given showers, and one elephant even held a paintbrush with his trunk and created quite a pretty abstract-art painting. Our guide explained that the sanctuary was necessary because the habitat for wild elephants in Malaysia was rapidly shrinking. More and more of the forest land was being turned into farms or urban developments, and many of the elephants had no place left to live. Homeless or injured elephants were brought to this sanctuary and were used to help educate Malaysians about their native wildlife.

We learned, for instance, that Malaysia had once had a large elephant population roaming their tropical forests, and they also taught us how to tell an Asian elephant from an African one. African elephants have much larger ears than their Asian cousins, so Julia and I decided that Disney's famous character, Dumbo, must surely have come from Africa since he was born with such enormous ears. Visitors could also take rides on the elephants and were offered a choice between a wet ride, which included getting dunked in the river, or a dry one.

I wasn't sure which ride I wanted to take. It was so hot that a dunk in the river didn't sound too bad, so we walked over to the elephant-loading area near the riverbank to watch how it was done. The elephants would take several visitors on their backs and walk along the bank of the river, then turn and step down into the river itself. After a few meters the elephants would squat down and tumble their riders into the chest-deep water.

Felix was all ready to take the wet ride and urged me to join him, but something made me hesitate. While it looked like fun, I didn't find the clay-colored water all that appealing for a swim. As we waited and watched other people taking their rides, I noticed there were little puddles of red water all over the ground. I had seen them here and there throughout the sanctuary, but they were especially numerous here along the riverbank. They were about five or six inches in diameter, and for some reason they just made me uneasy.

As we watched people coming up and out of the river, I noticed three young adults laughing and talking excitedly as they exited the river. Suddenly the two women started looking nervous and lifting up their soaking-wet *abayas* (Muslim dresses) to inspect their legs—very unladylike and provocative for Muslim women, which is why it caught my attention. I gasped when I realized why. Both women had leeches clinging to their legs, and their male companion had two big ones on his chest! Stationed nearby was a sanctuary employee who had the unenviable job of helping the river-dunked visitors pull the leeches off their skin. The bloodsucking worms were then thrown on the ground, and as people walked to and fro they got squashed underfoot. *Now* I knew why there were little red puddles scattered all over the ground! It was just gross, and I knew there would be no wet-elephant rides that day for me or my family!

After that our group set up a potluck picnic buffet with foods packed by each employee's family. We had many typical foods from Malaysia, but also dishes from the cuisines of China, India, France, Germany, and of course, Mexico! It was delicious and lots of fun. Too bad we all got together so rarely. After lunch, some of the men decided to try their luck and cross the river on a swaying "footbridge" made of three steel cables—one cable for the feet and one for each hand. It reminded me of something Indiana Jones might have encountered on a jungle adventure. All the men made it across without falling into the river, but I stayed high and dry on the riverbank and let them have their fun. There was absolutely no way I was going to risk taking a tumble into *that* water.

Chapter 30
Our Chinese Uncle and a Mexican Serenade

As I discovered on my first day as a new resident of K-L, Malaysian society has three distinct ethnic groups: the Chinese, the Malays, and the Indians. A majority of the people are Muslim (60 percent), with significant minorities that are Buddhist and Christian. Happily, everyone seems to get along pretty well in spite of such tremendous diversity. At least that is how it seemed to me, coming into the country as a new resident.

With the passing of time, however, I learned that the true situation was not quite so rosy. After a couple of years in K-L, I began to see things more clearly. The Chinese minority had the economic power, the Malay majority had the political power, and most of the Indian minority were poor and struggling just to have a decent life. Under the surface I often detected a feeling of resentment toward the Malays on the part of the two minority groups, who said that the Malays were lazy and given more benefits and protection by the government. Was my assessment accurate? I certainly don't claim to be an expert on socioeconomics, but I kept my eyes and ears open while dealing with Malaysians from all walks of life, and that is what seemed to be going on to me.

I had an up-close and personal window into the wealth of the Chinese citizens of Malaysia from my upstairs neighbor, Mr. Chang. He was a white-haired, elderly gentleman who lived alone for most of the year. Like many upper-class people in Malaysia, he had studied in the UK and spoke English with a lovely British accent. He still went to his office each morning for a few hours, but at home he seemed to interact with just three people—Edna (his Filipino housekeeper), his chauffeur, and an Indian nurse who came at night to monitor his diabetes. He never had any other visitors. We did not meet his wife for quite some time because she spent most of the year in England.

For some reason I cannot fathom, except perhaps loneliness, Mr. Chang just fell in love with my two kids. He actually met Julia first. Gaby had gone to pick up Julia at her *tadika* one afternoon shortly after we arrived, and they encountered Mr. Chang and Edna in the lobby of our building just as he was returning from his office. Later that afternoon he sent word through Edna to Gaby that he would like to meet Julia's mother and little brother, too. So we paid them a formal visit the next day. He found my kids funny and cute, and as time went by we visited each other quite often. We even found ourselves eating dinner with him from time to time.

Mr. Chang was, to put in bluntly, filthy rich. His father had been extremely wealthy, and when he died he left half his fortune to charitable causes and the other half to his eight children. Still, with only one-sixteenth of his father's fortune, Mr. Chang was reputed to be one of the richest men in Malaysia. This seemed crazy to me when I first heard the gossip because I knew from our many visits that his four-bedroom apartment was practically empty. He had only the most basic pieces of furniture and no decorative items whatsoever on his walls. His floors were white marble, but plain, and his kitchen could only be described as "utilitarian." It was a simple and, to me, boring space, although the view from his panoramic windows was every bit as beautiful as ours.

As I spent more time in K-L, I learned that Mr. Chang's home was not that unusual. Most people in Malaysia were not particularly interested in having beautifully decorated homes. It seemed foolish to them to waste money on something that only a few people would ever see. Instead, they preferred to display their wealth and status where everyone could see it—in their cars. Not surprisingly, the imported-car market in K-L was booming. Mr. Chang owned at least eight cars, including several Bentleys and Rolls-Royces, plus a Ferrari. His cheapest car was an elegant Mercedes. To drive all these cars, Mr. Chang employed a chauffeur. Every day, this gruff-looking chauffeur would drive him to his office and then to the "wet" market, where he purchased only enough fruit, fish, or meat to prepare his meals for that day. He never ate "old" food, only fresh food purchased daily. He often bought gifts of fresh fruit for Julia and Sebastian, who truly enjoyed their visits with him and began to call him "uncle," as Malaysians are accustomed to do with anyone they feel close to. Once he even offered to share a durian with me. I felt very rude saying "no thanks" to his "king of the fruits," but I just couldn't risk barfing in front of my dear Chinese neighbor. In time we even began to celebrate our birthdays together. He loved buying the kids toys on their special days, and one year Julia and I baked him a birthday cake using artificial sweetener so as not to affect his diabetes.

I must admit that at times I was more than a little jealous of Mr. Chang—not for his money, which did not seem to bring him any joy that I could tell, but for all his cars. I sure could have used one of those cars to help me with my errands. Besides my regular shopping errands, I also had to make frequent trips to the pediatrician since both kids continued to suffer from asthma and allergies. Now it wasn't the cold, polluted air of Shanghai that caused their breathing difficulties, but the humid, tropical air and the pollen spewed by all the tropical plants and flowers. Our change of countries had not brought much benefit in the kids' respiratory health, as I had so fervently hoped—one more way in which our big move had not improved my life at all.

Another reason I lusted after his cars was the daily weather. It rained a lot in K-L. Even a day with scorching tropical sun could, without warning, bring a cloudburst of rain that would suddenly inundate the streets with floods of water. It reminded me of what happened inside Robin Williams's house in the movie *Jumanji*—it was that bad. When the rain hit, traffic turned chaotic and all the taxis immediately filled up, often leaving me and the kids stranded for an hour or two wherever we happened to be. And then there was the "winter" monsoon season, from mid-November to March, when it was still very hot but rained heavily every single day. No matter how hard I tried, I still couldn't get Felix to let me drive. He took our car and parked it for twelve hours inside the parking garage at his office, but I couldn't use it because he considered it "unsafe" for me to drive in K-L's left-hand traffic. I thought this was nonsense, pointing out how much more dangerous it was for me and the kids to be driven around in beat-up old taxis without seat belts. "Wouldn't we all be safer," I asked him many times, "if I could strap the kids into proper children's car seats and drive around inside a sturdy, well-maintained car or van?" Felix had access to such vehicles through his employer.

But he resisted all my pleas and my logic, insisting that I would surely crash and kill our kids and any pedestrians who happened to be in the area. I was furious, and silently resolved that this was a battle I was going to win sooner or later. Someday, somehow, I was going to drive again, I promised myself, and in preparation for that day I made a clandestine visit to the Petaling Jaya Traffic Department to get my Malaysian driver's license. I was going to be ready when the time came! My parents would be visiting us in a few months, and perhaps with their lobbying for my need to drive, the three of us could convince that stubborn Frenchman I married to listen to reason.

Another sore subject about the weather in Malaysia was Felix's aversion to air conditioning. That had not been such a big problem in Shanghai, where it was hot only during the summer months, but K-L was deep in the tropics, and it was fiercely hot every day year round. Still Felix balked at turning on the AC even when the kids and I were covered in sweat, even when we had guests. It was a torment for all of us, but Felix remained adamant. He did not like it and claimed it was an expensive and unnecessary luxury. I tried pointing out that his employer paid our utility bills and would have leased a car for us at no cost, but Felix would not budge. Sometimes I would turn on the air conditioning when he was away at work, but if I ever forgot to turn it off before he got home he would be angry and temperamental for the rest of the evening.

The monsoon rains were something that affected all of our lives in K-L, and I remember them vividly. The amount of water that fell to earth was just incredible, and they could be very scary when experienced from the fourteenth floor! I remember watching the aftermath of the storms from the terrace of our apartment. We had a 180-degree view of the city, and sometimes I could see smoke from the fires that lightning had caused. The next day I would read about the trees, apartment buildings, or shops that had been destroyed. When we first arrived, I did not know how dangerous these storms could be, but later on an ex-pat woman I met advised me to stay away from my windows and to not take a shower or use a landline phone during these storms. It just wasn't safe, she told me.

One of the most comical, and ultimately to me most useful, things I discovered about the citizens of Kuala Lumpur was their utter fascination with a particular television soap opera. Every weekday at 1:00 p.m. the city would come almost to a standstill as seemingly every Malaysian stopped whatever he or she was doing to watch *Rosalinda*, a soap opera that was filmed in . . . Mexico! I couldn't believe it! I knew our Mexican soap operas, called by us *telenovelas*, were extremely popular in both North and South America, but I never expected they would captivate people living on the other side of the world. Here was an unexpected bit of home, and I would tune in to watch it from time to time. Every single man in town seemed to be in love with the beautiful Rosalinda, and the traffic noticeably diminished at one o'clock as people tuned in to follow the trials and tribulations of the poor but lovely Mexican señorita and her rich but faithless lover. Typical story, right?

I was surprised that the soap opera was not dubbed into either of Malaysia's official languages; instead, it was broadcast in Spanish with subtitles in Melayu, the local Malaysian language. Nobody even spoke Spanish in Malaysia, but due to the popularity of the lovely Rosalinda, everyone now seemed to consider Spanish the language of beauty, love, and romance—as I was soon to find out.

Taxi drivers, despite their usually gruff and grouchy demeanor, seemed to be especially crazy about Rosalinda. Almost every time I got into a taxi with my kids, if I happened to say something to them in Spanish, the drivers would perk up their ears. They would look at me, and then at my blond, Western-looking kids, and then ask me where I was from. When I told them that I came from Mexico, they would get so excited they practically ran off the road, and they would always ask me to please, *please* say something more in Spanish. I could say anything—a comment on the weather or a snatch of poetry—and they would be so thrilled! It felt like Spanish had become for them the new language of love, sort of like French has been for Westerners.

It was kind of fun, and it gave me a way to have a more pleasant interaction with the taxi drivers I was forced to deal with day in and day out—and I needed all the help I could get. In the beginning I met many rude, sullen drivers and endured a lot of uncomfortable rides while trying to keep track of my kids, my packages, and my ever-sulking maid. I didn't really blame them for their bad moods. It was hot and their shifts were long, and things got even worse for everyone during the month of Ramadan, when most of the drivers had to do without food from dawn to dusk. *Rosalinda* gave me a way to connect with the drivers, so to speak, and soon I discovered an easy way to get even better service from them.

Early on, a couple of the drivers who enjoyed listening to my Spanish babble asked me if I had ever met Rosalinda or knew where she lived. Well, of course I hadn't, and at first I said so. But one time, feeling particularly mischievous, I told one of the drivers that Rosalinda was my neighbor back in Mexico. I have no idea what prompted me to say such a thing, but his attitude changed completely and he instantly became much more friendly and helpful. He gallantly assisted me with my diaper bag and packages, unfolded Sebastian's stroller, and even helped me settle my son inside. Wow! What an advantage it was to be a friend of Rosalinda!

From that day on, I took full advantage of my imaginary relationship with Rosalinda whenever the opportunity arose. On some rides Rosalinda might be my high school chum, instead of just my neighbor, and on others she became my mother's cousin. It got to the point where I had to be careful since I would sometimes meet the same driver again at a later date (they often had specific driving zones), and I had to think fast to keep my story straight. Finally, I settled into one story—that Rosalinda was my cousin—and it became the survival strategy I used to sweeten all those hours I spent in the backseat of K-L's taxis. I know it was a bit conniving on my part, and I did feel a bit guilty about it sometimes. But my regular drivers became so much more cheerful when they saw me, and since it seemed to brighten their day as well, I decided it benefitted us all. For about a year, I "applied the Rosalinda act," as I called it, all over town and reaped the pleasant rewards of my notoriety.

As much as Rosalinda helped smooth my transportation issues, the *telenovela* heroine couldn't do much to help my homesickness for real family and friends. One day about seven months after we moved to Kuala Lumpur, I was feeling particularly low. Felix had been working very long hours, and I was lonely for my family, for my *tai-tai* friends, for *anyone* with whom I could have a long, comfortable chat. I kept asking myself what on earth was I doing here—living atop a tower in a city in the middle of a jungle (all right, a *rain forest!*) on the far side of the earth. The thought of going out in the oppressive heat without a car to buy groceries just seemed too much to bear.

I finally managed to move my butt and left the apartment to go to Cold Storage supermarket. I was walking listlessly up and down the food aisles when my ears latched onto several voices coming from the opposite side of the store. My heart started to pound when I realized what I was hearing. It was a loud, animated conversation between several men—not only were they were speaking to each other in Spanish, but they were using that very particular slang tone that comes only from Mexico!

At first I thought I must be so lonely that now I was even beginning to hear voices, but I quickly realized that no, these voices were real, and that meant there had to be real Mexicans right here in Cold Storage! I abandoned my shopping cart and began a frantic search to find them. I knew my instincts were right when I finally spotted a guy wearing a T-shirt with the logo of the Las Chivas soccer team on it. I ran right up to them and introduced myself. I was so excited that I think I even hugged them and kissed them all on the cheek as if we had been "amigos" our whole lives. I soon found out that these three guys were part of a seven-member band from San Luis Potosi, a city to the north of Mexico City. They had been hired to play for six months at one of Malaysia's biggest and best beach resorts.

I was so thrilled to meet them that I invited them all to my house that night for dinner, and they accepted! I called Felix at work to tell him what had happened—for once he was available when something important was happening to me—and asked him what kind of meat he would like to grill for my new Mexican friends. Then I completely reorganized my grocery list and rushed home to prepare for my unexpected party.

That evening all nine of us—Felix, me, and seven musicians—had the most wonderful dinner out on our terrace. The weather was perfect. The Petronas Towers and city skyline had never seemed as lovely as they were on that night, or maybe it was just being in such great company. Felix, ever keen to show off his prowess at the grill, cooked a delicious dinner of lamb chops and beef, and we drank the tequila that we had brought all the way from Mexico and served only on special occasions. After dinner, two of the guys brought out their guitars and played song after song of great Mexican music. It brought tears to my eyes and left a great big lump in my throat. It was so beautiful.

Before they left, we brought out the embroidered silk flag of Mexico that my father had given us (to remind us to keep Mexico in our hearts wherever we roamed), and we took pictures of each other posing with the flag. What a great evening! The guys left for the beach the next day, but we kept in touch via Facebook for quite a while. Our lives had touched for a brief moment in such an extraordinary way, creating a unique memory for all of us.

Chapter 31
Finally, I Make a Friend

In another of my attempts to meet other ex-pat mothers and to socialize a bit, I joined an organization called Ibu, which means "mother" in the Malaysian language. The group had its headquarters in a small house in our Bangsar neighborhood and sponsored classes in childcare and nutrition. It also organized playdates for the mothers and their kids. Since the members were all ex-pats or locals married to foreigners, I thought it looked promising, and I joined with high hopes. But after the kids and I attended a few of the get-togethers I was completely discouraged and ready to quit. Most of the ex-pat moms were British, and they were weird beyond belief. Very snobby and unfriendly. I found their attitudes and their turkey-breast white skin completely unappealing. But on the last playdate I forced myself to attend, I got lucky and met Sandra.

Sandra came from the Malaysian island of Penang, which had been an important port during the country's colonial days. It was now well known as a beach resort and was located northwest of K-L about three hours away by car. She was married to a foreigner, a friendly and outgoing Australian guy named Kevin. They had met when Sandra was taking university classes in Melbourne, Australia. He fell so deeply in love with her that he followed her back to Malaysia and convinced her to become his wife. Lucky for me, she had a little girl just about Julia's age, named Angelique. Sandra and I seemed to get along well from the first moment we met, and I was thrilled to learn that she lived close-by. She was friendly and supportive, and our three-year-old daughters got along reasonably well during their playdates.

No more dull and uncomfortable Ibu meetings for me—I had finally found a real friend!

The most interesting thing about Sandra was her heritage. She was Malaysian but did not label herself as Chinese, Indian, or Malay. Instead she invented the word "Chindian" to describe herself. Her father was Chinese and her mother Indian—an uncommon combination—and she was fiercely proud of this, following the traditions of both her parents equally and enthusiastically. Even though Malaysia has its three ethnic groups, there was little intermarriage between them, and most Malaysians looked down on children of mixed backgrounds, calling them hybrids—just like the Chinese did to me in Shanghai. One more thing that we had in common!

To me, Sandra looked even more exotic than anyone else in the already exotic land of Malaysia. She got her dark skin from her Indian mother and her typically Chinese eyes from her father. Sandra was a woman with charisma, but I wouldn't consider her a beauty. In fact, she wasn't even pretty—she was rather fat and walked with a limp. Her beauty came from within. She always had a positive attitude, and her personality was very outgoing and friendly. She had friends and acquaintances all over town. I admired her for that and was so thankful for the cheerful guidance that she gave me about so many things in Kuala Lumpur.

Sandra introduced me to a variety of shops, restaurants, and even doctors in K-L. She helped me get to know the city and served as my referral service and survival guide. Her friendship was, to coin a phrase, balm for my soul. Our daughters were close in age, but as alike as salt and pepper. Julia was thin, blond, and rather quiet; to me, Angelique looked like a typical Mexican girl. She was definitely more talkative and plumper, and she had olive skin and soft, dark hair—a real cutie pie. After a few playdates together, we decided that it would be fun and economical to schedule some of the girls' learning activities together. Felix could be very tight with his money, but he was always agreeable to anything educational for Julia. He considered her to be super intelligent and wanted to enhance her status as a global child at every opportunity. So getting his consent for classes was a snap.

First we tried ballet lessons, which were okay but not great, and then we moved on to swimming lessons, which turned out to be great fun. My apartment building had a lovely pool, and Sandra managed to find a swimming instructor who actually made house calls. He was Chinese and went by the name of Carter Wong. He would arrive twice a week on his motor scooter, dripping wet, with his wet suit rolled down to his waist. Both girls loved "Uncle Carter." He had a great way with kids, funny and noisy, but firm with them when needed. As hot as the air was in K-L, the swimming pools were all unheated and very cold. Our girls came out of the pool as blue as Smurfs, but Uncle Carter was prepared for this Arctic-like water and always wore his wet suit. Apparently Uncle Carter had plenty of students and spent the day motorbiking from pool to pool as he taught ex-pat kids from all over the world how to swim—nice work, if you can get it! He was probably the darkest Chinese guy I have ever seen since he spent so much time in the sun—totally different from the Chinese I met in Shanghai, who hid from the sun like moles.

Another activity Sandra suggested for our kids after a year or so was English lessons, and I heartily agreed. Many Malaysians speak English, but they often do so with a very peculiar and strong accent. It was important to keep the kids from sliding into this Malay-accented English, which would be hard to understand back in America and Australia. Their teacher, "Miss Shirley," called her lessons "phonetics class" and used flashcards with pictures to help each girl practice speaking correctly.

Perhaps the best thing Sandra introduced me to was acupuncture. Sandra underwent acupuncture treatments regularly with a very well-known Chinese acupuncturist in the Petaling Jaya area of town, and one day she asked if I wanted to give it a try. "It will help bring your body systems into better balance," she told me one day after I had been complaining about how the stress of my marriage and daily life seemed to be taking a toll on my health. At that point I was ready to give anything a try, so I said yes.

The clinic was always crowded with patients, but thanks to a reference from Sandra, I was able to get an appointment on the same day and time as her next one, and we went together.

The acupuncturist was named Mrs. Wang. She was very friendly and chatty, which helped calm my nerves considerably. During the first session, she had me lie down on a comfortable examination table and began to examine my feet. She squeezed and manipulated them all over, top and bottom, with considerable force. Then she compressed them between her fingers, massaged them, and stroked various parts of my feet and toes between her thumb and fingers. From time to time she would pause and write some notes down on paper. It was a thorough but strange exam—halfway between pain and tickling. Finally she sat me up, looked me right in the eyes, and delivered her diagnosis.

"Let me start by telling you what I have found," she said. "You have blood-sugar issues; in fact you are hypoglycemic. Your tummy is not okay—you have gastritis. You suffer from dryness of the eyes, and you have so much stress that you have developed bruxism, which is grinding of the teeth. I feel there is a great sadness in your soul, and you are not as happy as a young woman your age should be."

By the time she finished speaking, my mouth was hanging wide open in amazement. How could she have known so much about my life just by examining my feet? It was as if she had read a book about my physical and emotional health written right on them! My family does have a history of diabetes, and my stomach becomes quite sensitive whenever I feel upset, which was happening ever more frequently in K-L. I had noticed that my eyes felt tired and sticky when I read or worked on the computer, and I had been wondering why my lower jaw ached in the morning. If this woman, whom I had just met, could deduce so much about my stress and health in so short a time, I felt like I would be foolish not to give her treatments a chance. She recommended acupuncture treatments twice a week, and I signed up immediately, hoping with all my heart that she could heal my damaged body and soul.

Mrs. Wang started her treatment by inserting about fifteen needles in specific spots on my face, hands, belly, and feet. It wasn't too painful to have most of the needles put in, but in two places—between my thumb and index finger and the joint where my lower jaw connects to my upper jaw—she could barely get the needles to insert, and it was unbearably painful. She explained that the points that hurt the most are the ones with the biggest problems. They need to be worked on more than the others. Not surprisingly, she told me that my two most painful spots were indicators of emotional stress.

When she had finished placing the needles, I thought the worst was over. Then I noticed her beginning to attach small electrodes to the end of each needle, and I really freaked out. She calmed me down, explaining that adding the electric current would not hurt and was vital to the treatment. Then she turned on the power. She was right, the electricity was not a problem, but as I lay there for half an hour or so, I had another one of my reoccurring episodes of self-doubt. *What in the world am I doing here?* I wondered for what must have been the hundredth time since I arrived in Asia. *Here I am in the capital city of Malaysia, in the office of a Chinese healer, covered with needles connected to electrodes, and hoping the experience might improve my life. What am I—crazy, or just totally desperate?* Sometimes when I look back on it now, my life then feels like something I dreamed, something that didn't really happen.

With Sandra's encouragement I didn't give up on the acupuncture, even though it weirded me out at the beginning. After about a month, ten sessions or so, I did start to feel better and noticed a distinct difference in my mood and energy. Was it the acupuncture, or was it just hanging around with Sandra that made me feel so much better? I'll never know for sure, but I do know that one of the best things about undergoing those acupuncture sessions was going out with Sandra for lunch afterward. Sometimes we would go to a regular restaurant (Sandra knew so many!), but usually we would just go to one of K-L's "banana-leaf restaurants." These tiny food stalls served traditional Indian food on banana leaves, not plates. You would eat with your fingers, or sometimes with a piece of Indian bread called *naan*, which is cooked with spices inside a large, clay pot. I just loved the banana-leaf stalls. They were fast, tasty, and fun! It was such an adventure with Sandra as my gastronomic tour guide! She was as in love with food as I was, so we definitely found a shared passion.

I also developed quite a taste for *char kway teow*. This dish consists of flat, fried noodles made of rice and topped with spicy sauce. The best thing about *char kway teow* was that it could be made with pork, chicken, veggies, or seafood according to the tastes—or religion—of the customer. And believe me, this was an important consideration in a country with three ethnic groups. The Malays don't eat pork and require meat that is *halal*, the Indians don't eat beef and many are even vegetarian, and then there are the Chinese, who, luckily for restaurant cooks everywhere, eat pretty much anything that swims, crawls, or flies. As for me, I think I found *char kway teow* so appealing because it reminded me of a popular Mexican dish called *chilaquiles*, a poor-man's food cherished throughout our country for its ability to quell hangovers.

Wherever Mexicans travel, we are always on the lookout for two types of foods—those with a spicy zing to them, or soups with a rich, robust broth. Both of these remind us of our native cuisine and help us survive our traditional binges with tequila. That must be why I fell in love with *laska*. This lovely soup, available everywhere in K-L, was always served piping hot (in temperature), but its flavor was so hot (in taste) that I would only eat it in restaurants with strong air conditioning. The broth had a coconut base, in which were swimming noodles, soy, pieces of prawn, and boiled egg. It was delicious, and I became quite fond of it.

Then there were the times I developed a craving for the Spanish dish called *paella*. Since Mexico was a Spanish colony for three hundred years, Spanish food is beloved throughout Mexico. In case you are unfamiliar with *paella*, it is spicy rice dish that features bits of chicken, sausage, and seafood tucked into golden-colored saffron rice. Served in wide, shallow pans, *paella* is lovely to look at, has a heavenly aroma, and I love it! Malaysia actually has a pretty fair substitute for *paella*. It is a group of rice-based dishes that can be prepared with slightly different ingredients to appeal to each of Malaysia's three ethnic groups. *Nasi* means rice, so *nasi lemak* is the Malay version of this popular dish. The rice in *nasi lemak* is cooked in a broth of coconut milk and pandan leaf, then topped with a very spicy chili sauce to which are added fried anchovies, chunks of fried fish or chicken, and salted peanuts. Usually it is served with a boiled egg on the side and some slices of cucumber, which are there to cool down your palate if needed. Tiny restaurants, just stalls really, would wrap up the *nasi lemak* in a banana leaf and offer it as a takeaway meal. Some diners even preferred it that way, insisting that the banana leaf enhanced the flavor.

Nasi goreng is the Chinese version, in which the rice is be fried, sweetened with soy sauce, and served with chunks of fried chicken, chicken satay, or fried egg. The egg version seemed to be the most popular, especially with kids. It was certainly Julia's meal of choice whenever we were out and about in the city. I think she first tried it because she saw Sandra's daughter, Angelique, snarfing it down one day. After that, she was a *nasi goreng* girl through and through.

Finally, *nasi briyani* was the recipe that appealed to K-L's Indian population. This one was prepared using long-grain rice freely spiced with saffron. It could be left vegetarian and served with cashews, green peas, and lentils, or it could be embellished with chicken, lamb, fish, or shrimp, but it was always spiced with garlic, cardamom, and coriander. Unlike Julia, I could never decide which *nasi* dish I liked the best. They were all yummy and a great way to have a cheap meal that included something from every single food group!

Just like the food vendors in K-L, Felix and I had to take care to offer the appropriate foods whenever he invited new people to our home for dinner. Yes, Felix was still inviting his coworkers and business acquaintances over to show off his skills as a gourmet cook and grill master. In fact, the big terrace that overlooked the city from our apartment was definitely his favorite part of our home, and he would invite people whom he met at business meetings to dine with us about twice a month. Most of his guests were local businessmen and therefore Muslim, so we had to make sure all the foods were *halal*, and of course he could never serve them pork. Some Muslims were so strict about their diet that they would actually question us about our food preparation, asking whether we had cooked pork on the grill recently, and if so, had we had cleaned the grill carefully afterward? *That* could get awkward! Indian dinner guests were easier, requiring only vegetarian meals, and the Chinese were easiest of all—no restrictions whatsoever!

Felix just reveled in his role as the gourmet host. It was a pleasant way to spend an evening, I suppose. He was actually more interested in showing off his cooking prowess than getting to know his guests, so I rarely saw the same people twice. I also had to do all of the shopping and most of the preparation, except for the actual cooking, so my duties as hostess would take up considerable amounts of my time whenever Felix decided to throw another dinner party.

With his spending so much time at the office and on business trips, I often asked him why we couldn't just spend some time together, just the two of us, when he was home. Why not leave the kids with Gaby and go out together on the weekends? But he preferred to be the "host with the most," and said that he did not want to spend the money it would take to go out to restaurants. That made no sense, since the price of groceries for six or seven people was about what we would pay for two at a restaurant, but that was what he wanted to do.

Chapter 32
Asian Influences

Living in a foreign country changes you—ask anyone who has lived abroad for a while, and they will tell you it is true. But some people change more than others. I was interacting with Malaysians on a daily basis, but only in brief interactions each day. Felix worked with Malaysians all day every day (and weekends, too!) at his company, and Julia attended the Malaysian-run *tadika* every morning. So it shouldn't have been a surprise for me to see them changing and evolving in ways that I was not, but it did. Some of these changes were amusing and easy to handle; others were more difficult, even sinister.

Julia loved attending the *tadika*, so it was worth it to me to make the rigorous climb up and down our hill each day so she could play with kids her own age. As time passed, she began to copy certain behaviors she saw there. Many Malays eat most of their foods with their fingers, and I wasn't surprised to find that Julia did, too. After all, what small child wouldn't want to eat foods the simplest way possible? But I had to insist that at home she "eat like Mommy" with a fork and spoon so she could blend in at family dinners when the time came for us to return to Mexico. She also learned at the *tadika* to clean her bottom with a water hose after using the toilet, and she would ask me why we wanted her to use toilet paper when she was at home. "You are a Mexican girl," I had to remind her over and over. "At school you do what the teacher tells you, but at home you must behave like a Mexican girl and clean yourself with toilet paper, just like Mommy does, okay?"

Julia's teachers also wore the traditional and colorful Malay *abaya* and covered their hair with scarves, so eventually Julia wanted to wear a scarf, too. Not wanting to try to explain religious differences to a four-year-old, I finally managed to talk her out of it by appealing to her vanity. "The Malaysian ladies' hair is not a pretty as yours," I would tell her. "Yours is blond and extra pretty, so you don't need a scarf to cover it up." Okay, so that was kind of lame, I'll admit, but it worked and gave Julia a boost of self-esteem in a place where she looked quite a bit different from most of the people she saw.

Felix was changing, too. His new job seemed to take over his life, and we rarely spent much time together anymore, and when we did, I had a hard time recognizing the man I married. He had made new friends at work, which was good, I thought at first, but why did he have to take it so far?

He began eating lunch with Mandy, the woman in the human resources department, and her friends at work. She was Buddhist, and they apparently got into some deep philosophical discussions during their lunch hour. Before long, my husband, who had never had more than a passing interest in religion, decided that he must attend Buddhist training sessions every Tuesday and Thursday evening after work. What?! We hardly saw each other as it was, and now he was coming home extra late twice a week. Then he began to bring home statues of Buddha to decorate the corners of our apartment. That wasn't a big deal to me—they fit in with the Asian-inspired decor in apartment. But I really got annoyed when he insisted on swapping out our evening television shows, *Grey's Anatomy* or *Nip/Tuck*, for DVDs of Buddhist chanting and prayer sessions. They were incredibly boring and repetitive, and put me to sleep almost immediately.

The moment I knew things had gone too far was the evening we actually went out to dinner together at a seafood restaurant. We ordered from the menu, and the waiter grandly told Felix that he would have the "privilege" of selecting his dinner from one of the live fish swimming around an aquarium in the center of the restaurant. Felix suddenly looked nervous and uncomfortable. He finally told the waiter that his wife would pick out the fish. I asked why, since it had always been his decision before.

"*Chou-chou* [darling, in French], I really prefer that you pick out the fish. I am afraid to kill one fish in particular because we believe that it will give me bad karma."

Oh my gosh! *We* believe? It is you who believes such things, my dear! That was just too much. I laughed out loud and went to select the fish without remorse. But later, as I thought back on the incident, I was more concerned. He now truly believes this stuff, I realized with a sinking heart, and even worse, he didn't even seem to care whether I might get bad karma, only whether he would. What does that say about him? About us? About our future?

The next step Buddha took into our family came when Felix wanted to send Julia along with Mandy's daughters to "Buddhist Youth" gatherings at a local temple. That's one time I put my foot down. She was only four years old, and it seemed insane to me to leave her with people I did not even know to do I didn't even know what for four hours every Saturday. When I opposed this, Felix got very angry and criticized me for not being open to new ideas. *Excuse me*, but if I was not an "open" person after all I had been through in the last four years, what was I then? Of all the accusations he could have hurled at me, that one was the most absurd.

Thinking back on it all now, I realize that the man I married was very much a chameleon. He changed his colors to blend into whatever environment he entered. As a Frenchman newly arrived in Mexico, he enthusiastically embraced Mexican culture, bravely swallowing our spicy foods and decorating our apartment in Mexican colonial furniture. Then when we moved to Shanghai, he began to brew his own tea concoctions and comb the antique markets to fill our apartment with Chinese art and furniture. Now in Malaysia, his metamorphosis continued. He added figurines of Buddha to our household décor and guarded against bad karma with chanting and temple visits. What next? Would he ever settle on one true identity? Could he?

It wasn't just Buddha that captured his heart and soul in Malaysia. One day about a year after we moved, he made a comment about how beautiful he found the Malay women's dress, the *abaya*. I just heard it as just a random comment and didn't pay it much attention. Although I found their clothing colorful and exotic, I actually pitied the poor Muslim women who had to cover themselves so completely in a climate as hot and humid as Malaysia's. His comments continued from time to time, and I continued to pay them little mind, until one day he made an announcement. "I would really like it," he said with emphasis, "if you started to wear the abaya. They are so beautiful," he continued, "and they come in such lovely colors, you know? Adela," he said, looking me right in the eyes with that charming smile of his, "you would look so beautiful. Wouldn't you like to wear them?"

One more time, I could not believe what I was hearing!

"There is no way I would wear those things!" I told him. "No way! When you met me I was clearly Mexican. You fell in love with me as a Mexican, and I am still and always will be Mexican, even if I am living on the other side of the world. I may dress more conservatively here, in deference to Malaysia's Muslim population, but there is absolutely no way I am going to go about my daily life dressed up as a Muslim—no way!"

I was adamant about this on principle, but also because I had actually tried it one time, and I knew I would find it unbearable. An American woman I knew briefly in Kuala Lumpur, named Laura, invited me to visit the National Mosque with her. It was very interesting, but all women who entered the building, not just Muslims, had to wear special garments to achieve the appropriate level of modesty. We were shown to a special room and given a blue *abaya* to wear and a blue *chador* (scarf) to cover our hair. I didn't mind the additional clothing since I would be entering a religious and holy place. But Laura and I both practically melted in the heat, swaddled as we were, and could handle it for only about thirty minutes. I knew I could never survive the tropical heat dressed like that, and why should I even try? It is not my religious tradition.

My significant other was slowly becoming a total stranger to me and the kids. We lived in the same house, slept in the same bed, but as the months in Malaysia came and went, we led ever more separate lives. He was always too tired or too stressed out to listen to much of anything from his wife and kids. And then there was his boss, Bernd, and his after-work partying.

To keep on Bernd's good side, Felix had to accompany him from time to time to the bars and restaurants. To the credit of my husband, I could tell that Felix really did not want to do this very often. He complained to me but still had to go along. Bernd eventually found his way to a joint called The Beach Club, which was really dangerous, I heard from gossip, because it was full of Filipino and Chinese women on the prowl. Bernd loved the nightlife at The Beach Club, and not surprisingly he was reeled in one night, like a fish on a hook, by an experienced young Filipina on the hunt for a sugar daddy. She moved into Bernd's lovely penthouse apartment, and for a while she kept him so busy at home that working hours at Felix's office relaxed a little bit. That made life for all the employees somewhat less hectic, and everybody breathed a sigh of relief.

I remember how much Felix laughed at his boss and criticized his *affaire* with a woman he actually had to pay for companionship. He had learned from Bernd's chauffeur that he gave the woman a monthly stipend and also paid for her trips back to the Philippines to see her family. This was all kept secret from his wife back home in Germany, of course. Felix pumped the chauffeur for details and learned quite a bit about this boss's new home life, which he always reported to me with a sneer.

I was glad that Felix was feeling a little bit less stressed at work, but the whole thing really turned me off. I actually felt bad for the wife back in Germany. I had met her a few years ago when we were all still in Mexico. Felix made such fun of Bernd behind his back, even though he needed his support and friendship at the office. It was not a real friendship, obviously, and made me feel less warm toward my own husband. If only I had more fully understood the chameleonlike nature of Felix's true personality! But at that point I did not—I should have been much more worried.

Chapter 33
Asian Oddities

Our Chinese neighbor and "uncle" continued to be a part of our lives—well, at least part of mine and the kid's lives—as long as we lived in K-L. He always greeted us warmly and seemed genuinely pleased to interact with my two little Franco-Mexican kids. The highlight of our friendship was the day we celebrated his birthday with a sugar-free cake baked and decorated by Julia and me. He seemed surprised and so pleased that we had not only remembered his birthday, but also his struggles with diabetes.

I knew he had a wife, because he mentioned her when we first met, but why was she absent? From his comments it did not sound as if he and Mrs. Chang had divorced, but where was she? I was afraid to appear too inquisitive, so I did not ask him outright, and a number of months passed before we learned the answer. It turns out she was in England, and she lived there most of the year. She disliked the tropical heat of Malaysia, claiming that it was bad for her skin, so she rarely came home to her husband.

Eventually we did meet the elusive Mrs. Chang. Our first clue that something had changed upstairs was the convoy of trucks that delivered dozens and dozens of boxes of bottled Evian water to their apartment. Our maid, Gaby, knew exactly what that meant since she was good friends with Mr. Chang's maid, Edna. Gaby told us that Mrs. Chang believed her skin to be so sensitive that she would use only Evian water to take her baths. In fact, she used Evian water for everything, including the laundering of her bed linens and towels. She was not as friendly as her husband and did not stay in town very long during her visits, so we seldom saw her. But each time we did, she was dressed entirely in the color purple, just as

Gaby told me she would be. Apparently she and Mr. Chang lived separate lives even though they were still officially married. According to the gossip from Gaby, Mr. Chang met her at a restaurant where she used to work. They fell in love, married, and with Mr. Chang's financial help, she opened a company that imported food products from Italy. It was successful, and she became rich in her own right. Maybe that is why she felt she could come and go as she pleased.

Early in our friendship, I was surprised to see Mr. Chang on the sidewalk one day stooping over to pick up a Malaysian penny near the entrance to our building. You wouldn't think that a man as rich as he would bother with coins only worth a cent or so, but he did. He smiled and told me, "I always pick up any pennies I see because if you have ninety-nine cents, you don't yet have a dollar. Every single penny counts if you want to have a dollar."

Although the currency was called the Malaysian ringgit, for some strange reason I never understood, everyone talked in terms of dollars. And nobody seemed to value a dollar quite as much as our lovable neighbor, Mr. Chang.

His chauffeur was another story, however. We saw him almost every day driving his boss back and forth to the market, and I could tell he did not like me one bit. I tried to be extra pleasant to him whenever our paths crossed, but it didn't help. He continued to give me ugly looks whenever his employer was not around or not paying attention. One day I was waiting outside our building for a taxi. I was alone and dressed very nicely since I was going to meet Felix for dinner. My dress was long and white, and I considered it quite modest since it reached down to the middle of my calf. When the chauffeur came out of the building and saw me there, I could tell something snapped inside him. He stomped over to me, obviously upset.

"Lady!" he said, as a year's worth of pent-up anger boiled over inside him, "could you *please* cover up your ankles!"

I was stunned at first, but then understood what had been our problem. The chauffeur was Malay and obviously Muslim. While I was at home or wandering around the apartment complex, I often wore comfortable clothing, sometimes shorts or short sleeves, and I had obviously been upsetting his Muslim sense of decorum. His facial expression on that particular evening was so harsh that I immediately sat down on the steps to hide my provocative ankles. Thankfully the taxi arrived shortly after that. Oh, well . . . at least I finally knew why he disliked me so—in his eyes I was a wanton woman!

It was hard living in a Muslim country sometimes. Women had to be very careful not to upset the conservatives in the population, or they would be rebuked as I had just been. I tried to be sensitive to this and carefully considered the clothing I wore when out and about the town. But here was a guy who had gotten upset with me for how I dressed inside my own apartment building! I admit that I was more than a little peeved and wished, not for the first time, that they would just back off and mind their own business.

Extra care was required whenever we attended social events in Kuala Lumpur, especially for me as a woman. After a few months in Malaysia Felix had gotten plenty of experience interacting with local businessmen, but my role as a housewife had not prepared me nearly as well. Take, for example, the one "high society" wedding we were invited to attend.

The eldest son of a prominent Malay family was being married off in high style. Bernd and several other men from Felix's office received invitations, which included their wives. I was thrilled to be included, but puzzled by the dress code indicated on our invitation. It said something like "formal sarong *kebaya* required." I didn't have a clue what that meant, but no problem—I called my Chindian friend, Sandra, and she explained it all. Men who were foreigners could wear a standard business suit and tie, so for Felix things were simple. However, all the women, both foreign and domestic, would need to wear a robe-like dress inspired by the traditional *abaya* of Saudi Arabia. Since I had no idea how to go about acquiring such a garment, I asked Sandra if she would come with me to buy one, and she did. We finally settled on a beautifully embroidered *kebaya* in a soft beige color. It covered my body completely from the neck down. Malaysian etiquette does not require foreign women to wear a veil covering their heads, which was a great relief to me since I already felt like an extra from the cast of *Lawrence of Arabia*.

On the appointed day and time, we arrived at the site of the wedding reception—the huge Kuala Lumpur Convention Center—which had a gorgeous view of the Petronas Towers from its entry plaza. The front reception room was crowded with wedding guests from all three of Malaysia's ethnic groups, plus a few foreigners like us. As I surveyed the colorful scene, I checked around me, and yes—every single woman there had politely followed the required dress code. Okay, so far so good.

But then I made an obvious faux pas as I followed Felix's lead and attempted to shake hands with several people to whom we were introduced. Wrong! People stared at me and my extended hand, then abruptly turned around and left me hanging there as if they had just seen the devil himself. A quick look around showed me that no women were shaking hands. Instead they would simply nod in a shy way and put both hands on their chest, making a very slight bow. So I just began to play copycat, and things quickly got much better as I learned the proper way to mingle with K-L's crème de la crème.

After about an hour, and several rounds of highly sweetened beverages, we were all ushered into the dining hall, which was a huge room elaborately adorned with golden decorations. Felix and I were directed to our table and were seated with Felix's colleagues from work. At this point I noticed two immense chairs, resembling thrones, that were situated at one end of the room on a dais under a beautifully decorated canopy. All of a sudden the bride and groom entered the room, and everyone stood up to honor them. They made their way slowly toward the two thrones, pausing from time to time to greet various guests as they went. The last tables they reached were the ones reserved for the immediate family members of the bride and the groom, but they did not join them. Instead, they each took a seat on one of the thrones. Everyone sat down, and the meal began.

To my surprise, the bride was dressed in a Western-style white wedding gown. Every other woman in the room was cloaked in a flowing *kebaya*, but the bride would not have looked out of place in New York or London. The dress itself was stunning, although quite discreet. Only her face and hands were visible, but what caught everyone's eye was her sparkling tiara and diamond bracelets, undoubtedly real.

We were served a variety of traditional Malay dishes that were quite spicy and hot. To my Mexican palate they seemed quite delicious, but I noticed several of the European guests at our table had a little problem enjoying the distinctive flavors. Since the family was Muslim, no pork was served, although I am quite sure that all the meats we ate that night were *halal*. The drinks we were offered included sodas of many sorts and a bright-pink beverage called rosewater, which was sugary and very aromatic. It just did not seem right to me that we should be toasting the bride and groom with something as ordinary as soft drinks, but Muslims abstain from all forms of alcohol, so champagne was out of the question. Almost as strange was the bridal couple being confined to their thrones for the entire meal. They just sat there and watched everyone else enjoying dinner—no merrymaking for them!

After the meal was finished and dessert served, we heard a band begin playing some really great music. *Oh boy!* I thought. *The dancing is about to begin.* The band was from the Philippines, whose musicians are famous throughout Asia for their wonderful dance music. Which way to the dance floor? People began to stand up, so I took Felix's hand and practically pushed him in the direction that everyone was heading. My Latin soul was ready to dance!

I was incredibly disappointed to find the wedding guests had all left their tables merely to walk past the bride and groom, giving them their best wishes before leaving the room and heading home. Literally, the wedding guests ate, drank, and left—I could not believe it! The music was so great, but nobody danced, they just left. So with great surprise and disappointment, that's what we did too.

☼

Yes, life in a Muslim country could be quite dour at times, but it had its compensations. One of the things I came to enjoy the most was, ironically, the evening call to prayer, which came at about eight o'clock each evening. This was actually the fifth call to prayer of each day, but the noise of the city generally drowned out all but the first and last ones. With the kids already put to bed, I loved to prepare myself a glass of red wine (French influence) or hot chocolate (Mexican influence) and go out to sit on my terrace and enjoy the coming of the night. It was so soothing to watch the Petronas Towers reflect the changing colors of the sunset. Then, whenever possible, I would stay to watch the other city skyscrapers begin to glow as the incredibly beautiful view spread out before me . . . so relaxing to simply sit, chill, and feel the calming call of the Muslim prayers.

I did not know what was being said, but it didn't really matter. Sometimes the prayer seemed melancholic, other times very passionate and devout—or maybe it was just my own mood that made me interpret it one way or another. After the first few months, Felix rarely joined me for these evening meditations. He was seldom home early enough, or if he did manage to leave work early, he would usually rush over to his Buddhist meetings, or come home with just enough time to pack his suitcase for a working trip to Singapore or even Europe.

I can still recall the many aromas that wafted up to my terrace in the evenings. The smell was ripe with exotic spices, and I often imagined all the many women cooking dinners in their apartments nearby, then sitting down with their families to eat together and share stories about their day. As time went on, it would bring me tremendous sadness. Why couldn't my family be like that? Why did I always seem to be home alone? I felt more like a single mother or a rich widow in our beautiful penthouse in the sky. In Kuala Lumpur I felt much more like a bird in a golden cage than I ever did living in Shanghai.

I know that his job was important, and I know he worked to provide for his family—at least that's what he kept saying. But we were becoming a family he hardly ever saw or even knew much about. When he did come home, he was usually exhausted and paid very little attention to anything I said to him. After a while I tried calling him at work, but he was always too busy to take my calls. Then I tried to send him e-mails several times a week, but very soon I realized he considered other e-mails far more important than mine. My husband was becoming a stranger to me and the kids, and I did not know how to turn the situation around. We had once been so very, very close—and now, we may have been sleeping in the same bed, but we communicated hardly at all.

A couple of times, under the influence of the red wine, I suppose, I would stand up at the railing of my terrace and close my eyes. I would click my heels together three times just like Dorothy in *The Wizard of Oz* and say, "There's no place like home. There's no place like home. There's *no place* . . . like home!" Even though I put my whole heart and soul into it, I always opened my eyes to the disappointment of finding myself not back in Mexico, not back in the happy home of my parents, but all alone in my lovely golden cage on the far side of the world. After that, I would usually just watch some TV and go to bed, tired of waiting for my significant other to return.

Then one day my chant actually did come true—well, sort of, anyway. My sister Pilar, who had come to Shanghai to help me when Sebastian was born, was getting married, and the wedding would be, of course, back home in Puebla! There was no way Felix could get out of taking the family back to Mexico for the wedding of my sister. My wish had been granted—I was going home!

Chapter 34
Pilar's Wedding

I was so happy to be back home, to be around people who loved me and actually wanted to talk with me, that I didn't mind the long, long plane ride at all—not even with three cranky people in tow, Felix not included. I would be staying in Puebla for two months, so I brought Gaby along with me to help manage the kids. Felix, with work always uppermost in his mind, decided to come to Mexico just for the week of the wedding. At that point, I hardly minded. It was August 2007, and I had been living in Asia for four years, in K-L for eighteen months.

The wedding was beautiful. Pilar had decided to have the wedding ceremony in the same small, baroque chapel where Felix and I had wed, Nuestra Señora de la Candelaria y Guadalupe. But for the reception afterward, she and her fiancé chose a magical location, a downtown hotel located inside the cloister of a seventeenth-century Franciscan convent. All the hotel rooms are situated around the convent's enormous, colonnaded courtyard, which has a central fountain and is open to the sky. Nearly all the wedding guests chose the convent as their lodging, and the entire weekend was just one big, happy party. It was historic, romantic, beautiful, and very, very Mexican.

For the evening wedding reception, the courtyard was filled with forty white-clothed round tables. Each one was adorned with a candlelit arrangement of flowers and set with Talavera plates, Puebla's colorful signature ceramic. Family members and friends ate, drank, and danced the night away in celebration. And yes, we toasted the bride and groom many times, but I can guarantee you one thing—they were toasted with champagne, or even tequila, and not some wimpy pink punch! The only note of sadness, which my parents tried valiantly to mask, was the knowledge that Pilar, like me, would not be settling down somewhere close to home. She had met her fiancé in Shanghai's ex-pat community when she came to help me with the birth of my Sebastian. Her fiancé was Australian, and she would be moving with him to Melbourne.

One thing I hoped to accomplish during my two months in Puebla was to help Julia improve her Spanish. Felix and I had agreed we would stay in Malaysia no more than three years, and then return to Mexico. I wanted Julia to be well prepared when yet another enormous upheaval came into her life. I decided to enroll her in a mornings-only summer day camp, which would also give me some much-needed time to help with the wedding preparations. At that point in her life (age four, plus a few months) Julia understood quite well everything I said to her in Spanish, but she rarely used it to answer me in return. In her kindergarten, she heard mostly English, and that is the language she was transitioning into. No problem, the day-camp teachers all spoke sufficient English.

Julia had been enrolled barely a week when the camp director requested that I come in for a meeting. I did not understand what could be possibly be the problem until she explained that my little blond darling was telling everyone who would listen that she was a Chinese girl from Shanghai. Other times she would describe how she lived in the jungles of "Kuala Dumpur" where there were monkeys in the streets.

Well, no wonder they were befuddled and confused. I had not bothered to give them a heads-up about my daughter's upbringing as a "global child." I just did not think it would be an issue, but it clearly was. After her years as a rather quiet toddler, Julia was rapidly maturing into a friendly, talkative child. She was apparently quite enjoying all the extra attention she got from her autobiographical "tall tales," but would become upset when people did not seem to believe her.

Of course, the director and her teachers thought Julia was inventing these stories. But no, I explained, it was all true, at least in the mind of a child. She really had lived in China for three years, and many of her first words and phrases were learned in Mandarin from our beloved Xiao Tian. And it was equally true that her new home, Kuala *Lum*pur, Malaysia, was as infested with monkeys as Puebla was with pigeons.

I told them how we would encounter the crafty primates coming out of trash bins as we walked down the street or see them hanging from palm trees lining the road. After our terrifying incident with the monkeys that chased us in the park, I did not like to get too close to them, but Felix would occasionally buy bananas and amuse Julia and Sebastian by feeding them to the monkeys in our neighborhood. In fact, many of the houses in K-L had iron bars decorating the windows as we do in Mexico, I explained to them. They served not only to keep out burglars—something the teachers could readily understand—but also to keep out monkeys, who could easily jump in an open window to steal food or cause lots of damage to people or property. The director was surprised and also a bit relieved, I think, to find out that Julia was not delusional, no matter how bizarre her stories had seemed at first.

Yes, our little Julia was growing up and coming into her own. Like most kids she learned by example, and since she was growing up in Asia, what she considered normal often came as a surprise, even to me. One time during our stay in Mexico Felix and I took her shopping with us in the department store at a local mall. They had on display a lovely collection of decorative items from Asia. As we walked toward it, Julia got very excited—here was something she recognized from home.

"Look, Mama, look! It's Buddha!" she said in a loud, happy voice and ran right up to the statue. But what she did next startled even me. She placed her hands on her chest and began to salute the four cardinal directions—north, south, east, and west. I had not taught her to do that, nor had I ever seen her do it before, but somewhere, somehow, she had learned the proper way to act when entering a Buddhist temple. Her little ceremony caught the attention of the other shoppers and store clerks, who watched her with surprise, some of them laughing and others dismayed. I can still remember how much she loved the smell of incense as a small child, and how frustrated she was with the straws she found in her drinks in the restaurants of Puebla. She kept trying to use them like chopsticks, and they just wouldn't work!

One thing she certainly did NOT absorb from Asia was the role of the submissive female. She was becoming quite headstrong, and we were having regular mother/daughter confrontations by the time we traveled together to the wedding. My sister, Pilar, although incredibly busy with wedding preparations, was the one who discovered the most effective way to rein her in. It involved the Disney Princesses, a line of toys that was becoming very popular right at that time. Julia was enthralled by the idea of being a princess, and Pilar could get her to behave in just about any way she wanted by telling Julia that "this is what princesses do."

It worked, and for a while Princess Julia could be enticed to behave herself, most of the time. I say "most" because it did not work at all the first few days after we (foolishly) let her watch some programs during Shark Week on the Discovery Channel. Princess Julia was replaced by Shark Julia. To this day, several wedding guests still remind me about the time they watched Julia get down on her hands and knees on the sidewalk and bite one of my aunts on the leg. She was not amused.

Chapter 35
I Get to Drive Again

Our two months in Mexico passed swiftly by, and all too soon I found myself back in K-L in my lonely tower in the sky. Things were slightly better now. My mother had come to spend some time with us several months before the wedding, and she could not help but notice how difficult and isolated my life was becoming. She had always had good relationship with Felix before we moved to Asia, and she achieved what I alone could not. She convinced Felix to let me drive!

Unlike my father, whose personality can be quite volatile, my mother never loses her cool. In her own low-key manner, my mom confronted Felix one evening when I was busy elsewhere in the apartment. She politely but firmly reminded him that he had married an intelligent woman—one who had a college degree, spoke several languages, and had years of experience driving in the busy, crowded streets of Mexico.

"She's never even had a traffic accident," my mother reminded him, "and she has lived in K-L long enough now to know her way around. She *needs* to be able to drive in order to keep up with the family's errands, and your children *need to be protected*. Riding in their car seats would be *much safer* than riding unsecured in the backseat of a rickety taxi." Without even raising her voice, she had maneuvered Felix into a corner. Either he could let me get behind the wheel of our car again, or he would have to confess to my mother that he considered her daughter stupid—and no amount of French charm could make my mother accept that bit of nonsense!

Hallelujah! I did not have to walk and push a stroller up and down steep hills to run even the simplest errand! Nor did I have to rely on my relationship with Cousin Rosalinda to get decent taxi service! Not anymore. I could drive again!

Three things immediately got better in my life. I could now be a more equal partner in my friendship with Sandra, I was able to travel more easily to a great gym and sports club I had recently discovered (thanks to Sandra), and I was able to move Julia out of the *tadika* kindergarten and enroll her in preschool classes at the British school when she turned four.

What having a car did not do was improve my relationship with my husband. He had succumbed to pressure from my mother, but grudgingly. He resented the whole idea of my being able to leave our apartment and have some sort of life on my own—like I was going to run wild in the streets or something! I never understood what his problem was about my doing things outside the home. I never gave him any reason to doubt my love and devotion to him and the kids. In fact, I would have loved for *him* to spend more time at home, but that was out of the question apparently. Without the companionship of the *tai-tais*, I needed outside activities and friendship more than ever, but he never seemed to understand that at all. Thank goodness I never had a traffic accident in K-L, or at least one that was my fault. One time I was idling the car at a traffic light when another driver hit me. It was totally her fault, but I'm still so glad that Pilar and her husband were visiting us that week, so they could vouch for my innocence. Otherwise, knowing Felix, he just might have taken away the keys once more! The only danger I truly worried about was urban wildlife on the roads. I had plenty of experience watching out for dogs on the road while driving in Mexico, but in Malaysia drivers always had to be on the lookout for dog-sized lizards! Monitor lizards would sometimes wander out into traffic and seemed totally clueless about what cars could do to them. I remember one time even having to stop my car abruptly in the middle of the road and wait, with my warning lights blinking, while this BIG monitor lizard slowly made his way back into the bushes.

About a year after we moved to K-L, I thought I discovered a really good solution to my loneliness. I found an apartment for lease in a different building, a more modern place with lots of ex-pat families in residence. I was quite excited about it. I felt certain that I could make many more friends if we moved there.

Although I liked our penthouse in the sky, we only discovered after we moved in that nearly all the other residents of our building were Chinese! That might have been all right, except they were all speakers of Cantonese and not the Mandarin version of Chinese that I had learned to speak in Shanghai. So my family and I were truly strangers in a strange land! As time went on, I discovered that our apartment building had been planned specifically for Chinese residents. Each apartment was designed according to the principles of fêng shui, a Chinese philosophy that stressed the optimal flow of energy into and through residential space. It was only after we moved in that I noticed how the windows and doors were placed in odd arrangements and that no floors were numbered four or fourteen, which are considered unlucky in China. The building I tried to persuade Felix to move into was more modern, more Western, and had a lovely heated pool so we wouldn't turn blue each time I took the kids for a swim.

I thought this new residence would be a significant improvement for me and the kids, but Felix would not even consider it. Why? The only reason he would give me was that moving to the new building would add another ten minutes to his ten-minute commute to work. In Shanghai his commute had often been one to two hours each way, but now he couldn't even handle an extra ten minutes?! I had the impression that he vetoed the move just because he had the power to do so—or maybe he just preferred having a lonely, bored, and depressed wife.

I couldn't tell what he was thinking any more. And when he did give explanations, they seemed frivolous, like his refusal to move or his choice of schools for Julia. The reason he insisted on the British school for her instead of the American school had nothing to do with academics or teacher-pupil ratios. He chose the British school because on the day we visited their air conditioning was not as strong as it was in the American school.

Thankfully, Julia seemed to do well at her slightly warmer British school. While the curriculum emphasized the English language, what I remember most vividly about her year there was the staff's enthusiasm for multicultural holiday celebrations. The first one Julia encountered was "Be Proud of Your Country Day." Everyone was supposed to come to class dressed in the typical clothing of their homeland—a great idea since most of the students and many of the teachers were ex-pats. Well, that was no problem for us. My parents had given Julia a tiny *China Poblana* outfit the year before, and it still fit her. She looked so cute in her green, red, and white skirt and puffy, white peasant blouse. But what really bugged me was that nobody at the school could recognize that she was representing Mexico. With her blond curls, she looked nothing like Dora the Explorer, a famous cartoon character at the time. Dora was definitely the stereotype everyone had for little Mexican girls, and I must have explained "my daughter is dressed as a Mexican" twenty times that day at her school.

Each of Malaysia's three ethnic groups had their own holidays, and the school celebrated each one with gusto. The Indian community celebrated Deepavali (or Diwali) around the end of October. Known as the Festival of Lights, it symbolizes the victory of good over evil as one of the gods and his wife return from exile. I figured that wrapping Julia in the yards and yards of cloth that make up a sari would be too impractical for a four-year-old, so I bought her an outfit worn by the Punjabi people of northern India. It consisted of loose pants topped by a very long blouse, both in shiny, blue-purple fabric. Metallic sandals and a long, decorated scarf completed the outfit. She looked great and was still able to run and play with the other kids at school. However, I think there was another, more personal reason I opted for the Punjabi attire. Ever since I arrived in Malaysia, people would look at me and immediately decide I must be from the Punjab. Apparently the women there have light-brown skin, light-colored eyes, and black hair—which describes me to a T. To complete the comparison, Punjabi women like to wear deep-red lipstick, which is what I often wore in those days since it was Felix's favorite.

The Chinese New Year, which usually falls in February, was also celebrated by dressing up. Again, this was another easy one for us. Julia loved to wear her Chinese *qipao* dress—and tell everyone she was from Shanghai. Teachers introduced the students to Chinese traditions and customs during their lessons throughout the day. Of course, Christian holidays were well represented at the school, thank goodness. I felt quite honored when Julia was chosen to play the part of the Virgin Mary in the kindergarten's Christmas pageant. She managed to appear appropriately reverent as she cradled my Cabbage Patch doll lovingly in her arms. That doll was a gift from my American aunt, who lived in Atlanta at the time, and I had brought it with me as I traveled across the Pacific. For once, Julia did not look completely out of place in her role, even though the rest of the Nativity players came from all over the world. Our Joseph was a little boy from Saudi Arabia, while the shepherds came from Singapore, Pakistan, England, and Australia.

With all these different influences, I sometimes wondered just how "global" my little girl could afford to be. She was already experiencing a push-pull at home between my own Mexican/Catholic traditions (in Spanish) and the European/now-Buddhist influence (in French) coming from her father. Now the school was throwing bits and pieces of diverse cultures at her almost every month. So far she seemed to be handling it all just fine, but in my heart I was relieved that in another year or two she would be back to a more stable environment in Mexico.

The fourth big celebration day at school was Hari Raya, which marks the end of the Muslim month of fasting, called Ramadan. It usually falls during late summer. Malay families gather after the sun has set to celebrate the end of the fast with a big dinner—a feast, really—and of course, the kindergarten students mimicked the real thing dressed in *abayas* and other traditional garb during their day at school.

We were invited to a Hari Raya dinner during each of the two summers we lived in Malaysia, 2006 and 2007. The spicy food was delicious, but I must say it felt a bit odd to sit with everyone on the floor, especially when I was wrapped up in several layers of cloth. I wanted to honor our host family and wore an *abaya* to each celebration. I felt myself just melting and cannot fathom, then or now, how the women can survive such heat. I remember being amazed that so many people could go all day long during the month of Ramadan without eating or drinking *anything* between sunrise and sunset—especially in that fierce tropical heat! Needless to say, by late afternoon people would be flocking to restaurants or food stalls or their kitchens at home to wait and wait, literally counting the minutes, until they were finally able to slake their thirst or feed their hunger. The only Muslims exempt from this month-long fast are small children, pregnant women, and construction workers (because they could faint and fall from buildings to their death). I really had to admire their devotion to their beliefs. I honestly don't think I could have done it.

Now that I could drive, it was so much easier to get to a gym I really liked. Sandra had recommended it to me as a popular one, although she herself did not particularly enjoy exercising and rarely went. The young man who processed my gym application noticed I was from Mexico and said, "Wow, just like Salma Hayek!" I laughed out loud and gave him a big smile, but didn't think much more about it. The next day, when I came to work out, the same guy saw me walk in and shouted out, "*Selamat datang* [Welcome], Salma Hayek! Have a good workout!" Everyone in the gym turned around to look at me and from that moment on, every time I entered the gym or took a class, I would be greeted as Salma Hayek. At first I would laugh nervously when anyone said it, but after a while I got used to my nickname and rather enjoyed it. I mean, what Mexican woman would NOT want to be compared with the beautiful Salma? Besides, for me it was quite a step up—with my new driving privileges I had been promoted from "cousin of Rosalinda" to one of the most glamorous women in the world. If only Salma had known . . . surely she would be pleased to know she had helped another *mexicana* so far from home!

Speaking of other Mexicans, during my time in Malaysia I only met three, far fewer than in China. The first one had worked as a stewardess for Malaysia Airlines. She later moved to K-L and opened a small restaurant called, appropriately enough, "La Mexicana." I would go there sometimes when I was feeling homesick. The second was an older woman who worked at the Mexican consular office. She was married to a French guy, too, but our similarity as couples did not seem to foster any special bond between the four of us. The third one was married to a British guy whose job transferred him to K-L. Unfortunately, I had been living here for quite some time before I met any of them.

As hard as I was trying to make friends in this city, my workouts at the gym produced only one, but she was a good one. She was a very nice woman from India who was living as an ex-pat in K-L, which is quite a different situation from someone who had grown up here as part of the resident Indian population. I think it made her more outgoing and eager to make new friends. She was very chatty, and we met while working out on adjacent treadmills—so boring! We hit it off right away, and soon we were making plans to coordinate our exercise times so we would be sure to see each other. Her name was Meher, and she was a little older than me. She had a teenage daughter and another eight years old. She had a beautiful face but was carrying at least twenty kilos (forty-four pounds) of extra weight, which she was determined to lose. She told me she had been a flight attendant for British Airways. During one flight, while working in the first-class cabin, she met a young bank executive. They fell in love, got married, and her husband's successful banking career had brought them to K-L.

In spite of our exercise goals, what really brought Meher and me together was food. We were both foodies and loved eating and trying all kinds of new cuisines. Although I loved Indian food, I had never tried to cook anything Indian. She had never sampled any Mexican food at all, so I invited her to my house for a traditional Mexican meal. She asked so many questions about ingredients and technique that the luncheon turned into a cooking lesson.

I had found one small supermarket in K-L that sold imported foods. Unfortunately it was on the other side of town in the Ampang area. I used to phone the market every week or so to find out whether they had received a new shipment of any special ingredients that I needed, like tomatillo sauce or squash-flower blossoms. That week I was in luck and managed to buy enough "exotic" Mexican supplies to prepare and teach two meals. She was an enthusiastic student, and in just a few weeks she had learned to make chilaquiles with green sauce, enchiladas in red sauce, stuffed chili peppers, tortilla-and-bean soup, and of course, refried beans. She was so excited about her Mexican meals that she decided to take some home to share with her husband and kids. Her family really liked them and were surprised to find out that Mexican cuisine uses a lot of coriander, just like Indian food.

Soon it was my turn for a lesson. Meher had little trouble purchasing the wide variety of foods and condiments typically used in Indian cuisine since Malaysia has such a large permanent Indian population, and anything she couldn't find would be brought to her by family members visiting from India. She showed me how to make several types of curry as well as a pastry called *samosa*, and *roti*, an Indian flatbread similar to tortillas. They were all delicious, and it was very interesting to watch her prepare them, but I quickly learned that Indian cooking is far more complicated than the rather simplified Mexican dishes that I was able to teach her.

I remember one time Meher and her husband decided to give a dinner party for some of their Indian friends, and she asked me if I wanted to participate in the preparation to see the process from beginning to end. I said yes before I realized that my friends would be starting the cooking process a week before the event! Oh well, I thought, I certainly had the time. What a culinary education that was! Her preparations went methodically step by step, and I watched as she ground spices and flavorings that my eyes had never seen before and my nose had never smelled. Leaves, seeds, herbs—she prepared them separately and combined some of them with others, each time giving every single ingredient its proper timing and grinding style. It was like she was the master and I was her apprentice on those daily sessions. Her way of prepping, cooking, and organizing her kitchen reminded me so much of a movie I liked, *The Mistress of Spices*, which starred the famously beautiful Indian actress, Aishwarya Rai. The final product was a wonderful and amazing meal, and I was honored to have assisted in its preparation. I think Indian food appeals to me so much because the curries remind me of the complex and aromatic sauces (*mole*, *pipian*, and *adobo*, for example) that are so much a part of the Mexican cuisine I grew up with.

Well, all the food we were enjoying was wreaking havoc on our weight-loss dreams! Actually, Meher was the one more in need of drastic weight loss, and she was the one who first broached the idea of plastic surgery. We had both been watching the TV show *Nip and Tuck*, which was very popular at the time, and we suddenly realized there might be a better way to lose weight than killing ourselves in the gym day after day. Plus, we were definitely in the right place at the right time. Malaysia and Thailand were becoming the plastic surgery meccas of Asia, and medical tourism was booming. People were arriving from the US, the UK, France, Germany, and Australia to have makeovers done by doctors trained in Europe or the US. Why had we not thought of this before?

We did a little investigating and found the prices were quite affordable. Liposuction and a tummy tuck would cost about four thousand US dollars, breast implants about three thousand, and that's for the complete package—hospital, doctor, everything! I decided to make a "look and see" appointment with one of the plastic surgeons at the Pantai hospital, a Dr. Fan. I would have a little Botox work done since that was the simplest thing of all, and then get all the preliminary information about getting breast implants. Ever since I had been forced into being a patriotic mother and breastfeeding my son Sebastian, my breasts, always a perky 34-B, were left looking like two fried eggs. Maybe it was time to do something drastic.

Dr. Fan was Chinese and had a pleasant demeanor. When he realized that I was Mexican, he gave me an enormous smile and said I was the first patient he had ever had from Mexico. He then jumped up and went to change the CD he was using for his office music. To my surprise, the next thing I heard was the unmistakable voice of one of Mexico's favorite romantic singers, Luis Miguel.

"I don't have a clue what this guy is singing about," he told me, "but I think his voice is just beautiful. I've never heard anybody sing like that. The music lifts me into the clouds, and I feel so inspired."

Wow, I thought. *One more time someone in Malaysia is telling me how much they love to hear Spanish. It really is their new language of love.* I couldn't help but wonder if this wasn't one more example of the effect "Cousin Rosalinda" was having in Malaysia. Who knows? I decided his enjoyment of Luis Miguel must surely be a sign from heaven that this man was the doctor for me!

When I asked for information about breast implants, Dr. Fan told me that the implants he uses were made in Scotland and that they came in two shapes, spherical and teardrop. He said that American and Australian women usually chose the spheres in order to get the sexiest cleavage, but European women usually wanted the more natural-looking teardrop shape.

He then looked at me and paused, and I guessed that he was wondering just what shape his first Mexican patient would choose. But then he went on to say that the life-span of implants was between ten and fifteen years, and after that they must be replaced. Well, that surprised me. God only knows where I would be a decade from now and whether I would have the money or the opportunity to replace them. So as much as I liked Dr. Fan, I decided not to get the implants. It turned out to be an excellent decision. When my son turned three, my long-gone 34-B boobs came back, just like my Canadian *tai-tai* friend Diana told me they would back in Shanghai!

My friend Meher decided to go ahead and have Dr. Fan give her a tummy tuck with liposuction. It turned out to be quite an ordeal, but I supported her all the way and helped take care of her in the hospital during those times when her husband couldn't be there with her. She stayed three nights in the hospital, curled up like a shrimp for the first two days because she was in such pain. She came home afterward wearing a heavy girdle that covered her from just below her rib cage to her knees, and she carried with her a big glass jar of "souvenir" fat and sagging skin, just as if it were a trophy.

But I must say it was so worth it because she looked gorgeous after she emerged forty days later from that girdle. To celebrate, she organized another one of her famous Indian dinner parties. Meher wore a beautiful sari to show off her new figure, and she lent one to me to wear as well. "Mine" was bright blue-turquoise embroidered with gold. I felt so beautiful and exotic that night, although I remember it was quite heavy to carry around—about seven meters of fabric were wrapped around my hips and draped over my shoulder. Sure enough, all her friends remarked how much I looked like a woman from Punjab. Dressed in that sari, they declared, I could have walked the streets of Punjab and nobody would ever suspect that I was an imposter from half a world away!

Part 6

The Beginning of the End of Asia

Chapter 36
Our Trip to Penang and Its Aftermath

Sometime in the fall of 2007, Felix had a long weekend off from work and decided to take the family to visit Penang, a resort island only about a three-hour drive from K-L. It was famous for its beaches, its history as a British colonial trading post, and its many temples. We decided to bring Gaby, our housekeeper, along with us to help manage Julia and Sebastian, who were then ages four and two. I was hopeful that this would give Felix and me some adult time to reconnect with each other—heaven knows we needed it. It did not work out that way, however. In fact, I think back on it now as one of the worst vacations of my life and the beginning of the end of my marriage.

It started off happily enough. The drive wasn't too long and we all arrived in a good mood. We were staying at the Shangri-La, a beautiful hotel with both a great location on the beach and several swimming pools. Julia was really looking forward to hitting the pool and, for once, so was I. Ever since we moved to Asia I had not been able to find a swimsuit that fit. My Latin/Spanish body is typically pear shaped, while Asian women are notoriously thin as string beans. I even noticed the clerks in clothing stores in China would laugh sometimes as they watched me looking through their merchandise. Without a hint of mercy, they would tell me, *"Waiguoren ni tai pang,"* which means, "Foreigner, you are very fat." Some of them would even add, "We don't have any clothes for people like you."

So it was a relief to be able to find stores that carried Western sizes when we moved to Malaysia. I really lucked out one day when I found a lingerie shop that specialized in Spanish brands. It was called Women's Secret.

Finally! Clothes designed for a body like mine. After a year of hard work at the gym, I felt I was ready for some new clothes and had purchased a bikini I *really* liked. It not only flattered my figure, but was relatively modest (for a bikini). I was as anxious as Julia to get down to the pool!

The first thing we did poolside was to initiate the sunscreen-application ritual for all four of us. (Gaby was not into swimming.) As we all buttered up, I got a creepy feeling that people were staring at us, but I ignored it and concentrated on making sure the kids were well protected from the tropical sun. To allow time for the sunscreen to be properly absorbed, I took Julia for a walk around the edge of the pool. At first I thought the people were remarking on Julia and her blond, Western appearance, but then I realized it was not Julia they were all staring at—it was me! Maybe it was my cellulite, I thought self-consciously, but no—these people were shocked and upset. There was no mistaking their facial expressions.

As Julia and I completed our circuit of the pool, I finally noticed there was not a single woman in the pool, only men and children. The women were mostly seated back under the pool umbrellas, with just a handful of them near the water, taking pictures of their kids or talking to their husbands—and they were all dressed in flowing, black robes! Suddenly I understood. Lots of families from Saudi Arabia were currently staying at the Shangri-La, and every single one of them must have been down at the pool that afternoon. I was the only nearly naked Western woman anywhere in sight. I could not understand the words they were saying, but the looks they were giving me said it all.

I practically ran the last few steps back to where Felix was sitting with Sebastian and hissed, "Quick, give me your T-shirt. Now!" He looked up at me indignantly and said he needed it to keep from getting sunburned.

"It's my bikini!" I told him. "It's making these people really upset, so just give me the damn shirt, okay?" Felix took a look around him and, feeling the scorn and scrutiny, took off his shirt and handed it to me without another word.

So much for feeling good about my newly toned body and great suit. (Sigh . . .)

The next day we did some sightseeing in George Town, the main city and colonial center of the island in the nineteenth century. My friend, Sandra, who was the very proud product of a Chinese and Indian marriage, was born in Penang, so I wasn't too surprised to find that most of the shops, markets, and small eateries we saw seemed to be either Chinese or Indian, and not from Malaysia's other ethnic group, the Malays themselves. The island had a distinctly different personality than the capital city where we lived.

What impressed me most on our sightseeing tour, however, was the Snake Temple. Built over a hundred years ago to honor a Buddhist monk, it was renowned for healing the sick. The temple looked typically Chinese on the outside, like dozens we had seen in Asia. But on the inside, nothing was the same. The floor was literally covered with snakes—lots of them—and the air was saturated with fragrant incense. Legend says that snakes began arriving from the surrounding forest soon after the temple was built. The monks believed this was a good omen and allowed them to take up residence. Most of them were pit vipers, which are venomous and often aggressive, but inside the temple they seemed completely docile. Every year the temple receives thousands of devotees from all over Southeast Asia who come here to pray. We could see several such pilgrims offering quiet yet fervent prayers. They held burning sticks of incense in their hands and lifted their heads up to direct their gaze toward heaven.

Visitors could walk to the back of the temple along a path between the sleepy snakes. Incense burners were lined up along each side of the path at intervals of about five feet. This was supposed to keep the snakes in a state of torpor, and it did seem to be working, so we decided to take a quick tour. I carried Sebastian, while Gaby and I scurried down the path as fast as we dared. Felix strolled nonchalantly along behind us, carrying Julia. At the back of the temple was a pool with fruit trees around its edge. Although it wasn't obvious at first, if you looked closely, you could see more vipers coiled on the branches of the trees.

In the main hall hung a large six-hundred-pound bell made in China during the Manchurian dynasty (1880s). It is rung on the first and fifteenth day of each month of the Chinese calendar to remind the faithful to come and pray. Near the entrance to the temple, we noticed an enterprising photographer who appeared to be making a good living by taking photos of tourists holding one or more (if they dared!) snakes. It made my skin crawl to watch as Felix took his turn holding what the guy said was a viper and a python. He wanted me to hand over Julia so she could be in the picture, too. But hell no, I wasn't going to let that happen!

After the temple we went to the Botanic Gardens. While it was a pleasure to walk the shady paths under the trees, it wasn't long before I began to feel really strange. My legs started to itch, and when I looked down I saw several spots on my calves that looked like mosquito bites. I remember thinking that my capri pants had been a poor wardrobe choice that morning, but we kept going and toured a market devoted to spices. The air was thick with the aroma of many exotic spices, some pleasant and others not so much. We kept on walking and entered a street of small shops. By this time the itching was bothering me even more, and I felt my lips getting numb. I stopped at one of the small shops to look at myself in a mirror and almost fainted. My lips and face were so swollen I looked like the human version of a parrot fish.

I told Felix we needed to leave the sightseeing group and look for a doctor. This was something much more than just mosquito bites. We found a small clinic near our hotel. The doctor told me I had a case of hives, probably in reaction to some plant or spice that I had come in contact with that day. He had no idea what it might be but gave me some antihistamine pills to take three times a day to control the itch and swelling. Unfortunately, the pills made me so sleepy that I spent the rest of the vacation in bed, just like Sleeping Beauty—except by that time I was covered in hives and looked more like a sleeping troll than a beauty.

So I didn't get to go to the beach, or ride the fun little funicular train up the mountain, or sample any of Penang's famous cuisine. I did not even get

The Beginning of the End of Asia

to accompany Felix to Kek Lok Si, the largest Buddhist temple in Malaysia. I slept nonstop for two days. I couldn't stand up or even keep my eyes open for any longer than it took to go to the bathroom, and I remember I couldn't breathe very well either. Thank goodness we had brought Gaby along to help Felix with the kids! I stopped taking the antihistamine the morning of our departure so I would at least be able to walk to the car, but even so I felt like a zombie during our drive back home.

It was storming and raining heavily when we reached K-L that Sunday evening. Felix sent Gaby home while I put the kids to bed. Then my symptoms suddenly got much worse. The itch had increased and become so unbearable that I wanted to pull off my skin. My eyes were swollen almost shut, and I began to have even more troubling breathing. My face looked like I had lost a match with a prizefighter. I was frightened and asked Felix to take me to the Pantai Hospital, only about ten minutes away. But he said that he was tired and that I should just take another one of my pills and go to sleep. Tomorrow, if I did not feel better, I could take myself to the hospital after Gaby arrived. The kids were sleeping, he said, and shouldn't be disturbed.

"Well, those kids are going to be orphans soon," I remember telling him. "It's getting harder and harder for me to breathe!" Felix told me to calm down and not get all hysterical, but at that point I just couldn't be rational anymore. I felt like I was in a fight for my life. My first thought was to call a cab, but there was not a single one available on that stormy Sunday night. So in total desperation, I put my passport, my cell phone, and my wallet with some cash and a credit card into a backpack. I left Felix asleep in the apartment and went by myself to try to find a taxi somewhere on the streets below.

I can still recall how soothing the heavy rain felt on my itching and burning skin. In some spots it was actually bleeding because I had scratched so much. It was already dark, and I remember reciting quite a few Hail Marys in the hope that I would not be struck by lightning along the way. After about twenty minutes I managed to reach a shopping center with some open businesses, but the cab-loading area was empty.

I started looking around. Maybe I could find someone and ask for help—somebody who looked nice and safe. I noticed a middle-aged Indian couple on the sidewalk and approached them, imploring them to help me. I must have looked awful—soaking wet, my face swollen, my skin bumpy and red with hives and bloody patches. They looked frightened at first. Then they looked at each other, and back at the pitiful creature before them.

"Please help me," I begged them. "I am a Mexican tourist. I think I have food poisoning, and I can barely breathe. Please take me to the hospital." I showed them my passport, and that kind, wonderful couple drove me in their car to the Pantai Hospital emergency room. They gave me a presentation card with their names on it. I was so thankful for their help that later on, when I felt better, I invited them to lunch at a restaurant nearby.

Anyway, back at the emergency room, they took me in right away and asked if I had a doctor who knew me at the hospital. I wrote the name, Dr. Mahendra Rash, on a piece of paper and gave it to them because at that point my throat was closing and I could hardly speak. I was focusing all my energy on breathing. That dear man, the same doctor who cared for me when I had my nervous collapse over a year ago, came in to see me. At first he did not even recognize me, but then the emergency room doctor told him I was Mexican, and I could see the recognition flicker in his eyes. (I mean, how many young Mexican women do you meet in Malaysia?)

"Oh, my little Mexican patient," he said to me. "Here you are again! Don't worry, my dear, we will take care of you. Just relax, everything will be all right." And now that he was there, I knew I wouldn't die. He supervised the whole thing and made sure I was treated well. They put an IV tube into my arm, gave me oxygen and several shots, and I fell into a deep sleep.

When I woke up the next day, I could not remember where I was or what had happened to me for several minutes. That was pretty scary. Then someone came to bring me breakfast and answer questions about my current situation. My arms were covered with scratches and my lips were still numb, but my eyes felt less swollen.

About noon Felix called on my cell phone to find out where I was. He had left the kids with Gaby when she arrived that morning at 7:30, and then gone straight to work. With tears running down my cheeks, I told him I would need to stay several more days in the hospital to treat this terrible allergy. His response was, "Well, I didn't realize it was *that* serious. I hope you get better soon because I am worried about leaving the kids at home for such a long time with the maid." Then he hung up the phone, excusing himself because he had to hurry over to a meeting.

That really broke my heart. His main concern was leaving the kids with Gaby, not whether his sick and missing wife was safe or not. The next day (Tuesday) he stayed home from work because he was "so exhausted from having to care for the kids for two days in Penang (with Gaby's assistance!) and then drive back home in the rain." He did manage to rouse himself and bring me some fresh clothes at the hospital Tuesday evening. The ones I wore the night I checked in were a mess.

It took three days in the hospital to get my allergy symptoms under control. When Dr. Rash came to dismiss me, I was so in need of warm human contact that I hugged him as I thanked him for taking such good care of me. Felix had a couple of important meetings with clients that morning, which, of course, he did not want to cancel, so I had to go downstairs to the business office and handle the paperwork myself. A nurse took me down in a wheelchair with the IV tube still attached to my arm so I could pay the bill and check myself out of the hospital.

Chapter 37
Advice from Friends and Relatives

My stay in the hospital had given me plenty of time to think about my life, my marriage, and the kind of person I had become. It was all pretty depressing. I had once been an active, vibrant young woman in love with life and with my husband. Now . . . well, now what was I? Who was I? I lay in that hospital bed and analyzed my situation over and over.

I was the mother of two young children.

I was a deluxe housekeeper and hostess for my husband.

I was a lonely and isolated expatriate who had managed to make only two semi-close friends during my two years in this exotic and distant land.

The real me, the person I looked at in the mirror each day, that person felt completely empty, vacant—constantly busy but never getting anywhere or doing anything that mattered. At least, mattered to me. I felt stranded—marooned, actually—so far from my home, my people, and my place in the world.

What was missing, I told myself, was the love, warmth, and attention of the person I had once felt so very close to—my husband, the man I had once been 100 percent sure was the love of my life.

For some time, I had been thinking that I needed to make some changes, that I could transform myself into a better wife for Felix, that we could regain what we had lost—and I had really, really tried. I had tried to make myself more beautiful by coloring my hair or getting electronic Korean perms. I had tried to make myself a little sexier by exercising to tone my body and grooming my nether regions with painful Brazilian waxing. And I had tried to be more communicative by sending him e-mails, phoning him during the day, or attempting to engage him in pleasant conversations at home. None of it worked. We had become strangers in every sense of the word. But to make it even worse, we were strangers existing side by side on the far side of the world.

What would happen to us? The last morning I sat in that hospital bed, I thought back to my conversations with that wise ex-pat woman who had already lived ten years in Shanghai when I met her—the Mexican woman who had invited me and my parents over for a breakfast of *machaca con huevo*, the one whose maid was absent that morning because she had been ordered to attend the execution of several criminals in her neighborhood. Her name was Judy, and I suddenly remembered how she said ex-pat families did one of two things as they faced the day-to-day struggles of living in a foreign land. Either the husband and wife learned to support each other *inter*dependently, or they did not. This cooperation and interdependence strengthened the marital bond, and the couple thrived. If they failed to achieve this, the marriage would not survive the stresses of life abroad.

Oh my God! Was this what was happening to Felix and me? Was our marriage going to fail? What could I do? We had two small children! The prospect of divorce, even with the problems I knew we had, was horrifying to me. Divorce was unthinkable! There must be some way to turn our lives around.

A few days after I got home from the hospital Felix announced that his mother and her boyfriend were coming for a visit—again. But with the thoughts I had been having lately, this news now gave me hope. Surely the mother of my husband would have some good advice on how to handle my now-opaque husband! To my surprise, I actually began to look forward to their arrival.

Having houseguests always means extra work, but this time it was rather pleasant to have them around. Their presence helped me feel less alone, and I didn't have to struggle so hard this time to find acceptable food for them since Malaysian supermarkets carried a wide variety of organic products for their macrobiotic diet. Unfortunately, their personal hygiene had not changed. The boyfriend still had the world's stinkiest feet. My mother-in-law still drank only one cup of water a day and still did not believe in using deodorant, so her body odor was as pungent as ever. To make things worse, like many French people I met in Asia, they simply hated air conditioning—Felix wasn't fond of it either—and in the tropical heat of Malaysia, it was painful sitting next to them in the apartment—and worse still in the car. Julia would claim that having them in the car with us made her feel like throwing up. Lucky for me, she decided to announce her observations in Spanish, so they never realized what she was saying. But for years afterward she would refer to my mother-in-law as "the grandma who smells."

They enjoyed sightseeing around K-L with me, and as starved for companionship as I was, I enjoyed the outings as well. They particularly liked being able to converse, at least a little, with the Malaysians they met, something that they were never able to do in China. However, they apparently believed that all Asian merchants must like to haggle and bargain as much as the ones they met in China. I remember one time we toured the Royal Selangor factory, where they make and sell beautiful items made from pewter. I had to stop them from trying to bargain down the prices of some souvenirs they wanted to buy in the factory's famous gift shop. "Come on, guys," I implored them. "This is not China, and you are trying to pay in euros, not the local currency. Please don't do this." They looked surprised, but didn't push it.

One weekend Felix joined the family for trip to the Batu Caves. This Hindu pilgrimage site is located just north of K-L. It attracts thousands and thousands of devotees during the holy ceremonies of Thaipusam, which occur sometime in January depending on the date of the full moon. Although we made sure never to visit anytime even close to Thaipusam due to the crowds, I've heard that the ceremonies are very dramatic. Pilgrims carry brightly colored displays of flowers, and some of them pierce the skin on their backs with silver hooks to carry or drag heavy offerings up to a temple inside the cave.

The main cave was simply huge, and an enormous golden statue of the god Murugan stood tall (140 feet) to greet visitors just inside the cave. From there visitors must climb 272 steps up a wide staircase to reach the temple. All six of us managed to make the climb, with Felix carrying Sebastian and Julia holding my hand. Besides the ordeal of climbing all those steps, we had to beware of monkeys along the way. They would jump over the handrails and boldly snatch any bit of food that a tourist or pilgrim might be carrying. We saw one woman actually knocked down by one of the monkey-thieves. She rolled down several steps and came to a stop right in front of us.

When we reached the temple, it appeared small and definitely anticlimactic inside the dark, gloomy cavern. But its exterior decorations were elaborate, and statues of Hindu gods adorned the interior. Inside the temple, we once again caused a scene because several local people were attracted to our blond, paled-skinned kids and wanted to touch them or pat them on the head. Sometimes Julia and Sebastian cooperated with interested strangers, but often they did not. Julia would usually scowl up at them, and Sebastian would cry and hide his face in Felix's shoulder. It felt really weird and uncomfortable to encounter people paying more attention to our kids than to the religious icons they had supposedly come to worship.

A couple of weeks after my in-laws arrived, after she had had plenty of time to observe how things were going between Felix and me, I put the kids to bed early and sat down to have a woman-to-woman talk with Felix's mom. I described how Felix worked all the time, how lonely I felt raising two small kids as if I were a single mom, and how we were essentially now living separate lives. It all came pouring out, and you know what? She wasn't any help at all. Even the spice-market allergy ordeal raised no sympathy in her for my predicament. She basically said that I just needed to get used to it and do the best I could. "That's just what French men are like, *cherie*," she told me. Her advice was to hang in there, wait until the kids grew up, and then get a divorce like she had done from Felix's dad. She refused to do anything at all, refused to even talk with her son on my behalf. What a disappointment that was! And just like in the French movies, my emotional appeal changed nothing about the rest of her stay. We kept up our daily activities and went on behaving just as if nothing had happened, even though she knew how miserable I was. I will never understand the French! They must have ice water in their veins.

Just a few weeks later we got a big surprise. Felix's boyhood friend, Michel, came to visit us! He was the one who had helped us get settled when we first moved to Shanghai. He was now working in Russia and residing in Stalingrad. We knew he and his wife had divorced—no surprise there—but when he walked through our door, I could not believe my eyes. He had totally reinvented himself. He had lost a lot of weight, ditched his glasses for contacts, whitened his teeth, and updated his hairstyle and wardrobe. The slob I had once known was gone, and—there's just no other word for it—Michel was HOT!

That evening over dinner, he told us all about his new life. His ex-wife had moved back to the US with their young son. She had gotten a restraining order against Michel so that he could not even enter the country without her permission. He became deeply depressed, which is what finally motivated him to make all the changes in his personal appearance. He was now dating a Russian woman named Anastasia. He was deeply in love with her, he said, but she was driving him crazy. After all his wild affairs with Japanese, Korean, and Chinese women during his ex-pat years in Shanghai, this Russian would not let him take the final step and actually make love to her. He was quite certain, however, that he would soon be the victor in their battle of the sexes. (In my experience with the French, the biggest interests in their lives always seemed to be either food or making love.)

He even took out his computerized version of "the little black book" and showed us his spreadsheet of all the women he had ever slept with. His long list included the name of each woman and the details of when, where, and how, plus he told us lots of funny stories about them. Anastasia was number sixty on his list, and the line with her name was marked with "???" and the letters TBD—to be determined. I couldn't stop laughing (and blushing). He was a great storyteller and so nonchalant about the whole thing. Felix, on the other hand, nodded his head now and then, pretending to pay attention, but most of the time his blue-gray eyes just stared out the window at the Petronas Towers. Hanging out with Michel and listening to his kinky adventures used to be one of my husband's favorite pastimes, but this time his mind seemed a million miles away.

The next morning Felix packed his bags and flew to Europe for five days on business. Even though his friend had come to visit from so far away, he didn't even try to delay his meetings. That left me and Michel together all week, and boy did we have fun! I took him sightseeing during the day (by this time I was an expert guide), and in the evening we went to nightclubs and some sensational bars overlooking the city skyline. But most of all, we talked—as only old friends can talk. He told me all the details of his "extreme makeover," and I told him about the troubles I was having with Felix.

One afternoon I took him to a restaurant that was known for *teh tarik*, which is Malaysia's national drink. It's made from black tea and condensed milk, but the cool thing about it is how the waiters hold the teapot high above your head and pour the tea in a long stream back and forth between two cups to create a thick, frothy head of foam on the tea. It makes for quite a show. Anyway, while enjoying our *teh tarik* moment, Michel turned to me and lamented how truly bad he felt to see his best friend and me so sad.

"But don't give up, *cherie*," he said. "Let's make a plan to fix this situation. What you need is a total makeover, just like me, and then *mon ami* will fall in love with you all over again! I am sure of it. Let me be your guide, *cherie*—I know what men like."

I thought about it for a moment and decided I had nothing to lose—and who knows? Maybe my husband's best friend knew something about men, or Felix, or sexuality, that I didn't. God knows he had the experience. So we went shopping.

He decided I needed a more youthful look, so we went to Abercrombie & Fitch and Aéropostale, apparently now his favorite brands, and then moved on to Levi's, Express, Spirit, and Guess. Then the next day, following his *savoir-faire* French advice, he took me shopping for lingerie. Now, I knew that Felix had never cared much about lingerie, but Michel refused to believe this. He considered it a sin against the French national character for a man not to love lingerie. So off we went to the lingerie boutiques I had seen at the Kuala Lumpur City Center (KLCC), a mall located at the base of the Petronas Towers.

It was clear that Michel was a man on a mission. He was determined to find the perfect sexy costume that would drive Felix back into my arms. He picked out several sets of lingerie, and then sat outside the dressing room like a fashionista waiting for me to model them. I was more than a bit apprehensive to let him see me in such skimpy and erotic attire, but I finally decided, "What the hell," and walked out for his critique.

The first outfit was white, but he decided that one was too innocent. "This is not a Madonna video," he said. Then I tried a red one, but no, that one was too slutty. The third one, all black, was the charm.

"*Voila, cherie!* That is the one we need for my best friend to fall in love with you again! *C'est magnifique!*" It was a black-lace corset with a garter belt and black stockings. The black-lace panties were the smallest ones I had ever put on. Never in my life had I ever worn anything remotely like this, but for the sake of our mission, I agreed to do it. The last day we stopped at a beauty salon and got my hair styled in a layered cut to add even more drama to my "femme fatale" look. Michel was so pleased with the results of "our" makeover that even I began to believe it might help turn around my marriage.

Waiting for Felix to arrive home, I was kind of excited and felt like a young woman about to be "naughty" for the first time. But I decided his first night home would not be a good time to unveil the new sexy me. Felix usually came home so tired that all he wanted to do was take a hot shower and go right to bed, so I decided to wait. When he came in the door, Michel and I were watching *Grey's Anatomy* on television. I asked him if he was hungry, and he said no. Then much to my surprise, he said, "But you know, *chou-chou* [a pet name for me that he hardly ever used anymore], it is time for you to come to bed with me."

I responded that I really wasn't tired yet and would like to stay and watch the end of the program, but he said sharply, "I don't care. You are coming to bed with me right now." He gave me such a cold, calculating look that, to keep the peace, I left Michel in front of the TV and went to join him in our bedroom. He then told me to undress because he felt at that moment that "he had needs." Well, that was surprising because he hadn't "had needs" for quite some time. He was generally too tired or not in the mood to make love to me, even when I tried to be seductive. Yet now, after a long international plane ride, he suddenly decided that he "had needs"!?

But instead of a kiss or an embrace, he began to inspect my body up the front and down the back, as if checking for evidence like a detective. He apparently did not find what he was looking for and tried to cover up his suspicious behavior by saying that he really was tired after all, and if I wanted to make love to him then I could do what I had to do.

That's when it hit me—he was giving me a physical inspection because he thought I must have been cheating on him all week long with Michel! I was so humiliated and upset that I couldn't do anything but put on my nightgown and cry myself to sleep.

The following morning at breakfast Michel invited Felix to have a boy's night out with him after work that evening. They went to a Japanese restaurant at the Hilton Hotel. Michel did his best, he told me later on, to talk with Felix about how lucky he was to have such a pretty wife who loved him and supported him. He described how horrible and sad his own divorce experience had been, and told Felix that he really needed to make a sincere effort to be more present in our marriage, or he may come to regret it, and soon.

Michel told me the next morning before he left for Russia that Felix had not said a word in response to his plea. He just looked quiet and sad, as if he were about to cry, and then changed the subject. I was really sad to see Michel go back to Russia. I would miss the companionship of having a "big brother" hanging around, and we had certainly had fun together. As he went out the door, Michel gave me a big hug and said he hoped his words would be a wake-up call for his friend, and he asked me to e-mail him and let him know how we were doing. When I closed the apartment door, I felt optimistic about the nice chat he had had with Felix, and I prayed, I actually said a prayer, that this guy-to-guy chat would open Felix's heart and get us back on the right track. At that point we had been married ten years.

Chapter 38
The Agony of Defeat

The weekend finally arrived, and I decided it was time to implement Michel's strategic weapon for improving my marriage—the lingerie. To be honest, I was nervous about it, but Michel had been so enthusiastic. He assured me that the black lingerie looked so good with my tanned skin and black hair that Felix would find it (and me!) irresistible. And he was Felix's very best friend, right? I applied the burgundy-red lipstick that I knew Felix liked and gave myself two shots of tequila to loosen up and relax.

Finally, I heard Felix open the door and walk into the apartment. I looked up to give him what I hoped was a seductive smile, but he did not respond in kind. He just looked me up and down very slowly and said with a low snarl, "So, how much of my money did you spend on *that*?"

To say I was crushed would be an understatement.

His heart was not for his wife anymore, or even for his family, as he had said in the past. His heart now belonged to his money. I guess I knew that by then, but with Michel at my side, I had hoped there was a chance I could draw him back. My new makeover and sexual allure were complete and total failures. The next morning, I e-mailed Michel and informed him that our efforts had made no difference at all. Felix and I resumed the pattern of our daily lives—him working practically all the time and me taking care of the family he claimed to love but generally ignored.

Over the next few weeks I did a lot of thinking about "his money" and where my life was heading. I came to the realization that I needed to find a path for myself. I needed to get back into the world beyond my apartment walls. I realized that my intelligence, my skills, and my knowledge of languages were being wasted by staying at home and supporting Felix's dreams and career. I came to the conclusion that he did not see me sharing in his success. He did not value my contributions to making our family successful. He was "the family" and I was a lowly subordinate.

Well, if money was the most important thing, then the only way I could be worth anything to him, it seemed to me, was to generate money. I had had a good job in Mexico and had (stupidly, I now realized) left it to pursue the dream Felix, not I, had desired. It was time for me to get back on track!

Yes, indeed! And I knew just how to do it, too. I grabbed the phone and called Felix's boss, Bernd, to inquire about a job for me. Even though I had my reservations about Bernd and his difficult personality, this was the obvious solution—Bernd had told me several times over the years, even back in Mexico, that he wished I would come to work for him. I could have the job all arranged and present it to Felix as a *fait accompli* when he returned home because, as usual, Felix was out of town on another business trip.

Bernd didn't think twice about my request and invited me to meet him for dinner at a beautiful restaurant in the Ampang area of K-L, the district where most of the embassies and consular offices were located. Called Tamarind Springs, the restaurant was designed to make guests feel as if they were dining in the tropical forests of Bali. The décor was lush and exotic. Orchids and frangipani flowers were blooming everywhere, and the Indochinese food was a delight for the senses.

During that dinner we worked out the details of a very appealing and very convenient job for me. Bernd already had one administrative assistant (who, I swear to God, had the infamous name of Pussy), but he needed another who could speak fluent German and handle communications directly with company headquarters in Europe. I would be paid four thousand US dollars per month, and I even managed to get him to agree that I could leave the office at four o'clock every afternoon in order to get back to the kids and supervise dinner.

It was a fantastic job offer for me, both professionally and as a working mom. I was very excited and couldn't wait to tell Felix that I would start work about a week after he returned. With Felix's salary and now mine, we would have plenty, and I mean *plenty*, of money. Maybe now I would earn the respect and esteem I felt I deserved from him!

Never have I misjudged a situation so completely.

Felix totally flipped out when he heard my news. He started screaming that I was insane to leave my children unattended to go to work (we had a full-time, experienced housekeeper!) and that he could supply enough money for all of us (yet kept saying that so many things were "too expensive" for us). He shouted that he would never agree to this foolish plan, and then he grabbed me around the throat and slammed me bodily against the wall. Lowering his head down to look me right in the eyes, he growled, "Either you call Bernd right now and say you have changed your mind, or you can pack your suitcases and leave!" Then he let me go and slammed his fist into the wall several more times. His eyes were raging with anger, and I honestly feared for my safety.

What could I do? Walk off and leave my little kids with him? Where could I go, with nothing in my pockets except "his" money? So I gave in to him. I felt as if I had no other choice, no control whatsoever about my own life. I felt like a complete idiot as I called Bernd and told him I had changed my mind.

Felix did not speak to me for days except to say yes, or no, or pass the salt. Then a couple of weeks later, he started a conversation as if we had just been chatting instead of living our lives in silence. Out of the blue, he told me how much he loved me, but that I should understand that if one day he had sex with other women, it would be only sex, not anything important, and that I would still be the main woman in his life.

And that's the moment everything finally made sense to me. Finally. No wonder he arrived home so late and was always tired and not interested in making love. No wonder he didn't mind being away for so many corporate weekends, or why he had stopped letting me use his cell phone—I think he was even taking it into the shower with him by that time. I felt totally broken at that moment, speechless. I foolishly wasted time and energy wondering who this other woman might be. A woman in his office was a former Miss Malaysia—could it be her? *Who could have competed for Felix's attention with a former beauty queen?* I tried to console myself.

It may have taken a few hours, or maybe it was a few days—I don't remember which—but eventually I was able to acknowledge that my marriage was over. It had taken me so long to admit that Felix did not love me anymore. I had been in denial so long. I couldn't believe how blind I had been—and how blindly I had loved him. My love for this charming Frenchman had paved the way for my own personal disaster. Now I had to confront the crushing reality that I was far, far from home in a dead marriage with a man whose love of money was far greater than any love he might have for me.

What should I do? What *could* I even do?

A few days later, I gave Felix a little speech I had prepared. "You know what, dear? I know now that you don't love me, and I don't love you anymore either. You can sleep around and do as you please. I just don't care anymore what you do outside our home," I told him calmly. "But for the sake of the kids, let's just pretend we're friends. Let's raise them with love, giving them the best we can. You support me, and I will support you, even though our hearts and minds are somewhere else."

Felix just stared at me. His eyes grew big and wide, but he did not say a word. I had decided the advice Felix's mother had given me a few weeks earlier had not been so bad after all.

Things might have continued as they were in our ghost marriage for quite some time. After all, there didn't seem to be much I could do to change anything. I had lived in Asia for more than four years but had remained a Christian. I didn't have any belief in karma. Felix was the one who had picked up that bit of Buddhism. But maybe it was karma after all. The day I gave him my "let's just raise the kids with love" speech, Felix and Bernd were about to run afoul of the Malaysian government.

Chapter 39
My Asian Adventure Comes to an End

December 2007 had arrived, and despite my blue mood, I was gearing up for Christmas. The kids and I had decorated the Christmas tree, and presents for everyone were all wrapped and ready for the holiday. My parents would arrive in just a few days to spend Christmas with us in K-L, and then we would all leave for a holiday trip to Singapore. While my mom had visited us previously in Malaysia—which resulted in my finally getting a car (hallelujah!)—this would be the first visit here for my dad. I was looking forward to the diversion their visit would provide in my increasingly lonely life, and they were eager to see their grandchildren again. I even remember what I was planning to serve for Christmas Eve dinner that year. Five pieces of my favorite Australian lamb shanks were safely tucked away in my freezer, ready and waiting.

Early on the morning of December 12, Felix's cell phone rang. I particularly remember the date because in Mexico it is the day we celebrate our national patroness, the Virgin of Guadalupe. It was Bernd calling from Europe. He ordered Felix to get out of our apartment immediately, then call him back as soon as possible on the "safe international phone number" they both knew. He was not to call Bernd back on our house phone nor use it for any more business calls—because it was probably under surveillance, he said.

I suggested that we call my friend Meher on his cell phone. We could ask to use her house phone, saying that ours was broken, and that is what Felix did. When he returned a short time later, I could tell at a glance that something was very wrong. His hands were shaking, and his face was contorted into a mask of fear. We sat down in the living room and he told me, "I must leave Malaysia and fly to Europe—today. Bernd's secretary, Pussy, is making the necessary flight arrangements right now. Your job," he continued, "is to cancel all the holiday plans we have made with your parents and wait here for further instructions."

"Whaaaaaat?" I said in both alarm and anger. "Why? What is happening?"

Felix would only say that there had been a misunderstanding with the Malaysian government, and for his safety, he needed to leave the country. If he did not leave, and soon, it was entirely possible that he could be arrested, and perhaps me, too. Felix hurried to his office and saved certain computer files onto a disk. He then erased all the files on his computer and returned home to bring the disk to me, begging me to keep it with me at all times no matter what. He instructed me to call him from a safe phone after he had had time to leave Malaysia, and then he was gone. He left us in the apartment and flew out that evening to Europe.

That's right. He LEFT us in K-L. With Felix's demeanor and abrupt actions, I felt more confused, frightened, and alone than ever. The next morning, I returned to Meher's house, asked to use her phone again to call Felix, and got the surprise of my life. He told me to buy three business-class airline tickets for me and the kids, pack our essentials into six suitcases, and leave the country—immediately and probably forever.

"What about our furniture, our rugs, all our nice stuff . . . our memories?" I asked him, distraught. He simply repeated coldly to "pack as many essentials as possible and fly yourself and the kids to Singapore, or somewhere else, somewhere safe. But most importantly, get out of Malaysia. Don't tell anyone you are leaving, not even Gaby. Don't tell anyone we are not coming back."

This sounded crazy—even bizarre—to me, and I asked him to tell me what the hell was going on. "Tell me something, at least!" I insisted. "Why is my world suddenly turning upside down?"

All he would say was that the company had a problem with some fake invoices that were created to avoid paying import taxes, and the Malaysian government found out about it. He blamed everything on Bernd, of course, but I'm sure Felix was implicated as well, although he did not admit it. I thanked Meher and returned home, overwhelmed by what I had just heard.

Following his instructions, I called to get the airline tickets, and I began the agonizing task of deciding what was worth packing to take with me and what was not. I practically had a panic attack every time the phone rang or the doorbell chimed. I felt extremely anxious and trembled constantly. I could hardly eat or sleep, and I was terrified that people were watching me or following me whenever I left the apartment. Plus, I had to do all this while trying to act totally normal, not letting anyone, even Gaby, suspect that anything was different in our day-to-day life.

Then, to put the cherry on top of the sundae, two-year-old Sebastian came down with a mild case of diphtheria, a respiratory disease seen most often in tropical climates, and he passed it on to me. Really! In the middle of all this, I had to deal with a very sick toddler. I managed to get some antibiotics for the two of us, but we were unwell for days.

Finally, on the night of December 15, three long, miserable days after we received that life-changing phone call from Bernd, I left my home like a thief in the night. I held Julia with one hand and carried a coughing and feverish Sebastian with the other. It was ten o'clock. Gaby had been sent home, and I saw no witnesses lurking about our apartment building. A van pulled up near the lobby of our building and out stepped Bernd's assistant, Pussy, who had been summoned to drive us and our luggage to the metro station where we could catch a train to K-L's international airport.

She told me—sincerely, I thought at the time—how sorry she was that we had to leave the country. "But it is necessary now, for the safety of your family," she said. "So take care, okay? You know we love you, and the kids!" Then she gave me a hug and a kiss. Later on, I would find out her charade was nothing but the kiss of a Judas.

Before leaving the apartment that evening, I had allowed myself a few minutes for one last walk around the rooms that had been both my home and my golden cage—one long, nostalgic look at all the things I was leaving behind. I remembered how we had transformed the cold, white walls with soft-yellow paint, adding deep terracotta on the accent walls. I gave every piece of furniture its own farewell, recalling how it had come into our lives. The cabinet from China, vases from Bali, statues of Buddha, and silk bedding from Shanghai—each had its own story, and together they told a rich tale of our many adventures in Asia.

Yes, the apartment's décor was as eclectic as its owners had become over the past few years. We had managed to combine all of our treasures into a lovely Asian-themed home in the sky—if only our lives could have meshed as harmoniously! It took all the self-discipline I could summon not to break down and sob as I pondered all that I was leaving behind, all that just would not fit into six pieces of luggage. I saved the best for last—our lovely terrace overlooking the Petronas Towers and the city skyline. It was so beautiful and had witnessed so many of my tears.

This time I didn't need to click my heels like Dorothy to go home. This time I knew I was truly leaving, and I was not coming back. I would not be sharing my life with Felix any longer—that part of my life was over. Felix had told me to flee to Singapore or "someplace safe." There was nothing for me in Singapore, except a return flight to an empty life.

I had not told anyone, but I was heading someplace I knew would be truly safe. The tickets I had purchased would fly us to Australia, where the children and I could recuperate in the home of my sister Pilar. Then, when I was healthy and could manage a trans-Pacific flight, I would take my children home to Mexico. This was the end of my life in Asia and the end of my marriage. Felix had left me to fend for myself too many times—in the hospitals, isolated at home, and now under threat of arrest by the Malaysian government. As Pilar, and later my parents, all said: What kind of man escapes to safety and leaves behind his wife and children?

After four and a half years in Asia, it was time for me to go home. I wasn't just fleeing K-L—I had found the opportunity I needed to escape.

Epilogue

Felix and I never lived together again, but he did wage a long campaign of harassment from across the Pacific Ocean. Our children became the focus of his revenge, and he tried for years to wrest them from me. To take them where, and do what? I never understood his motives. They had become strangers to him long before we left Asia.

Oh, and remember Pussy and her kiss of Judas? Felix was back in K-L within a month or so and brought Pussy and her daughter to live with him in our apartment. I know this from Gaby, who continued to work for Felix and would gossip with one of my former neighbors in the apartment building next to ours, a woman whose son had attended the *tadika* with Julia.

How much of the "dangerous situation" in K-L was real, and how much was a manipulation by Felix to get his girlfriend beside him?

That is something I will never know for sure. But it just doesn't matter anymore. I have finally lost interest in him. I now devote my life to my kids, my church, and as of three years ago, a job that I find quite rewarding.

About the Author

Susan McDonald has worked as a magazine journalist in Atlanta and an educator in Raleigh, North Carolina. She currently lives on the side of a mountain near Huntsville, Alabama, with her husband of many years, who was born and raised in Mexico. When not traveling or writing, she enjoys working in her backyard fern garden.